MASKS
AND
FAÇADES

By the same author

SHERIDAN

SCOTLAND UNDER MARY STUART

1. Sir John Vanbrugh (painting by Sir Geoffrey Kneller—*c.* 1704–10; National Portrait Gallery)

MASKS AND FAÇADES

Sir John Vanbrugh
The Man in his Setting

MADELEINE BINGHAM

LONDON
GEORGE ALLEN & UNWIN LTD
Ruskin House   Museum Street

NA997
V3
B56

Printed in Great Britain
in 12 pt 'Monotype' Barbou type
by W & J Mackay Limited
Chatham

ACKNOWLEDGEMENTS

I am indebted to a great many people who have given me help and advice when writing this book, particularly to those still living in Vanbrugh's houses; to the Earl and Countess of Ancaster and Mr George and the late Lady Cecilia Howard who gave me a detailed view of Grimsthorpe and Castle Howard; and to Mr C. S. Lewis of Kimbolton School and Mr M. V. Morton of Vanbrugh Castle School, who interrupted their schedules to show me round. Also to Mr Hetherington at Seaton Delaval and Mr Drayson of Stowe School, the Staff of the Police College at King's Weston, to Mr James Stevens Curl, Sir Dermot Morrah and Dr Conrad Swan of the College of Arms, to the staff of the National Buildings Record, the Enthoven Collection, the Prints and Drawings Department at the Victoria and Albert Museum, the County Library and Record Office at Chester, the German Institute Library, and, of course, the staff of the London Library.

Madeleine Bingham

ACKNOWLEDGEMENTS

CONTENTS

ILLUSTRATIONS

Good manners and soft words have
brought many a difficult thing to pass

JOHN VANBRUGH

CHAPTER I

The Burgher Background

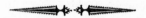

Some men are fortunate in the moment of their birth. Whether the times make the man or the men make the times is one of those problems difficult of solution.

There are certain ages which breathe an optimistic air, as if the world were in bud and opening and everything ready to be written and to be discovered. Vanbrugh's was one of those ages. An age before specialisation closed minds and industrial-isation furrowed the countryside. An age which still believed that mankind was perfectible, that men of sense and sensibility could penetrate the secrets of the spheres, perfect palaces, forge new political systems, and spread across new continents.

It is easy to point to the condition of the peasants, the misery of the urban poor, the wretched conditions in the army, and in the ships afloat, in the prisons, in madhouses and brothels and to say that this was a wretched century of hunger and poverty.

This may be true. But what men believe is sometimes what they can achieve, and in Vanbrugh's age achievement in many spheres seemed, like Newton's apple, ripe to fall into men's hands.

Vanbrugh was born in 1664, when the euphoria of the Restoration had not given way to later disillusion. His talents came to their full fruition when the Glorious Revolution had already driven the Stuarts away to the Continent. He was born into the age of the enlightened amateur, when aristocrats like Buckingham and Etherege could write comedies. When it was possible to be an astronomer and mathematician like Wren, and turn to building the greatest Cathedral in London. When poets were drawn to scientific experiment, and scientists wrote like poets. He lived on into the age of Queen Anne and the Hanoverians, when talented amateurs like the Earls Bathurst and Burlington were lending their taste and patronage to the development of Georgian architecture.

Vanbrugh was above all a man of many parts, an architect who wrote witty comedies, a comedy writer who designed a great palace for a general, a wit who satirised genealogy but became a King at Arms, and presented the Order of the Garter to a future King, a soldier who never fought a war, and a prisoner from the Bastille who brought many French comedies to the London stage. He was a man who moved easily through his times and about whom few of his contemporaries, even the bitter tongued Pope, spoke a word of malice. If he laughed with others, they in their turn laughed with him.

In many ways both the arts he practised were in styles of transition. His comedies, though they looked backwards to the Restoration, also stretched forwards to the novels of Fielding and Smollett.

Although the continental Baroque style of architecture was later swept aside by the all conquering and classical Palladian, yet it lingered on into the nineteenth century, and many a pompous Kensington tradesman's villa still sports stucco urns or cannon balls which echo the details of Blenheim.

The various arts he practised were studies in contrasts. The grandeur of his palaces sometimes seems to sit uneasily in the English landscape, as if they demanded a foreign city about them. But his comedies, though they were influenced by and often adapted from the French, have been completely transformed by his wit and firmly rooted in English soil, which appears to be their natural habitat.

Although Vanbrugh's name has woven itself into the theatre and architecture of England, he was, like so many English artists, not of English stock. Wars, revolutions and persecutions, like hurricanes, can decimate cities and lay countries to waste. But occasionally, like stray seeds borne on the wind, they can blow human beings about the world, and produce a harvest of talent far from the country of its origin.

The grandfather of Sir John Vanbrugh was born in Ghent in Flanders, Gillis van Brugg, and was said to have fled to England 'during the reign of Elizabeth'. The Flemish background explains a great deal in the character of Vanbrugh. Flanders was a bourgeois country, probably the first to exist. It was an independent country, and it was a rich country given to extravagant building, to display, and to a lush appreciation of the good things of life. The Flemish burghers had little respect for kings and princes, with their wealth they were always aware that kings could always be in need of money which could be lent at high rates of interest. In an age when kings depended on fighting mercenaries of various nationalities, they were dependent on the money they could raise from the burghers to pay their armies.

The Low Countries, from which the Vanbrugh family sprang, was not a nation in the modern sense of the term, but a series of independent cities, provinces and duchies. Because of this fact, the people of the Low Countries had developed an independence of thought and action different from that pertaining in other countries where the divine right of kings ran as a paramount writ. This sturdy independence of thought and action were traits which Vanbrugh was to inherit.

Ghent, the town from which the Vanbrughs, or van Bruggs came, was one of the richest cities of a rich province. Erasmus once remarked that 'there was no town in all Christendom to be compared to it for size, power, the political constitutions, or the culture of its inhabitants'.

As the wealth of a town like Ghent had been built by the hard work, industry and ingenuity of the inhabitants, the burghers were in some measure correct in thinking that they were safe from oppression. Their self-governing guilds, tribes of weavers, and gentleman living on their investments, were protected by the strong walls of Ghent, which were nine miles in length.

But the riches and independence of Ghent split on the twin rocks of the religious fanaticism of Spain, and the rise of the Calvinists. The strong walls fell to the money hunger of the Spanish Crown. The downfall of Flanders in general, and Ghent in particular, was caused by Philip II and his father, who bled the city to pay their mercenaries.

Vanbrugh's grandfather, who came to England in Elizabeth's time 'for the enjoyment of the reformed religion', was one of the persecuted Protestant minority. He may have come to England any time in the late 1580s, or possibly after the final defeat of the Spanish Armada, when he could have been about eighteen. If this were the case, the family must have endured much of the worst persecutions of the Spaniards, when the bodies of the Protestant citizens of Flanders hung from the trees 'like ripe fruit' and the rich cities were given over to devastation and rape for the greater glory of God.

Unfortunately, the flight of capital from the sacked towns added to the Spanish difficulties. The traders, including the van Bruggs were leaving. The foreign capitalists who had made Antwerp a trading city comparable with London in the nineteenth century, were slipping away. Not only did Spain ruin the Netherlands, but she ruined her own economy as well. Inflation became rampant in the mother country. Spanish trade dwindled into depression. Unfortunately for the State, it has always been difficult to convince the average trader that he should be working for the general good rather than for his family and his home. The van Bruggs were not so convinced.

When Gillis van Brugg escaped from the persecution and the depression of life in Flanders, he naturally slipped into the same sphere of trading merchants and guilds in the City of London. Here trade was expanding and even foreigners could set up in a fair way of business among the huddled houses and winding lanes. Although the conditions in the City, the filthy streets, the open drains, and the insanitary houses were to lead to the Great Plague and Fire of London, the riches of London were much admired. Their diet was equally admired. Londoners expected four meals a day, which no doubt suited the hearty appetites of the refugee Flemings. The city was fed by the farms and market gardens around its perimeter, although some families preferred to be self-supporting. One man in the City of Westminster was indicted for creating a public nuisance by keeping eight cows in his kitchen: the neighbours did not object to the cows, but mentioned that keeping hay in the bedroom was a 'fire hazard'.

It is not known what trading occupation Gillis van Brugg followed, but he settled down, married an Englishwoman, and had four sons, William, Giles (John's father, born in 1631), and twins James and John. Like many children of an English mother, living in England, they soon became anglicised, and in their turn settled down as merchants in the City.

In London the Protestant burghers from Ghent found an atmosphere to their liking, where money and trading were taken seriously, where independence of thought was cultivated, and where the worst excesses of religious persecution were slipping into the brutal past, although they remained in the folk memory of the family.

Vanbrugh's grandfather died at the end of the Civil War in 1646. His second son, Giles, Vanbrugh's father, married in 1659 at the age of twenty-eight, his sister-in-law, Elizabeth Carleton, one of the daughters of Sir Dudley Carleton. The Carleton family were connected with the court of Charles I, for Sir Dudley's uncle had been Secretary of State and Ambassador to Holland. He had been created Baron Carleton of Imbercourt near Esher in Surrey, and subsequently Viscount Dorchester.

Possibly because of the aristocratic connections of the girls they had married, it was said by the van Bruggs, that they came from a 'race of distinguished knights and burghers, one of whom was a praetor of Ypres in the fourteenth century'. But the prefix 'van' or 'vander' is so common in the Low Countries that it does not necessarily denote a family of aristocratic origin. People fleeing from their own country are often inclined to elevate their parentage in order to overcome the disabilities of being foreigners. Vanbrugh's uncles had complained that they found their un-English origins a disadvantage, for 'some out of spight goe about to hinder their trading, in regard their father was an alien'. The English, as a rule, do not take foreigners to their bosom, but now the family were in the process of marrying into the fringes of the English upper classes, and presumably being accepted.

John Vanbrugh was born at the end of January in 1664 and was baptised in the parish of St Nicolas Acons. He was baptised in his father's house, possibly because he was considered too delicate to be taken to church. At the end of the same year the first plague victim died in Drury Lane. By June of the following year the whole City was paralysed with fear, and the wealthier traders began to shutter up their shops and move away clandestinely. The Vanbrugh family, like many other well-to-do merchants, left the City of London during this time, slipping away before they were forcibly detained by the City fathers. They had fled the persecution in Flanders: now they fled the plague in London.

The town they chose to settle in was Chester. Possibly they may have had friends in the town, for Magna Britannia speaks of the trade of Chester as having been 'augmented by the ingenuity of a colony of Dutch'. In the seventeenth century 'Dutch' could have stood for German, or for Flemings (which the Vanbrughs undoubtedly were), or for the true Dutch as they are known today. The fact that the Vanbrughs' name was spelt arbitrarily either Vanbrugg, Vanbrook, or Vanbrouck is possibly due to the difficulty that foreigners have in pronouncing the Dutch or Flemish 'g'.

By going to Chester, the Vanbrughs were settling in an

environment which could foster their trading capabilities. At this date Chester was a thriving port doing a great volume of trade with Ireland, France, Spain and the Balkans. It was a tightly knit community of merchants who lived a comfortable and prosperous life behind the massive walls.

Even today it is easy to re-create the feeling of the town as it was three centuries ago. The churches, houses and shops huddle behind the walls, and the narrow roads and lanes lead to a maze of small 'wynds' and courtyards. It was a town protected by its walls two miles long, with the countryside stretching away outside the walls. In a sense Giles Vanbrugh had found a similar setting for rearing his family to that from which his grandfather had fled.

In the town of Chester, as in Ghent, the trading guilds were strong, and self-contained, keeping to their rules with the utmost discipline. The twenty-four guilds in the city exercised considerable control of their members. They not only had to buy themselves into the Guild, but they had to be Freemen of the City of Chester as well.

Here, in this self-protective trading community, Giles Vanbrugh set up as a sugar baker. This description of his trade is misleading, as it could give the impression that he was a master baker given to icing cakes. In fact he seems to have been in a fairly large way of business as a sugar refiner, the first to set up a factory in Chester.

Chester was at this date, before the silting up of the River Dee, a considerable port, and no doubt Giles was able to import his raw sugar by sea. Although he was the first sugar refiner in Chester, little seems to be known about his activities, although he must have had considerable capital because there were heavy expenses in connection with sugar refining. Two partners who set up a similar business in Bristol had to find over £1,000 each for workshops, bakeries, warehouses, cooperage, stables, besides drip pots, clay, lime and coal, and blue paper for wrapping the finished sugar 'loaves'. Sugar bakers at this time appear to have been manufacturers, wholesalers, and even retail grocers.

It would not have been possible for Giles Vanbrugh to set up business in such a large way unless he had already sown some foundations of his fortune, or had access to friends with capital who were prepared to finance him.

Giles' name appears in assessments for local taxes in the 1670s and 1680s, and in 1686 the Assembly Records for Chester show that 'Giles Vanbrugh Esq should have a lease for 21 years of a parcel of land called the Salt Grasse near the Starting stone for a fine of £5 and 20s yearly rent.'

The Salt Grasse is a large flat piece of land, formerly a marsh, now the Roodee, a local race course. But in Giles Vanbrugh's day it was the approach to the navigable River Dee, and could have been the site of Giles Vanbrugh's warehouses for his raw material, leading to his other property, the Sugar House, believed to have been in Weaver Street on the site of an old monastery.

Giles Vanbrugh was obviously in a prosperous way of business, and presumably well accepted by the local traders. He was one of the earliest members of the Congregation of Protestant Dissenters in Chester, a congregation which later became Matthew Henry's Presbyterian Chapel. Possibly these dissenters were also a closely knit group of traders enjoying simultaneously the comforts of the reformed religion and the fruits of godly enterprise. It had been remarked, with a certain hauteur, by the Catholics in Flanders that Protestants were 'more suitable for trading' than Roman Catholics. Possibly the same remarks could have been applied to the Chester Dissenters.

If the Dissenters had a narrow religion, they carried their restrictive ideas over into their trading. There were rules regulating the number of shops a man might own, and restrictions on traders owning shops in other towns. Tolls were levied on goods coming into the port of Chester, and even goods sold within the town limits were taxed. One wretched baker was sued by the Bakers Company because he 'sold spiced bread cakes which were much liked—but not subject to the assize'.

The traders of Chester were obviously solid well-heeled men who were intent on keeping their monopolies in the hands of their co-religionists.

It was a curious society and background for a high spirited boy to grow up in.

Giles Vanbrugh and his wife Elizabeth had nineteen children. John Vanbrugh was the fourth, although when he was born he only had one sister living, which would not have been unusual in the days of high infant mortality. Being surrounded by a large, happy and prosperous family may have made up, in some measure, for the narrow-mindedness of his father's religion. But the Puritanism which surrounded him in his youth was to leave Vanbrugh sceptical about ministers of Religion.

On the other hand, if the Vanbrugh family took a harsh view of Roman Catholicism, it was understandable, for it had largely wrecked their country and their way of life, and driven them into exile. The fact of their regained prosperity was due entirely to their intelligence, ingenuity and capacity for survival, all traits which John Vanbrugh was to inherit.

John Vanbrugh is presumed to have been educated at the King's School or Grammar School which was founded by Henry VIII. The original school had been within the precincts of the Cathedral and Monastery. The monks were put to flight, but a good grounding in Latin, the polite language of the learned, remained the basis of an education where boys from nine to fifteen were expected to learn to write and speak it correctly. There was a caveat, 'if any boy shall appear remarkably dull and stupid, and naturally averse to learning we will that that boy, after full trial, be expelled by the Dean and sent elsewhere, lest like a drone he shall devour the bees' honey'.

After the Dissolution of the Monasteries the headmaster complained that the 'schole was ruinous in so much that stones in diverse times dropping out of the walles have broken the schollers heads'. Presumably by the time John Vanbrugh was of school age, it had been repaired, and he was learning in the shadow of the great cathedral, and walked each day beneath the vaulted archways into the Cathedral close.

Chester in the seventeenth century must have been a town which would have influenced greatly an imaginative boy growing up within its walls. Behind the ramparts huddled the Elizabethan houses, but a walk round the walls would reveal the great world stretching away in the distance to the Welsh hills. Walls as a protection shutting out the world, and enclosing a dwelling must have been an idea which imprinted itself on the boy's mind.

In 1678, when John Vanbrugh was fourteen, the Popish Plot was alleged to have been discovered by Titus Oates, and the fears of Jesuits in every cupboard, and the machinations of the Pope behind every disaster, were revived. Not unnaturally having heard so vividly of the Catholics persecuting rather than being persecuted, Giles Vanbrugh, John's father, was solidly behind the establishment when it came to smelling out Catholics. He wrote to the Bishop of London outlining a plan for foiling the Catholics. Obviously the late 'horrid Plott' which had been discovered was hatched in Rome and furthered by the Pope. Giles Vanbrugh's plan was quite simple: it was to assault the City of Rome, on the side where the Vatican Palace stands, and 'bring away the library'.

Giles Vanbrugh had travelled extensively in Italy and France for three years improving his mind. But although his horizons may have been extended in some directions he retained his inherited hatred of Catholicism. It was not possible that a posse of monks and nuns would be able to organise anything in the way of defence. Rome was only a short march from the sea, and the enterprise could be quickly accomplished. Britain already had a fleet in the Mediterranean. Four thousand brisk men could be landed and make a sudden sally on the city of

Rome. Provided they were 'well arm'd and provided with scaling ladders, and Bombes to fire ye Citty in severall places at ye same time, it might accomplish ye Businesse.'

There was only one doubt in Giles Vanbrugh's mind: Catholics must be rigidly excluded from the British attacking force: otherwise they might ride ahead, warn the Pope and ruin the enterprise. This attacking force could also march to Loretto, raze that nest of superstition and 'bring away all its Treasure'.

There seemed to be no doubt that brooding on the persecution of his ancestors, and possibly also on the loss of their treasure, had kindled Giles Vanbrugh's imagination. He hoped that Charles II might be interested in the project, and he was willing to risk his life and fortune in this attempt to attack a nest of Roman vipers on their home territory. Nothing more was heard of this dashing enterprise. Giles went on with his sugar refining and bringing up his children behind the enclosing walls of Chester. Perhaps the idea of military exploits, of scaling walls and attacking Romish priests in their Vatican lair seemed a more exciting prospect than trading in sugar and bringing up his baker's dozen of children in the reformed religion. Many a military heart beats behind an appearance of respectability.

When he was nineteen John Vanbrugh went to France, possibly like his father to improve his mind and learn French, which was at that time growing in importance as a language of the courts and of trading.

It is sometimes said that John Vanbrugh had no training in architecture, and it may have been that he was sent abroad to become acquainted with trade on the Continent. Yet his father was obviously a man who still retained some connections with his continental past, and had travelled extensively himself, and it seems very hard to believe that John at this time did not receive some training in or study of the new architectural ideas which were then current in France.

In the late seventeenth century France was at the zenith of her power, and French architects, craftsmen, painters, and military engineers were the wonder of Europe. Even the great Marlborough had served in Louis XIV's army. France was the apex of the civilised world.

It was to this centre that Vanbrugh was sent at the age of nineteen. It is an age when the mind is susceptible to and receptive of new ideas, and it was not surprising if the French idea of architecture and of comedy should have flooded into the mind of an intelligent and perceptive young man.

When Vanbrugh went to France, it was only ten years after the death of Molière. French comedy was at its apogée, as in the Belle Epoque in Europe before 1914. It is perhaps only in periods of extravagance, when a leisured class flourishes, that comedy finds its best soil. It is one of the decorations of life. There can be little doubt that Vanbrugh was much influenced by comedy in France, for he was later to adapt not only plays by Molière, but also by Dancourt and Boursault, during his theatre career.

He may have had an instinctive feeling for art, but neither architecture nor comedy were to be his first choice of career.

John Vanbrugh returned to England in 1685, the year when Charles II died, when Monmouth landed and was defeated at Sedgemoor, Judge Jeffreys carried out his Bloody Assizes and James II was introducing Catholics into the Army.

Perhaps, like many bourgeois fathers, Giles Vanbrugh expected his son to find some lucrative field for his life's endeavours. Possibly John had inherited a streak of his father's adventurous and frustrated military nature. For about 1686 John Vanbrugh joined the Army.

CHAPTER II

The Captain Vanbrook

John Vanbrugh bought himself a commission in the Earl of Huntingdon's Regiment. At this time the army was in a state of uncertainty. After the Monmouth Rebellion, James II raised several additional regiments and various prominent noblemen were given the privilege, not only of raising the regiments, but commanding them, and amongst these noblemen was the Earl of Huntingdon.

Military historians, while praising the citizen army of Cromwell do not, as a rule, look with a favourable eye on the military prowess of the Stuart Army.

Sir Henry Everett, when writing the history of Vanbrugh's regiment remarks sharply: 'Had the Army of the Restoration inherited some of the virtues of the Commonwealth Army and less of the vices of the Stuart Regime, its records might have been more glorious.'

Vanbrugh's Regiment was raised in 1685 and in August of that year was inspected by the King, James II, who expressed great satisfaction with its efficiency when the regiment was encamped at Hounslow. He would doubtless have been less pleased had he known that three years later, in 1688, the regiment would turn its scarlet coat and support the landing of William III and the Glorious Revolution. Or that all the officers who had supported the Stuarts would be dismissed, and the noble Earl of Huntingdon, its founder find himself 'confined to safe custody where he still continues'.

The idea of allowing noblemen to raise regiments was, as a

veteran of Marlborough's wars, Humphrey Bland, remarked that 'those who had some stake in an established order of affairs of acknowledged integrity and reasonable substance would not bow their necks to a military dictatorship.'

This method was presumably a hedge against a repetition of Cromwell's regime. Once the regiment was raised, the colonel was given money for its annual upkeep, and the regiment then became his personal property and was known not only by his name, but carried his family coat-of-arms on the colours. There were, naturally, abuses which crept in as a result of the colonel being entitled to equip his men out of his grant. One colonel was known to have clothed his gallant followers with second-hand uniforms from another regiment.

The regimental agent sold the commissions and on conclusion of the deal he expected financial acknowledgments, both from the colonel, who had gained an officer, and the officer who had acquired a colonel.

As Commissions cost several hundred pounds and ensigns (second lieutenants) were only paid three or four shillings a day, the purchase of a commission would not, at first blush, seem to have been a good stroke of business acumen on Vanbrugh's part. But once a man had purchased his commission, he was entitled to half-pay when he was not actually serving with his regiment, so that the purchase of a commission was a way of buying an annuity for the rest of one's life. Possibly, like many a son of a bourgeois family, Vanburgh considered the purchase of a commission as a way of advancing his social status. Once commissioned he had a regular income, and could then look for an occupation, being a soldier was merely a stepping stone.

Or perhaps a conversation in his subsequent comedy *The Relapse* spoke for its author:

Lory, the servant, speaking of Lord Foppington says: 'Get him to redeem your annuity.'

Young Fashion replies: 'My Annuity? 'Sdeath he's such a Dog he would not give his Powder Puff to redeem my Soul.'

Lory: 'Look you, Sir, you must wheedle him, or you must starve.'

Young Fashion, as a Parthian shot, remarks that he will neither wheedle nor starve; he will go into the Army.

There is no evidence that Vanbrugh ever served abroad, and it is possible that he may have thought better of adopting the service as a means of advancement in life. Financially, it had many disadvantages. Not only had the aspiring officer to buy his original commission, but he had to buy his way up the army echelons. By the time he had become a lieutenant-colonel he could have paid out several thousands of pounds. Even by the middle of the eighteenth century the pay of a subaltern had only advanced to the princely sum of 4s 6d a day, although in the days of Marlborough's wars battles won could bring their rewards.

Officers of Vanbrugh's regiment had to buy their uniforms of scarlet coat, yellow breeches, worn with sashes embroidered in gold or silver with tassels. But the sashless foot soldiers were expected to march up to fourteen miles a day. In the winter of 1685–86 the regiment took sixteen days to march from Portsmouth to Hull. Deserters were shot out of hand, though occasionally a 'Russian roulette' form of leniency was shown. Three deserters were condemned to death in William III's reign; he decided to pardon two, and shoot one. The men were condemned to draw lots, the one who drew a blank was shot.

Deserters were advertised for, much as criminals today. In the summer of 1686 the Earl of Huntingdon's Own were advertising for one William Reyner, a deserter, who should have been easy to identify, since he had two fingers growing together on one hand, and six toes on his left foot, one of which 'always sticks out of his shoe'. This would seem to indicate a fairly low physical standard for the acceptance of new recruits. Blasphemy was punished by piercing the offender's tongue with a red-hot spike, and the cat-o'-nine-tails was used for other offences.

The army with its crowds of doxies, common law wives, and semi-prostitutes who followed the colours, was welcomed nowhere and cheated by all the innkeepers on the road. Married quarters consisted of a blanket over one corner of an attic in an alehouse.

Abuses were rife, and 'ghost squads' of soldiers put on borrowed uniforms only to appear to muster in order to allow the colonel to draw their pay, after which they silently melted away. Yet other ghost soldiers were the 'widow's men': these were soldiers who had gone to a better world but were still doing good service to others, their pay being drawn and pocketed by the company commander. In Vanbrugh's play *Aesop* there is a reference to false musters, which indicates that they were part of his army experience.

In short, the army may not have seemed a good venue for a gentleman of spirit and talent, and when Vanbrugh's regiment was ordered to garrison Guernsey he resigned his commission, presumably to draw his half pay. Vanbrugh used an occasional military phrase in his plays, but he never made the army the background for a comedy as Farquhar did in *The Recruiting Officer*. His short sojourn seems to have been a mere marking time occupation for him, swiftly entered, and just as swiftly discarded.

In 1689 Giles Vanbrugh died, and in his will he followed the continental custom of dividing his property between his thirteen children, Vanbrugh alone as the eldest surviving son receiving two of the fourteen parts. This left him at the age of twenty five with a small inheritance and no profession. As there is no correspondence connected with Vanbrugh's aims and ambitions at this date it is difficult to speculate what the ambitions of an intelligent and talented young man might be. Often a man of diffuse talents can misjudge his direction, as presumably Vanbrugh had done when he bought himself into the army.

The next time when Vanbrugh appears in historical records was when he was taken prisoner by Louis XIV. By 1690 rela-

tions between England and France had deteriorated. England
and Holland had joined the League of Augsburg, and fighting
had broken out. The Allies had been defeated at Fleurus. Vanbrugh was taken into custody at Calais.

Officially it was said that there were certain irregularities in
his passport, which were reported by a lady. The reason why he
was thrown into prison remains a mystery. Another playwright
—the first Englishwoman to write plays in the Restoration
period—Aphra Behn had been a spy in Holland at an earlier
date, and later Hogarth was arrested in the year of the Scottish
Rebellion 1745 for sketching the fortifications of Calais. There
are literary precedents for the theory that Vanbrugh was a spy.
The calling of spy, whether in a professional and paid capacity
or as an enthusiastic amateur, could have had a certain attraction for a young man who spoke good French and had a taste
for adventure which did not include being garrisoned in
Guernsey. Vanbrugh himself, according to Voltaire, professed
to be entirely astonished as to why he had earned the 'distinction' of being incarcerated by the Sun King. But had he been a
spy posing as a young gentleman of leisure, this attitude of
Scarlet Pimpernel *sang froid* would have been quite in tune with
his character. He was always a man who remained good
humoured in the most trying circumstances.

By September 1690 attempts were being made to exchange
Vanbrugh for some other, and more important, spy held in
London. By January of the following year, in spite of the fact
that King William III himself had made attempts to get Vanbrugh liberated, the French King had refused to compromise.
He wanted the French Officer who was held in Newgate and
no other. Nor did the King wish to reveal that this officer was
also a spy.

In February, M. Ponchartrain, Governor of the Bastille
writing to the Commandant of the Calais prison, said that he
had heard that M. Vanbrugh had been permitted to walk about
the town of Calais. The Governor of Calais prison was informed

that although M. Vanbrugh might give the impression of being an honourable man, he was an Englishman, and Englishmen did not merit the entire confidence of any Frenchman. The Governor was informed that, although his prisoner could be well treated, on the other hand he must not be allowed to escape.

The exchange of prisoners was not achieved and Vanbrugh remained in Calais gaol, but after certain complaints on his part he was transferred to Vincennes.

The account of Vanbrugh's arrest which was sent in July 1691 to M. Ponchartrain seems equivocal. It states that he was arrested at Calais 'on the information of a woman from Paris', that he was entering the country 'after the declaration of war' It appeared that this man [Vanbrugh] had 'produced the woman from Paris' for an English milord, a milord who seemed to have the liberty of Vanbrugh very much at heart. The suggestion of a *quid pro quo*, or a lady for Vanbrugh's liberty seems implied. A footnote in M. Ravaisson's *Archives de la Bastille* underlines the idea: 'The licence which pervades Vanbrugh's plays gives a certain veracity to the story that this Englishman was not, as the French would say, of an irreprochable morality.' Pots and kettles when writing to their superiors are apt to take on a lily-white complexion. It is only prisoners whose morality must be subjected to close scrutiny. Spies and their masters are not inclined to take a romantic view of their prisoners' motives or moral behaviour.

By October 1691 Vanbrugh's letters to his mother were being intercepted and M. Ponchartrain did not like them. He was afraid that his double agent, M. de Berteiller, who had been arrested by the English, might suffer from Vanbrugh's remarks on his treatment. The English must, at all costs, not be allowed to know that M. de Berteiller was being reclaimed in the name of the king, or that he was a spy. The Governor had decided to keep Vanbrugh's letter. His mother could remain in a state of anxiety.

2a. Inside the Duke's Theatre, Lincoln's Inn (Mansell Collection)

b. Lady with Fan and Mask (Cummington: *Handbook of English Costumes*)

3a. Fireworks in Covent Garden, performed at the charge of the Gentry on inhabitants of that parish for the joyful return of His Majesty from his conquests in Ireland, 16 September 1690 (Mansell Collection)

b. Scene from La Princesse d'Elide, a comedy ballet by Molière
(Mansell Collection)

A few weeks later Vanbrugh, ever resourceful, was trying to offer a ransom for himself through an intermediary. By November the King was complaining that he was receiving new complaints from Vanbrugh every day, that Vanbrugh did not seem to be a young gentleman easily intimidated; even in prison he retained his resource and courage. He complained about his bad treatment and the lack of firing for his cell. His Majesty conveyed the message to the Governor of the Prison that he must attend to Vanbrugh's complaints and to see that he was well treated. His Majesty was not disposed to be further importuned with these trivial complaints.

By January of the following year, 1692, Vanbrugh had succeeded, firstly, in getting permission to walk about the courtyard of the prison of Vincennes where he had been transferred from Calais, and secondly in achieving a transfer to the Bastille.

The Bastille has earned a reputation as a synonym and a symbol of oppression and torture. But according to some historians, amongst them the Hon. D. Bingham, who wrote a two-volume history of the prison, prisoners were treated much less harshly in the Bastille than in other prisons. There were enormous differences in the categories of prisoners, and according to their category they merited first class, or second class treatment, rather as if prisoners were starred like restaurants in the Guide Michelin. This was a logical attitude in a country which held so closely to protocol, and where the smallest details of behaviour were treated as of the utmost importance. According to Bingham, the greatest hardship which the prisoners suffered was the loss of their liberty. This is born out by the fact that on one occasion the prisoners asked the Governor to reduce their rations so that the Governor and the prisoners could share the economies on rations. As the King supplied all the rations, some prisoners were able to leave prison with a handsome savings account in their own favour, and the Governor, no doubt, was able to put aside his '*petites economies*' from year to year.

Spies were considered second class prisoners and de

Renneville, who was a spy (as presumably Vanbrugh was considered by the prison Governor), sketches the kind of menu which second class spies might have had to endure when incarcerated in the Bastille.

Dinner consisted of soup, entrée, entremet, dessert, three bottles of wine, two of them to be drunk during dinner (either burgundy or champagne) and the third bottle to be drunk during the day. De Renneville casually remarked that the reason for this good cheer was certainly that 'it was in the interests of the Governor to keep the men confided to his care—and for whom he was paid—in good health'.

It was the curious custom to incarcerate prisoners on similar charges in the same cell. Spies were shut up with spies, thieves with thieves, and poisoners with poisoners. Whether it was hoped that they might pass on information against their fellow offenders, or bore each other with their reminiscences, is not clear. Possibly it was the meticulous French insistence on categories of prisoners which produced this result.

Even the protocol for an arrest was strict. The agent who arrested the prisoner with the *lettre de cachet* touched him with a white wand in the name of the King. He was then conveyed to the Bastille in a closed carriage, taken before the Governor, who examined him, and here he was divested of his arms, his money, and his papers. An inventory was drawn up; this was signed by the prisoner and by the agent of the King. His category of imprisonment governed where he was lodged and the treatment accorded to him. The King granted him his food and prisoners were expected to furnish their cells at their own expense. Thus the official upholsterer to the prisoners of the Bastille ran a very lucrative business.

Prisoners were allowed to keep cats, dogs and pigeons. It is not known whether the combination of spies and pigeons was profitable, or if kindly visitors smuggled homing pigeons in to them.

The prisoners were allowed to buy and borrow books, they

were permitted pens, ink and paper to write on. Many of the prisoners, it is said, enjoyed carrying on their literary pursuits in the Bastille 'not unthankful for the quiet they enjoyed'. Presumably the quiet was due to the absence of wives and family responsibilities.

It was in the Bastille that Vanbrugh started to write his first play *The Provok'd Wife*. But apart from writing there were many other privileges. Prisoners who enjoyed the 'liberties of the Bastille' were allowed to stroll about, pay each other visits, play cards, chess, draughts, skittles and billiards. The only necessity was that a prisoner was expected to remain quiet, and if he did that, no one asked him to account for his time.

At first the only prisoners held in the Bastille were political prisoners, and presumably suspected spies like Vanbrugh. But later the number of charges was increased and they included swindling, debauchery, forgery, blasphemy, heresy, and even cheating at cards. Abduction and sorcery were other heinous offences, possibly these last two charges could run concurrently. There was also a mixed bag of religious offenders, Protestants, Jansenists, Quietists, and bad Catholics. Other types of person to whom Louis XIV took exception were prophets of doom, astrologers, witches, authors, vendors of pornography and journalists. If the Sun King's standards were applied to the modern world a great part of the literary and journalistic establishment would be accorded the liberties of the Bastille.

Alchemists who alleged that they could transmute base metals into gold were put into prison in order to try their hands at this experiment to the benefit of the Government.

This strange melange of eccentrics in a top class prison must have provided a rich vein of material for a future writer of comedies. The eccentricities of people under stress were likely to become wildly exaggerated.

Vanbrugh had been arrested in the summer of 1690 and was suddenly released on parole in November 1692, with a caution, having given a security of 1,000 pistoles against his escape. A

Monsieur de Lagny had provided the money, and as soon as he was released Vanbrugh went round in the carriage of a Monsieur de Besmaus to thank his benefactor. Obviously, in spite of his imprisonment, Vanbrugh still had good friends in Paris.

Voltaire, when he was in exile in England, writing about the people he had met, remarked that he had never heard Vanbrugh make any derogatory remarks about the French nation, although he had been imprisoned by them for two years. This seems to say something both for Vanbrugh's tolerance and for the treatment he had received in the Bastille. If you are to be imprisoned at all, it is clearly better to choose a prison for aristocrats.

In spite of its reputation, and its glorious fall in 1789, when the gates were finally opened on that first 14 July, no instruments of torture or skeletons were discovered. The number of prisoners was said to have been seven—four forgers, two madmen, and one prisoner who had been incarcerated at the earnest request of his family. English prisons were evil places at this time, and the conditions in the Bastille bore no relation to those at Newgate, where prisoners were fettered without exception and gaol fever was rife. Only violent prisoners were fettered in the Bastille, and there was no gaol fever. Possibly de Renneville was right. The rich diet of the prisoners and their three bottles of wine a day did keep them in excellent health.

Executions were carried out, but most of those executed were poisoners or manufacturers of poisons. During the reign of Louis XIV poisoning, as a means of disposing of unwanted husbands or wives or achieving financial independence, was a crime which became very prevalent. It was believed by many that Charles II's sister, Henrietta, had been poisoned by her French husband.

So in 1692, after two years of imprisonment, Vanbrugh returned to England, still without any settled employment. In his absence his younger brother Dudley, who was only fifteen years of age, had been in trouble in his regiment and had killed his colonel in a duel. His fellow officers had defended Dudley and alleged that his colonel had provoked him beyond endurance and that the Colonel had been killed in self-defence. Dudley, it was said—like his brother John—'was always of a peaceable quiet temper'.

Vanbrugh seems to have returned to the Army and then to have joined the Marines as a captain. Lord Berkeley wrote: 'I never preferred any officer upon my Lord Carmarthen's recommendation, but I promised him to make one Mr Vanbrook, a gentleman with him at sea last year (in the Marines) a Captain in my Regiment.' This dazzling post brought Vanbrugh £180 a year. It was probably a case of choosing a career which brought in some ready money, for neither the Army, the Navy, nor indeed the Marines were regarded by the general population as anything but a nuisance, only to be drummed up in time of war and dismissed without compensation or pension once the threat had receded.

It was said that 'A man only goes to sea when he can't get an honest job ashore; if there were more prisons there would be fewer sailors.' Presumably the same remarks applied to the Marines. If the general public did not revere the Forces, there was little love lost between the Forces themselves, which is made clear by a saying of naval origin, 'A messmate before a shipmate, a shipmate before a stranger, a stranger before a dog, and a dog before a soldier.'

Vanbrugh became a captain in Lord Berkeley's Marine Regiment of Foot, the date of this commission being 31 January 1696. But although the commission was granted the accompanying pay seems to have been more difficult to come by. In 1698 the Regiment was 'broke', as the expression was, but four years later in 1702 Vanbrugh was still trying to get his arrears of pay. He wrote to the Treasury claiming £128.13s 3d, which included his own and his servant's pay of ten shillings. The letter ended 'That the full clearing of the said Regiment has been delay'd upon some difficultys in the Accounts: But the said difficultys arising upon some matters transacted in the Regiment long before your Petitioner had his company therein, Your Petitioner humbly prays that his arrears will be met.' He signed himself 'Jno. Vanbrook, 14 July 1702.' An official wrote across the letter, 'He must apply to ye Collonel.'

But colonels of broken regiments, like husbands paying for ex-wives, are reluctant to accept the responsibility for services which they no longer enjoy.

It cannot be said that Captain Vanbrook's career in the army was either gallant or distinguished, and yet there was never any lack of courage in his attitude towards people or towards life It could have been that he constantly found himself in backwaters of military life, the seventeenth century equivalent of minor posts at Aldershot or Catterick. Unless a man has an obvious and dedicated penchant for the military life, he does not take kindly to its administrative role.

Later in his life, when Vanbrugh was one of the brilliant members of the Kit Cat Club, many of his friends were soldiers. It was possibly not to soldiers that he objected but the boring facts of military life in England. A career which kept a man in winter quarters in Dorset, Hull or Guernsey, and then refused to pay him for the inconvenience, would seem to have the disadvantages both of boredom and the lack of financial inducement.

But the army winter quarters provided a fortuitous meeting which was to launch him on the second of his several careers.

CHAPTER III

Vizard Masks
in Pit and Gallery

The beginnings of Vanbrugh's theatrical career are sketched in by the actor-playwright Colley Cibber. Cibber was not a universal favourite in the theatre; he was variously described as a coxcomb, sensible and observant, vain, witty, affected, humorous, and haughty. There are very few of the qualities ascribed to him which do not cancel out the others. But he seems to have conceived a great affection for the genial Vanbrugh which lasted over the years, perhaps because of the fact that he was gay, lighthearted and diverted the company 'with his odd sallies of humour'. Cibber and Vanbrugh had much in common, including the fact that they had their way to make in the world.

Captain Vanbrugh was stationed in Dorset near the home of Sir Thomas Skipwith. It is presumed he had helped Vanbrugh financially. In the days of patronage a struggling army officer of talent could have been considered a good investment by a man of quality. As Cibber puts it, 'Vanbrugh had happened somewhere at his winter-quarters upon a very slender acquaintance with Sir Thomas Skipwith to receive a particular obligation from him, which he had not forgot at the time I am speaking of.'

Sir Thomas had a share in one of the two theatrical patents, but he was not particularly knowledgeable about the conduct of business at Drury Lane. As a natural result of his lack of interest, his investment was not prospering. Actors and managers are not, as a rule, concerned about the financial affairs of baronets who interest themselves little in the conduct of the theatre. Vanbrugh conceived the idea that a way to reimburse his benefactor was to write a good comedy, which might not only improve his patron's investment but lay the foundation of his own fortunes. Then, as now, a lucky hit on the stage could be a short cut to achieving overnight success. He had already written part of a comedy to while away the two years of his imprisonment in the Bastille. Being a man of ready wit and fluent pen, writing plays seemed to him to be a swift way to repay old debts.

If, Vanbrugh's own words, his was a polite age in which a 'good deal of civility there passed between the sexes', the phrase was more neatly turned than the facts warranted.

The age was nothing if not outspoken, and the prologues and epilogues in which the actors spoke directly to their audience were as gamey as the people in the auditorium. Most of the audience at this date seemed to have been more concerned with finding bedfellows for the night than with watching the plays.

It is difficult to judge the plays of the period, and in particular the comedies of Vanbrugh, unless the nature of this audience is kept in view. They were, on the whole, a rough, bawdy, drunken, lecherous lot, and only the meatiest dialogue, the bloodiest spectacles, or the wittiest sallies could keep them interested and in their seats.

The nature of the spectators at the theatre is made abundantly clear in the prologues and epilogues, not only to Vanbrugh's plays but also in the many prologues which Dryden wrote both to his own plays and to the plays of others. As Dryden's net gain from these was from two to ten guineas per prologue or epilogue, it was perhaps not surprising that he took a low view of the men who frequented the pit.

'Who to save Coache hire trudge along the street,
Then print out matted Seats with dirty Feet;

And while we speak, make Love to Orange Wenches,
And between the Acts stand strutting on the Benches
Where ride a Cock Horse, making Vile Grimaces
They to the Boxes show their Booby Faces.'

In many cases these prologues of doubtful meaning were spoken by children of six or seven to add spice to salacity. In one case an epilogue to Powell's Bonduca was spoken by a little girl of six. She apologised to the assembled gallants in the pit for being unable, owing to her tender age, to gratify their desires, but hoped that, as soon as she was grown, to be able to comply with their needs.

A French traveller described a night at the theatre at the end of the seventeenth century:

'An amphitheatre filled with Benches without backboards, adorn'd and cover'd with green cloth. Men of Quality, particularly the young sort, some Ladies of Reputation and Vertue, and abundance of Damsels that hunt for Prey sit all together in this place, higgledy, piggledy, chatter, toy, play, hear, hear not, and just opposite to the stage rises another Amphitheatre which is taken up by Persons of the best Quality—among whom are generally very few men. The Galleries, whereof are only Two are fill'd with none but ordinary People, particularly the Upper one.'

The theatre of Vanbrugh's day was still the theatre of Pepys, a theatre of gusty disorder. It is easy to picture the hoi polloi standing up on their benches making rude faces at the 'quality' in the boxes, for the benches in the pit were raked until they were almost level with the ledge of the first row of boxes.

It was a theatre of comings and goings. Pepys, who had promised to meet his wife at the theatre, found that there had been a mistake and there was no play. Nothing daunted he went to two other playhouses to gaze up and down in the pit, thought neither of them worthwhile and took his coach home. This free and easy attitude towards visits to the theatre meant that some fly characters would see the first act of a play one day, the second act the next day, until they had seen the whole play for nothing by the old device of pretending to look for a friend.

Contemporary playwrights talk of fops who ran and rambled here and there from one playhouse to another, and 'if they like neither the play nor the Women, they seldom stay any longer than the combing of their Perriwigs, or a whisper or two with a friend.' Judging by other remarks in prologues and epilogues, the audience conversation very often rose above a whisper. This lack of manners, which was noted by Voltaire, was caricatured in the plays of the period. One comedy by Shadwell begins with the characters coming into the playhouse, chattering, running down the author and the play, shouting at the orange women, yawning, playing cards, or quizzing some 'fair Cyprians' (prostitutes).

Vanbrugh's was undoubtedly a civilised understatement when it came to the traffic between the sexes in the audiences for his plays. Most of the women were there to trade; the play was a side issue.

The contemporary prologues and epilogues are full of references to the prostitutes in the pit and gallery, and even in the boxes, where Quality could shade off into the raffish. The ladies of the town were called 'punk' or vizards. The latter name became current because it was the mode for women to wear masks, usually made from black velvet, which covered the whole face. It was an excellent disguise for other short-comings, as Dryden makes abundantly clear.

'But stay; methinks some Vizard Mask I see
Cast out her Lure from the mid-Gallery,
About her all the fluttering Sparks are rang'd;
The noise continues, though the scene is changed
Now growling, sputtering, wauling, such a clutter
Tis just like Puss defendant in a gutter;

Fine Love—no doubt; but ere two days are o'er ye
The surgeons will be told a woful story.
Let Vizard Mask her naked Face expose
On pain of being thought to want a nose.'

In another prologue he talks of bullies who enter drunk, invade the theatre, and 'grubble one another's Punk'.

Vanburgh was less explicit when in his play Aesop questions the young beau Empty.

> 'Aesop. Where do you live?
> Empty. In the side box.
> Aesop. What do you do there?
> Empty. I ogle the Ladies.
> Aesop. To what purpose?
> Empty. To no purpose.
> Aesop. Why then do you do it?'

Empty replies airily 'Because *they* like it, and *I* like it.'

The gallants fluttered round the ladies in the vizard masks and talked to them 'so wantonly and so loud—that they put the very players out of countenance. Tis a better entertainment than any part of the play can be,' as Lord Foppington remarked in Vanbrugh's *Relapse*: 'In that Side-box what between the Air that comes in at the Door on one side, and the intollerable Warmth of the Masks on t'other, a Man gets so many Heats and Colds 'twould destroy the Canstutition of a Harse.'

It was obviously not an easy task to keep such an audience entertained, or even quiet. For many of these so-called gentlemen rolled into the theatre straight from the taverns. 'You get your first load of claret by Seven, and then to the Playhouse where you reel about the stage, disturb the Actors, and expose yourself to the world.'

The entertainment given by the players appears to have been a very secondary consideration to the main traffic, which was the selection of a partner for the evening. In spite of its raffish behaviour, the audience was not disposed to accept fare to which it was not accustomed. Farquhar makes this clear in one of his prefaces, when he says that pit and gallery:

'Take all innovations for grievances and let a Project be never so well laid for their advantage yet the undertaker (i.e. author) is very likely to suffer by't. A Play without a Beau, Cully, Cuckold or Coquete is as poor an entertainment to some pallats as their Sundays Dinner wou'd be without Beef and Pudding.'

But if the noisy vizards, rakes and orange wenches were a difficult audience to entertain, the plays of the period were full of reflections of it. Good comedy strokes of misunderstanding were made from the fact that both fine ladies and whores wore their velvet masks at the play or in the Park.

Heroes awaiting their ladies remarked casually that, as the adored one had not arrived, they would divert themselves with a mask. The mask, of course, turns out to be the heroine in disguise.

Vanbrugh used this device in *The Provok'd Wife*, where the two heroines, Lady Brute and Bellinda, enter 'mask'd and poorly dressed', and the errant gentlemen remark to one another:

'How now, who are these? Not our Game I hope.' 'If they are, we are e'en well enough serv'd to come hunting here, when we had so much better Game in Chase elsewhere.'

Vanbrugh has reversed the usual situation where a well dressed lady is thought to be a whore merely because of her mask. 'Some punk lately turn'd out of keeping, her livery not quite worn out—she earns all the cloathes on her back by lying on it.'

The same comedy situation occurs in a play of Farquhar's, *Love and a Bottle*: the lady and her maid put on their masks

44

saying, 'the enemy approaches, we must set out our false colours.'

The heroine replies 'I dread these blustring men of war who are for boarding all masks they meet as lawful prize.'

Her maid takes a more physical approach: 'In truth, Madam, and most of them *are* lawful prize—they generally have French ware under their Hatches.'

The mistress reproves the maid for talking bawdy, but the maid reminds the lady that she has broken her stay laces 'with containing a violent tee-hee at a smutty jest in the last play.'

The black velvet masks which had been adopted with such commercial success by the despised punk had originally had a social purpose, and been used to spare the ladies' blushes at the rude jokes.

Cibber recalled:

'I remember the Ladies were then to be observ'd to be decently afraid of venturing bare fac'd to a new Comedy till they had been assur'd they might do it, without the Risque of an Insult to their Modesty; or, if their Curiosity were too strong for their patience, they took care, at least to save appearance, but rarely came upon the first days of Acting but in Masks (then daily worn and admitted to the pit, the Side Boxes and the Gallery) which Custom had so many ill consequences attending it, that it has been abolish'd these many years.'

It was the prudish Queen Anne who abolished the masks, but when Vanbrugh began to write for the stage, 'those dark disguised black-nosed few', who were also called fireships, were in full sail and he knew exactly the right mixture to purvey to an audience of punks, drunks and orange sellers.

The male element in the audience, apart from being noisy, restless and given to picking fancied whores, was equally ready to seize on real or imaginary insults, given to brawling and even killing. At the slightest offence swords were pulled from scabbards and actors or audience could be involved in fatal quarrels, which took place not only in the taverns around Covent Garden, but in the theatre itself.

Dryden mentions in one of his epilogues that prudent men paid their four shillings in order to sit safely in their boxes, hiding behind their ladies so that they could 'peep o'er the fan and judge the bloudy fray'.

Actors were as quick to fly to their swords as the sparks in front of whom they acted. Hildebrand Horden, one of the handsomest actors of his day, 'was kill'd at the bar of the Rose Tavern in a frivolous rash accidental quarrel'. The Captain Burgess who killed him was pardoned by the King. Possibly players were not considered to be so important as victims of gentlemen. Mountfort, whose voice was said to be of such softness that his words, 'like flakes of snow they melted as they fell,' was cut down at twenty-eight.

Mrs Verbruggen, the first Berinthia in Vanbrugh's *The Relapse*, seems to have had a liking for dashing gentlemen. Her first husband was killed duelling and her second was known as 'fiery Jack' Verbruggen because of his swiftness in flying to his sword.

Nor were these quarrels concluded outside the theatre. A press report in 1682 mentions that a Mr Charles Deering and a Mr Vaughan quarrelled in the Duke's playhouse, mounted the stage and fought. 'Mr Vaughan was secured—lest the wound prove fatal.'

The behaviour of the audience and of the actors seems to have born many resemblances to the Montagues and Capulets in Romeo and Juliet.

If the audience was coarse, the comedies which were purveyed matched its taste. If the audience was brutal, the dramas were equally bloody. Playwrights pandered to this taste. The theatre of the Jacobeans was dying but slowly. In one play by D'Urfey, a contemporary of Vanbrugh, *The Rise and Fall of Masamiella*, one scene opened with the trunk of the hero—headless and handless—dragged in by horses, his head and hands fastened to a pole with a suitable inscription, and behind this two further bodies on gibbets. As these dummy figures were carefully modelled in a Madame Tussaud waxwork fashion, and the mutilated members carefully coloured to match the living bodies, it could hardly have been a savoury scene. Many contemporary prints and illustrations to old plays show heroes and villains being broken on wheels, stuck with arrows, pierced with swords, or generally cut to pieces in various unpleasant ways. The modern taste for horrors on the English stage is hardly new.

But Voltaire, used to a more classical representation of tragedy, criticised the plays. Writing to Lord Lyttleton, he said:

'Your nation two hundred years since is us'd to a wild scene, to a croud of tumultous events, to murthers, to a lively representation of bloody deeds, to a kind of horrour which often seems barbarous and childish, all faults which never sullied the Greek, the Roman—or the French stage; and give me leave to say that the taste of your politest country men in point of tragedy differs not much from the taste of a mob at a Bear Garden.'

Not all Englishmen approved of this. Steele wrote that he found something very horrid in the public executions of an English tragedy:

'Stabbing and Poisoning which are performed behind Scenes in other Nations, must be done openly among us to gratify the Audience. I have been poor Sandford groaning upon a Wheel, Stuck with Daggers, impaled alive calling his Executioners with a dying voice "cruel Dogs and Villains" and all this to please his judicious Spectators who were wonderfully delighted with seeing a man in Torment so well acted.'

Apart from the coarseness of humour in the comedies, the technique used in the production of plays was geared to speed of action, much as the apron stage and the moving scenery is used in classical plays today.

In Vanbrugh's comedies, although there are swift changes of scene from one room to another, these entailed no clumsy moving of scenery carried out by stage hands. Once the curtain was raised, after the prologue, which was spoken on the apron close to the audience, it did not fall until the epilogue had been spoken. The various scene changes were carried out by means of scenes which were drawn either together or apart by means of grooves on the stage. The words in old plays, 'the scene is drawn' mean exactly what they say. By this means scenes were quickly changed. Characters moved forward on to the apron, the scene being quickly drawn behind them. Sometimes scenes were drawn off to show transparencies, groves, gardens, or scenes of battle. The techniques used in these plays were much more sophisticated and swift moving than they seem when they are read.

The usual exits and entrances were made by the use of the proscenium doors, which were a permanent architectural feature. These were set on each side of the apron stage. Sometimes there were four proscenium doors, and some contemporary prompt books show as many as six doors, but none of these would have been behind the proscenium arch. Over each door there was set a balcony, which was also a permanent feature.

In Vanbrugh's *The Confederacy*, when he writes 'Exeunt several ways', this would indicate that they went out by different proscenium doors, while 'puts 'em in the Closet' would also mean the use of a proscenium door to serve as a cupboard.

The fact that these doors were solid meant that they could be banged at, locked, unlocked, shaken, or rattled. There was no risk of the scenery collapsing. The balconies above the doors could represent the windows of houses on a street, balconies for lovers to sigh from, or for the less delicate art of throwing refuse on rivals. In farces, or in comedies like Vanbrugh's, they served as cupboards for hiding lovers, rivals or husbands, or for shielding virgins from irate fathers. They served all kinds of other purposes; garden gates, posterns to castles, or entrances to houses, as the exigencies of the plot demanded, and added a great deal of speed and bustle to a comedy.

The stage was richly furnished and part of the spectacle included the clothes. As Vanbrugh remarked in the epilogue to *The Relapse*, spoken by Lord Foppington:

'Who wou'd discauntenance you men of Dress
Far give me leave t'absarve good Cloaths are Things
Have been of great Support to Kings.'

Pope satirised this convention of grand clothes and splendid settings after the first night of Addison's *Cato*:

'Booth enters hark the universal peal
But has he spoken? Not a syllable.
What shook the stage and made the people stare?
Cato's Long wig, flowered gown and lacquered chair.'

Mrs Barry who acted Lady Brute in Vanbrugh's *The Provok'd Wife*, added the elegance of her dress to her intelligent acting. She was not, like other actors of the period, concerned with period accuracy. Her Queen Elizabeth in *The Unhappy Favourite, or the Earl of Essex*, was said to have been so approved by Mary of Modena that

'she testified her admiration by bestowing on the mimic queen the wedding-dress Mary herself had worn when she was united to James II, and the mantle borne by her at her coronation. Thus attired, the queen of the hour represented the Elizabeth with which enthusiastic crowds became so much more familiar than they were with the Elizabeth of history.'

Mrs Oldfield, another of Vanbrugh's comedy actresses, attracted equal admiration for her emulation of the style of the haute monde. The actresses added other fashionable appurtenances. It was said that 'in former times when the play was over,

49

the attendant boy used to call for "Mrs Barry's clogs" but now "Mrs Barry's chair" was as familiar a sound as "Mrs Oldfield's".'

The fashionable peruke, which the beaux and sparks are so often reproved for combing in the playhouse, was also worn by all the characters in the plays. Every stage character, whether Roman general, Greek philosopher, ancient Briton, mediaeval knight, or Elizabethan gallant, wore a peruke. In the comedies of Vanbrugh's time, these perukes were equally used for strokes of comedy. When women were supposedly disguised as men, the moment of discovery came with the falling of the peruke, should the plot hinge on a woman making love to a woman, mistaking her for a man, or a man duelling with his mistress, as in Vanbrugh's *The Mistake*. This fashion began with the re-opening of the theatres in Charles II's reign and continued as a stage convention until as late as 1720.

Perukes, masks and the sharp distinctions between the rich dress of the aristocrats and the drab of the hoi polloi added much to the variety of comedy, as did the swift action and equally swift scene changes. When Vanbrugh's comedies are read, the transparencies which overlay them are the brisk action and the excellent comedy acting of the period, and the coarse, brawling, noisy audience looking for women rather than wit.

But if they went to find women, they also found worldly wisdom in the plays, and if they went to laugh at their own wit, they stayed to enjoy Vanbrugh's.

CHAPTER IV

The Scene is Drawn

Vanbrugh's first play to be produced was not the first one he had written. He had begun *The Provok'd Wife* while in the Bastille. For it is generally supposed that Vanbrugh had read and seen many French plays when he had travelled in France as a young man, before he fell foul of the lady at Calais and spent two years imprisoned at the Sun King's pleasure. Later he was to adapt several plays from the French. But his first success on the English stage came from seeing an English comedy.

Colley Cibber, being like Vanbrugh, hard pressed for money, had written a play called *Love's Last Shift*, which had been very successful. Cibber says:

'Vanbrugh took a sudden hint from what he lik'd in the play, and in less than three months, in the beginning of April following [1695] brought us *The Relapse* finish'd; but the season being then too far advanc'd it was not acted till the succeeding winter.'

The aspect of *Love's Last Shift* which had quickened Vanbrugh's imagination was the character of Sir Novelty Fashion, played by Cibber, who had written himself the good and showy comedy part of a fop. But Cibber's sentimentality had given the play a happy ending. The unfaithful husband reformed and the couple lived happily ever afterwards. This did not appeal to Vanbrugh's mordant wit and the happy outcome of infidelity did not appeal to his bawdy humour. He did not believe in total reform, only in the fallibility of men and women.

51

Cibber remarked that Vanbrugh observed that most of the actors had acquitted themselves well in *Love's Last Shift*. By adding the word 'most' the actor playwright implies that certain of the cast could have done better by his own masterpiece.

Colley Cibber, the former Sir Novelty Fashion, played Lord Foppington, recently elevated to the peerage. Many critics including Johnson thought Cibber a poor actor, but in the part of Lord Foppington he scored a great success.

Critics said that nature formed him for a coxcomb, but by some men Cibber was considered a leader of fashion and by the women a *beau garçon* with his stiff embroidered clothes, rings, muff, clouded cane and a 'bawdy snuff box' with erotic enamels, mentioned by Vanbrugh in the epilogue.

Cibber took not only the part of Foppington to his heart, but he seems also to have taken the author to his heart.

He wrote:

'Sir John Vanbrugh's pen is not a little to be admired for its spirits, ease and readiness. There is a clear and lively simplicity in his wit, that neither wants the ornament of learning, nor has the least smell of the lamp in it. As the face of a fine woman, with only her locks loose about her, may be then in its greatest beauty; such were his productions, only adorn'd by nature. There is something so catching to the ear, so easy to the memory in all he wrote, that it has been observ'd by all the actors of my time that the style of no author whatsoever gave their memory less trouble than that of Sir John Vanbrugh; which I myself, who have been charg'd with several of his strongest characters, can confirm by a pleasing experience. And indeed his wit and humour was so little laboured that his most entertaining scenes seem'd to be no more than his common conversation committed to paper.'

It was a charming tribute from a grateful actor to an accomplished comedy writer. If this were the plain unvarnished truth, then it was not surprising that Vanbrugh was considered an easy man in his business and personal relationships. At the time of the first production of *The Relapse* he was thirty-two years old, an agreeable pleasant man of the world on the threshold of discovering ways to use his talents.

The Relapse was first acted in 1696 and the cast lived up to the play. Apart from Cibber as Lord Foppington, Mrs Verbruggen played Berinthia, the young and amorous widow. She was the child of actors and had been brought up to the stage from an early age. At a time when there was no restriction on the use of child actors, they were trained from early years, often starting to play the parts of young princes at the age of six or seven. By the time young men or women had reached seventeen years, they had already had ten years training, so that a Romeo or Juliet could be played by experienced actors, who not only looked the part but were the right age for it. A far cry from Romeo being played by a man of fifty with a paunch.

Mrs Verbruggen's husband William Verbruggen played Loveless. The violence of the stage had touched her life, for her first husband had been killed in a love quarrel over Mrs Bracegirdle. As Loveless in Vanbrugh's play, Verbruggen was said to have 'always had the words perfect at one view, and nature directed them into voice and action.' His voice was pleasing, being vociferous without bellowing. This last must have been a very necessary accomplishment in an age when actors had to compete with a good deal of noise from the brawling gallants and predatory ladies of the town.

Mrs Verbruggen, more brilliant than her husband, was noted for her playing of sharp comedy and had created the part of Melantha in Dryden's *Marriage à la Mode*. It was said of her that she could transform her whole being, body, shape, language, look and features into almost another animal. Her voice was round, distinct, voluble and various, and that nothing 'tho' ever so barren—if within the bounds of nature, could be flat in her hands.' From contemporary criticism she seems to have been one of those natural actresses brought up to the stage, knowing instinctively the value of the raised eyebrow, the tentative gesture, or the half-smile.

The part of the virtuous wife, Amanda, was played by Mrs Rogers, who was so prudish that she would only act parts where her stage virtue remained unsullied, which must have limited her usefulness to managements. She was said to be a competent actress. It was in this part of virtue assailed, but unsullied, that the heroine and her husband voiced Vanbrugh's views on the frailty of marriage.

> 'Loveless: The rock of reason now supports my love, the rudest hurricane of wild Desire, would like the breath of a soft slumbring Babe pass by and never shake it.
> 'Amanda: Yet still 'tis safer to *avoid* the storm. The strongest vessels, if they put out to sea may possibly be lost. I know the weak defence of Nature; I know you are a man—and I—a wife.'

The part of Lord Foppington's younger brother, Young Fashion, was played by a woman, Mrs Kent. It was a curious fashion of the age that audiences seem to have been fascinated with women playing men's parts. While it could possibly be said that the reason why women dressing as men was popular was because they could have the opportunity of showing their legs to the gentlemen in the boxes, it was certainly a more attractive custom than men playing women's parts. This was a vogue which still pertained at the beginning of King Charles II's reign, when sufficient women were not trained for the stage. One performance of *The Maid's Tragedy* was held up, the actor sending his excuses: the Queen had not yet had time to shave.

If Vanbrugh's *Relapse* is read with the idea in mind that Young Fashion was played by a woman, some of the exchanges between the pander, Coupler, and Young Fashion take on complicated facets of double entendre. Coupler says to Young Fashion: 'You, young lascivious rogue, let me put my hand in your bosom, Sirrah.' To which Young Fashion replies 'Stand off, old Sodom' and Coupler rejoins 'Prithee—don't be so coy. If you're not hanged before you come to my years, you'll know a cock from a Hen.' Coupler is making advances to Fashion (a woman) but, for the purposes of the play, they are homosexual advances, while on another plane, the real, they are the perfectly normal advances of a man towards an attractive woman.

At the end of the scene, Young Fashion says, 'I' God Old Dad, I'll put my hand in thy Bosom now.' And Coupler replies, 'Ah, you young hot lusty thief let me muzzle you. (Kissing him.) T'other buss and so adieu.' Coupler's remark, 'Ah, you young warm Dog you; what a delicious Night will the Bride have On't' takes on a completely new dimension when it is said to a woman playing the man's part.

The Relapse was an immediate success, and 'by the mere force of its agreeable wit, ran away with the hearts of its hearers'.

Vanbrugh did not take the play to be a great masterpiece and is characteristically modest in the Prologue, spoken on the first night by Miss Cross:

'Ladys, this play in too much haste was writ
To be o'ercharged with either Plot or wit;
'Twas got, Conceiv'd and born in six weeks space,
And wit, you know, 's as slow in growth as Grace.
Sure it can ne'er be ripen'd to your Taste;
I doubt, 'twill prove our Author bred too fast;
For mark 'em well, who with the Muses marry,
They rarely do Conceive, but they miscarry.'

The fact that the actress playing Hoyden was called 'Miss' indicated her youth. Obviously it was meant that the ingenue and diffident Miss Cross speaking lines which had sexual overtones was meant to add savour to the words. But she was not considered to be a good actress because of her lack of experience. The speaking of the Prologue was a very important part of the entertainment, and on the third night a new prologue had been written which was spoken by the star, Mrs Verbruggen.

'This is an age, where all things we improve,
But most of all, the Art of Making Love;
In former days, women were only won
By merit, Truth and Constant Service done,
But lovers now are much more expert grown,
They seldom wait, t'approach by tedious Form
They're for dispatch, for taking you by Storm.

She went on to castigate the manners and morals of the modern sparks in pit and boxes and ended with a warning:

'When I have seen 'em sally on the Stage
Drest to the War, and ready to engage
I've mourned your Destiny—yet more their Fate,
To think that after Victories so great,
It shou'd so often prove, their hard mishap
To sneak into a Lane—and get a clap.'

Unfortunately for Vanbrugh, and somewhat hypocritically, in view of the brisk nature of the trade in the theatre, there had been protests about Vanbrugh's *Relapse* which he discounts in his forward to the published play.

He begins by modestly deprecating his talents 'to go about to excuse half the defects this Abortive Brat is come into the World with, wou'd be to provoke the Town with a Long useless Preface.' He seized the nettle of the objections:

'But my modesty will sure atone for everything, when the world shall know it is so great. I am, even to this day, insensible of those two shining Graces in the Play (which some part of the Town is pleas'd to Compliment me with) Blasphemy and Bawdy.

'For my part I cannot find 'em out. If there was any obscene Expression upon the Stage, here they are in the Print—for I have dealt fairly—I have not sunk a Syllable.'

He added that when any of the polite ladies of the town have read the play, they will find it so innocent that it will be no affront to lay it on the same shelf as their prayer books. He was obviously smiling to himself as he wrote.

Vanbrugh then permitted himself a few witticisms at the expense of the Puritans, the Saints who were preparing to march forward to destroy his comedy.

'As for the Saints, I despair of them; for they are friends to no body. They love nothing but their Altars and themselves; they have too much Zeal to have any Charity; they can make Debauches in Piety, as Sinners do in wine; and are as quarrelsome in their Religion as other people in their Drink.'

There could have been an echo of his youth and a young man's observation of the behaviour of the Saints, and friends of his father at Matthew Henry's chapel in his native Chester. He could have heard the Presbyterians giving battle to one another, and fighting with their backs to the walls, down to the last biblical text. In *The Provok'd Wife* Vanbrugh had a sly thrust at this clinging to the text when Bellinda says to Lady Brute: 'Ay, but you know, we must return Good for Evil', and Lady Brute replies '*That* may be a mistake in the Translation.'

In spite of his sallies against the saints, even Vanbrugh cannot quite pretend that the play was as pure as a virgin's breast. He concluded his defence:

'One more word about the Bawdy, and I have done. I own—the first night this thing was acted—some indecencies had like to have happen'd but—'twas not my Fault.

'The Fine gentleman of the play (drinking his Mistress Health in Nantz Brandy, from six in the morning, to the time he wadled [sic] upon the Stage in the Evening had toasted himself up to such a pitch of Vigor, I confess I once gave Amanda for gone, and am since (with all due respect to Mrs. Rogers) very sorry she scapt; for I am confident a Certain lady who highly blames the Play, for the barrenness of the conclusion, wou'd then have allowed it, a very natural close.'

As Mrs Rogers had said in the play 'the strongest vessels may put out to sea and yet be lost.' Her words had come perilously near the truth. It was possibly Mrs Rogers to whom Cibber was referring when he said, 'I have formerly known an actress carry this theatrical prudery to such a height that she was—very near—keeping herself chaste by it.'

Vanbrugh's references to the trials of Amanda, played by the prudish Mrs Rogers must have amused the cast. The brandy-swigging gentleman Mr Powell, who played Worthy, Amanda's putative seducer, was well known for his drunken, brawling behaviour and inability to remember his lines. But he was apparently a good director, and had one great shining quality where managements were concerned—he kept the actors happy and cheerful on low salaries. It is a virtue which has always had a delicate appeal to the commercial side of the theatre business.

But like any good writer of racy comedy, Vanbrugh did not take his critics seriously. A good joke was a good joke and should stand or lie on its own feet. He tried to turn the criticisms against the critics by using and countering them in his dialogue. The technically virtuous Amanda in *The Relapse* remarks prudishly that although modern plays have charms they should restrain their loose encouragement to vice. Her husband speaking for Vanbrugh says, 'I would not leave the wholesome corn for some intruding Tares that grow amongst it.'

For the time being Vanbrugh had warded off the Saints' attack. But they were re-forming their forces. They were only biding their time, while *The Relapse*, by the 'mere force of its agreeable wit ran away with the hearts of its hearers' and went on playing to packed houses.

Vanbrugh made several adaptations from French comedies, and the first of these was Boursault's *Les Fables d'Esope*, which he turned into a comedy called *Aesop*. This was produced at

Drury Lane with Cibber playing Aesop, a part in which, as he complacently admits, 'I was equally approved in Aesop, as the Lord Foppington.' But as he shrewdly remarked that an 'auditor' does not like to see a wiser person than themselves on the stage, 'But when folly is his object, he applauds himself for being wiser than the coxcomb he laughs at.'

Others in the cast were Mrs Verbruggen playing a comic nurse, and the comedian Penkethman playing the Herald, Quaint. Penkethman was a comedian who played to the gallery. It was said of him that he had 'from Nature a great deal of comic Power about him; but his judgement was by no means equal to it; for he would make frequent Deviations into the Whimsies of an Harlequin'. He was a droll rather than an actor, but in *Aesop* he managed to get the most applause for a scene with 'Sir Polydorus Hogstye' which Vanbrugh had added to liven up the second part of the play.

It was perhaps a pity that Vanbrugh did not simply use the French plot and build on to it a new play of his own, for the speeches and fables which remain of the French original sit uneasily on the shoulders of Vanbrugh's bawdy lively people, who could have walked in from the cobbled streets of seventeenth-century London. The play seems ill-fitted together, as if a painter had not quite covered an old canvas, and the original landscape still shows through the fresh paint.

As always with Vanbrugh's writing he coarsens and quickens. The strokes which he adds make the play funny where the original is merely noble and sentimental. Vanbrugh had little use for noble sentiments and was keeping an eye on his restive lusty audience. They were not over-concerned with nobility and wanted to be entertained.

Vanbrugh makes no secret of the fact that he had not at all 'stuck to the original'. He begged the author's pardon, and added, 'though after all had I been so complaisant to have waited on his Play word for word 'tis possible that even that might not have ensur'd the success of it. For though it swam in

France it might have sunk in England. Their country abounds in Cork, ours in lead.'

Cork may be lighter in the hand, but lead has more substance and for the English reader, Vanbrugh's additions to *Aesop* smell of flesh and blood in a way which cannot be said of Boursault's original. A noble heroine became in Vanbrugh's hand an ordinary girl of flesh and blood, the classic *confidante* of the heroine, a cheerful Cockney, and a sad widow is turned into Aminta, a 'lewd mother'.

Vanbrugh was not the only English playwright to adapt plays from the French. The list of adaptations was lengthy and some of the adaptors were distinguished. Dryden, Wycherley and even Colley Cibber all trod the same path. The French considered the adaptations poor. Voltaire complained that the English have taken, disguised, and spoiled most of the plays of Molière. He attributed this lack of success to the fact that it is impossible to please an audience with portraits of people one neither knows nor understands. The only adaptation of Molière of which he approved was Wycherley's *The Plain Dealer* from Molière's *Le Misanthrope*.

Of 'Le Chevalier Vanbrouck' Voltaire says that his plays were more pleasing, but less ingenious than Wycherley's. This chevalier, he remarked, was a man of pleasure, and on top of that a poet and an architect. He added it was generally felt that he built, as he wrote, 'somewhat coarsely'. Voltaire wrote that this chevalier, having taken a trip to France before the war of 1701, was put into the Bastille, where he wrote a comedy, and 'what seems to me to be very strange, that there is no trace in the play of bitterness against the country which used this violence against him.'

This is an excellent comment on the essential ingredient of Vanbrugh's character and the character of his plays—good humour. Mr Bonamy Dobrée remarks on the same quality in Vanbrugh's comedies and comments on his robust vigour, sound commonsense, based on experience and real inventiveness. He adds, 'Vanbrugh had at least one of the qualities of a great comic writer an ingrained contempt for all cant and humbug, and added that with him 'the breeze of life swept into the theatre'.

Although Voltaire approved of English comedy, he did note that the English permit themselves expressions which would not have been heard in a French theatre—such as a woman, angry with her lover, wishing 'a pox on him', or Lady Brute in *The Provok'd Wife* pondering how she could cuckold her husband. 'These are expressions which gain much from being veiled in our theatre.' But the French theatre audience was not only more intelligent than the English audience, but the plays were written for a court which had different standards of behaviour, or at the least more correct ways of committing adultery.

Vanbrugh was always aware of his brawling audience and never more so than when he wrote the Prologue to *Aesop*:

'Gallants; We never yet produc'd a Play,
With greater fears than this we act to day
Barren of all the Graces of the Stage,
Barren of all that entertains this Age.
No Hero, no Romance, no Plot, no Show,
No Rape, no Bawdy, no Intrigue, No Beau . . .
But preaching here must prove a hungry Trade
The Patentees will find so, I'm afraid.'

Perhaps not surprisingly, *Aesop* was not considered to be very successful at its first showing, but in spite of this, or perhaps because of Vanbrugh's happy acting parts which he had written into the original, it was frequently revived during the eighteenth century. The last recorded production was in 1778 when Thomas Sheridan, the father of Richard, turned it into a farce. Old actors can frequently see the theatrical merit in old plays.

If Vanbrugh was fortunate in the moment when he wrote, because of the high standard of comedy acting, his players were equally happy in the lines and situations he gave them to act. This is brought out very strongly by Cibber, who, as a working actor, playwright and later manager was able to judge the effect practically as between actor, audience and play.

There was at this time great rivalry between the companies of players, the Duke's company under Betterton at Lincoln's Inn Fields, and the King's Company at Drury Lane. While it was admitted that Betterton and his company were more brilliant, the younger company were able to make a considerable stand against them. This began with *Love's Last Shift* by Cibber, and was continued with *The Relapse*. The new comedies and the young actors between them contrived to produce a new and more modern style of acting which obviously had a great appeal for audiences always seeking some new thing to tickle jaded theatrical palates. Methods of acting are constantly shifting, and Cibber and his contemporaries were coming up on the rising tide of Vanbrugh's wit.

The third Vanbrugh play to be produced was in fact the first one he had written, *The Provok'd Wife*, the fruit of his imprisonment in the Bastille. After the success of *The Relapse*, patrons were looking at Vanbrugh with new eyes.

Cibber recalled how 'Sir John' had steered a course, very correctly, between one patron and another.

'Upon the success of the Relapse, the late Lord Hallifax, who was a great favourer of Betterton's company, having formerly, by way of family-amusement heard the Provok'd Wife read to him, in its looser sheets, engag'd Sir John to revise it, and give it to the theatre in Lincoln's Fields. This was a request not to be refus'd to so eminent a patron of the muses as the Lord Hallifax, who was equally a friend and admirer of Sir John himself. Nor was Sir Thomas Skipwith in the least disobliged by so reasonable a compliance.'

The part of Sir John Brute was taken by Betterton, the greatest actor of the Restoration stage. He is considered by some critics to have been one of the greatest actors of all time. He was born about 1634, and was originally apprenticed to a bookseller who had a passion for the stage. His origins were humble, his father having been cook to Charles I.

At the time of the production of *The Provok'd Wife* he led the Company in Lincoln's Fields and was already in his sixties. Sir John Brute, the drunken, bored husband was a comedy part which fitted him like a well-cut suit and he continued to act it for many years after its first production. Yet Betterton had his own ideas on comedy. In an interview with Gildon, the old actor, in an obvious reference to his success as Sir John Brute, said 'I have attempted comical parts which the Indulgence of the Town to an old fellow has given me some applause for' and then he thought back on his triumphs and added, 'Yet tragedy is, and has always been my Delight. Besides as some have observ'd that comedy is less difficult in the writing; so I am apt to believe it is much easier in the acting; not that a good comedian is to be made by every one that attempts it.'

Nor, it must be admitted, is a good comedy easily to be written by every one who had a witty turn of phrase. But among the comedy writers whom Betterton praised were Congreve, Etherege and Vanbrugh. Of Vanbrugh, Betterton said, 'Mr. Vanbrook has shown Abundance of Rude, unconducted and unartful Nature; his dialogue is generally dramatic and easy.'

Betterton was a powerful actor who did not seek easy applause, or parts which commended by their attractions. Sir John Brute was hardly a part to attract that easy sympathy demanded by many actors. But his aim was always to keep the audience's attention by withholding his fire and force. The most telling tribute to an actor can be silence, and this he sought. Sometimes he achieved it on stage with less happy results. On one occasion his horror—as Hamlet—at seeing his father's Ghost reduced the Ghost itself to total speechlessness.

In *The Provok'd Wife*, Elizabeth Barry played his wife Lady Brute. She is considered to be the first real leading lady on the

English stage, and in her time she created over a hundred roles, playing many times with Betterton. She had played the heroines in Otway's tragedies, and all his life this playwright was hopelessly in love with her, to his own destruction. Unlike the chaste Mrs Rogers, her stage virtue was not reflected in her private life. She appears to have played cat-and-mouse with Otway, and to have driven him, quite literally, to drink. Finally she left him to become the mistress of the Earl of Rochester who considered it 'insolent' of Otway to make any attempt to reclaim his mistress.

Although Mrs Barry's first appearances were failures, she had been encouraged by Rochester on as well as off stage. It was said that though she had been trained by Sir William Davenant 'the flash of her light eyes beneath her dark hair and brows was as yet mere girlish spirit; it was not intelligence. That was given her by Rochester.'

In character she had a reputation for meanness over money, and violence with rivals. In a quarrel over a veil with another actress, as Roxana in *The Rival Queens*, the rage and dissension set down for the queens in the play were not simulated. Mrs Barry seized her detested rival and shrieking 'Die Sorceress, die! and all my wrongs die with thee'—she sent her polished dagger right through Mrs Boutell's stays; fortunately the stays being stout, the rival queen merely sustained a scratch.

By the time Mrs Barry came to play Lady Brute she was nearly forty, at the peak of her powers and able to match authority with authority when playing with Betterton.

The part of Bellinda was given to the charming Mrs Bracegirdle, a lady with whom it was the fashion of the sparks to fall in love. Although she was much sighed after, she seems to have escaped the tender traps of love herself and to have remained as chaste as Diana in her response. When Lord Burlington sent her a present of some 'fine old china. She told the servant he had made a mistake, that it was true the *letter* was for her, but the china was for Lady Burlington to whom he must carry it. Lord!

4a. Mrs Oldfield (painting by Richardson)

b. Mrs Barry (painting by Kettle)

(both portraits supplied by The Victoria and Albert Museum)

5a. Colley Cibber as Lord Foppington

b. Mrs Bracegirdle

c. Mr Betterton (Mansell Collection)

d. Laughing audience, by Hogarth

the countess was so full of gratitude when her husband came home to dinner.'

Mrs Bracegirdle had begun as a child actor, having played a pert page, Cordelio, in Otway's *The Orphan* at the age of six. According to some accounts she was taken into the home of Mr and Mrs Betterton, by whom she was trained.

She is described as having been of:

'a lovely height, with dark brown hair and eyebrows, black sparkling eyes, and a fresh, blushy complexion; and whenever she exerted herself had an involuntary flushing in her breast, neck and face, having continually a cheerful aspect, and a fine set of even white teeth; never making an exit but that she left the audience in an imitation of her pleasant countenance.'

John Downes, who was prompter at Lincoln's Inn Fields, wrote of her potent and 'magnetick charm—which caus'd the Stones of the Streets to fly in the Men's faces'. This natural phenomenon is difficult to explain, unless she caused them to leap on their horses in an excess of passion.

Her pleasant countenance must have added much to the character of Bellinda. It is often hard when looking at old theatrical prints, or when reading about old productions of plays, to recreate the atmosphere, the buzz and the excitement which contemporary performers had on the audience of their day. Charm is so evanescent a quality that even the records and films of our own day cannot call back the play, the performer, or the performance. The essential essence has slipped away with the falling of the dusty curtains of time.

At a time of wars and rumours of wars with the French, the villains in *The Provok'd Wife* were the foolish Lady Fancyfull, whose stage dialogue Vanbrugh has liberally sprinkled with French, as she talked to her lady's maid 'Mademoiselle', on whose intrigue the whole plot hinged. It would have been obviously popular, in the final unmasking, that the enemy to virtue should appear as a Frenchwoman.

The Provok'd Wife was the first play which Vanbrugh ever wrote and, unlike some of his other work, which was adapted from the plays or inspired by the ideas of others, was entirely his own creation. He had started it when he was still in his twenties and he put into it much of his own worldly philosophy and many of his own sentiments. In the play Vanbrugh builds up a picture of himself as a man who has a higher view of women's intelligence than of their kindness or their chastity. He writes, indeed, as a man who has learned much from his own experience and even more from the experience of others. He was aware of the intelligence, ingenuity and chicaneries of women, but, although attracted to them physically, was determined to evade their snares. These views are reflected in the dialogue of both the men and the women in the play.

The women in *The Provok'd Wife* are particularly well observed. They are as sharp as, if not sharper than the men. This is not a play written by a man who underrates the wit or wisdom of women. Nor is it one which clouds the traffic between the sexes with an aura of romance.

Lady Brute remarks: 'Men may talk—but they are not so wise as we, that's certain. We shou'd outdo 'em in the business of the State too; for methinks, they do and undo and make but mad work on't.' The two aspiring lovers in the play, Constant and Heartfree, would seem to represent Vanbrugh debating with himself over his experience of women, Constant representing the young Vanbrugh, and Heartfree the Vanbrugh who had been betrayed into imprisonment.

It is a great mistake, says Vanbrugh in the play, to believe a woman is a nymph or Goddess; tell her she *is* one, spend the night with her, but never believe her. Women are full of plots as to how to make men fall in love with them, only to use them like Dogs when their charms have achieved this object. Women are no different from men, they simply have a thinner, more tiffany covering, and use their bright virtue so that they can be lewd with greater security. Or possibly make their husbands fight, and so leave them happy widows. If the lover is killed, 'They cry "Poor fellow he had ill luck" and so they go to cards.'

Later, when questioned by Lady Brute whether he has ever fallen in love, Heartfree says he would fear it, if there were any danger of it, and repeats his aversion to being us'd like a dog. Lady Brute asks how he has come by his knowledge of love, and Heartfree replies—with Vanbrugh—'From other people's expence.' Although there were difficulties for a man 'with more flesh and blood than grace and self denial'. Female virtue was an obstacle to be overcome, but it had to be admitted it was something to be regretted. 'Sdeath that so genteel a woman as my dear mistress should be a Saint when Religion's out of fashion.'

Vanbrugh's ideas on the falsity of confusing technical virtue and chastity, which were current in the Puritan environment he knew so well from his youth, were clear cut. True virtue consists in goodness, honour, sincerity and pity, not in peevish snarling strait laced chastity. It has an intrinsic worth about it and 'is in every place, and in each sex of equal value'. Virtue is contrasted with continence that 'phantom of honour which men in every age have condemned and thrown amongst the women to scrabble for'.

It was an easy acceptable view of his world. As was the reply when Lady Brute asked why men recommend chastity to their wives and daughters—because they wish to keep their wives to themselves, and to dispose of their daughters to others. This was a pertinent social comment in an age when chastity was a commercial commodity.

Another reflection on sexual attitudes was Sir John Brute's reply when asked why he married the wife he was so bored with: 'Because I had a mind to lie with her and she would not let me.' When asked why he did not ravish her, his reply was practical: 'Yes, and so hedged myself into forty quarrels with her relations.' Seduction could be a very dangerous procedure if the lady had male relatives well trained in the art of swords-manship.

When Constant debates with his adored Lady Brute, the author puts both sides of the chastity question.

Lady Brute is setting a high value on her chastity so that he might be the more oblig'd when she makes a present of it.

The lady's attitude is that the present is so great that nothing can repay it. Her lover replies that he has no fancy for becoming an everlasting debtor, and the lady retorts that when debtors have borrowed everything 'they are very apt to grow shy of their creditors company'. The soothing male reply is:

'That Madam is only when they are forc'd to borrow of usurers, and not of a generous *friend*.' If creditors are chosen carefully, there will be no need to shun them. Possibly Vanbrugh had been able to borrow from several generous lady friends.

CHAPTER V

A Debauch in Piety

In his preface to the published edition of *The Relapse* Vanbrugh makes it clear that he was aware of the attacks on his bawdy jokes. He did not, as he put it himself, sink a syllable of what he had written and attacked the long faced Puritans with cheerful humour:

'As for the Saints (your thorough-pac'd ones I mean, with screw'd Faces and wry Mouths) I hope nobody will mind what they say. But if any man (with flat Plod Shooes, a little Band, greasy Hair, and a dirty Face, who is wiser than I at the expence of being Forty years older) happens to be offended at a story of a Cock and a Bull, and a Priest and a Bull-Dog, I beg his Pardon with all my heart, which I hope I shall obtain, by eating my words, and making this publick Recantation.'

But this off-hand airy pretence that *The Relapse* was fit to nestle next to a lady's prayer book had not deceived the sharp-eyed Puritans who, with the production of *The Provok'd Wife*, returned to the attack.

The Relapse still held the stage, but in 1697, the same year as the production of *The Provok'd Wife*, Mr Jeremy Collier's attack appeared. Entitled *A Short View of the Profaneness and Immorality of the English Stage*, it was an instant success amongst the Puritans who had won the Civil War but lost the peace.

Collier was a Non-Juror, one of those men who refused to take an oath of loyalty to the Crown. He had been on the side of the regicides and had even had the courage to give absolution to two foiled assassins of the King.

When Vanbrugh wrote plays and Collier attacked them, the Civil War had only been over for fifty years. The Puritans had been the dominant and victorious party and yet they had seen many of their ideas destroyed. The Restoration was less than forty years before, and with the Restoration had come many foreign ways disapproved of by the majority of the bourgeoisie. The French were not only our political enemies, but they represented Popery, foreign fripperies, actresses on the stage, free love, fornication and imported venereal diseases. Nothing good had ever come out of France, a view which was reinforced by the general view of the King's leanings towards Catholicism and the Duke of York's known Popery, and was backed up by the general view of the rapaciousness of the King's French mistress, the Duchess of Portsmouth. Years later when James had already been chased from the kingdom, these views still held good.

The Restoration stage was cheerfully carnal and references to the traffic between the sexes were frank and open. Vanbrugh's crudities are cheerful, natural and good natured. Collier's attack was crude and anything but good natured, and he singled out Vanbrugh's *The Relapse* for an especially detailed treatment, devoting one whole chapter to it.

If the *Short View of the English Stage* is read carefully, Collier seems to be more indignant about insults to the clergy than the other abuses which are touched on in his attack. Although he thunders against the light view of the relations between the sexes in general, and Vanbrugh's characters in particular, the utmost pitch of boiling rage froths over in Collier's mind when he examines the insults to the cloth.

The dissenting Minister wrote in a shrill, high moral tone, possibly because he was writing in the year when Vanbrugh's second play *The Provok'd Wife* was acted. It was not the affront to morality or to the Scripture which distressed him, but rather the affront to churchmen which drew forth the vials of his wrath—in particular, the scene in which Sir John Brute, on a drunken rampage about the town, steals a clergyman's gown from a passing journeyman tailor, is taken up by the watch, and still in clergyman's clothes proceeds to make speeches which suggest that all is not well under the black gown. 'My talent,' says the inebriated but clerical Sir John Brute, 'lies towards drunkenness and Simony.' This speech is followed later with a remark to the Justice of the Peace that he can give him a very good cure for the clap.

Collier attacked the plays of other dramatists—Congreve, Wycherley, Dryden, and even Aristophanes. Vanbrugh was in good classical company. But he devotes much Puritan attention to *The Relapse*, which he conscientiously picks to pieces, like an entomologist impaling and dissecting a mayfly.

The first charge he made against Vanbrugh is that in his preface to the play 'he swaggers and seems to look big upon his Performance'. Compared with Vanbrugh's modest and airy preface, Collier's is a pattern of conceited bombast. He even talks of throwing in a word or two to 'clear the sense, preserve the spirit of the original and keep the English on its Legs'. As he presumed to improve Vanbrugh and Congreve, he can hardly be said to err on the side of modesty in his own estimate of his writing.

The language of Vanbrugh's ladies is dismissed as too lewd to be quoted. Or Collier was possibly afraid that the jokes might be too good to make his points as clear as he wished. There is nothing like laughter to blur the edges of facts with which the critic wishes to shock, and Puritans have never been noted for humour.

A lewd character seldom wants good luck in comedy, Collier complained. Even the obvious stage device of Young Fashion's stealing Foppington's letter of introduction comes in for an explosion of anger: 'Had common *sense* been consulted upon this occasion, the Plot had been at an end and the Play sunk in the Fourth Act.'

A fact of which no doubt the playwright was only too well aware. Having demolished the plot, Collier 'had a snap', as Vanbrugh called it, at the characters. 'Foplington' [*sic*] cannot possibly have been as silly as he is painted; he had £5,000 a year, and would such a considerable man leave the choice of a wife to a pander like Coupler? There has always been a tendency on the part of Puritans to equate the possession of material wealth with the reward of virtue. Berinthia attracts equal censure. She lacks virtue and yet she is neither kick'd nor expos'd, 'makes a considerable Figure, keeps the best Company, and goes off—without Censure or Disadvantage.' Mr Collier was a forerunner of the Victorian school who preferred to see poor Nellie out in the snow with her shameful bundle.

For good measure, Collier accused Vanbrugh of plagiarising the playwright D'Urfey. This was one sin of which Vanbrugh was never guilty. When he adapted plays from the French he never made any pretence that they were other than adaptations, and in many cases was over-modest in his estimate of the scenes he added.

The final coup against Vanbrugh was that he neglected the three unities of the classic play. 'The scene,' says Collier severely, 'must not wander from one Town or Country to another. Long journeys in Plays are impracticable.' This view successfully eliminates many of the plays of Shakespeare.

When the *Short View* first appeared Vanbrugh, in his good humoured way, decided not to defend himself against so turgid, abundant and well-annotated an attack. As he says:

'I was far from designing to trouble either myself or the Town with a Vindication; I thought his charges against me for Immorality and Prophaneness were grounded upon so much Mistake, that every one (who had the Curiosity to see the plays, or on this occasion to read 'em) would easily discover the Root of the Invective, and that 'twas a Quarrel of his Gown, and not of his God that made him take up Arms against me.'

Even in his defence Vanbrugh cannot forbear from making jokes against the pious Mr Collier's sound and fury:

'The line in Rasor's Confession (The Provok'd Wife) which Mr. Collier's modesty ties him from repeating makes the close of this Sentence "And if my Prayers were to be heard, her punishment for so doing shou'd be like the Serpent's of old, she shou'd lye upon her face all the days of her life".

'All I shall say to this is, that an obscene thought must be buried deep indeed, if *he* don't smell it out.'

Vanbrugh added, 'Collier has a snap—as he goes by—at the Provok'd Wife, and here he's at foul play again. He accused Lady Brute for setting down as a Precept that the part of a Wife is to Cuckold her husband. Whereas her words are these: "In short, Bellinda he has us'd me so barbarously of late, I cou'd almost resolve to play the downright Wife, and Cuckold him."'

It was difficult for Vanbrugh to take such text-chopping seriously. 'This is indeed saying—Wives do cuckold their Husbands (I ask the Ladies Pardons for Lying): But 'tis not saying they shou'd do so; I hope Mr Collier will ask mine.'

The twenty or so pages of Vanbrugh's defence were written in a lackadaisical spirit, possibly in case the popularity of his plays should be affected.

Attacking Vanbrugh on the grounds of blasphemy was a vain pursuit, for he did not care enough about religion and regarded clergymen as fair game for caricature, as were Lord Foppingtons or Lady Fancyfulls, to be accepted or rejected on their merits. He had been brought up amongst Puritans and did not intend to take them as seriously as they took themselves. Possibly his sojourns in France, and his leanings towards French attitudes of thought, made him immune to the fuss and fury engendered by the contemporary Puritans.

On the charges of bawdiness he was on weaker ground. He had admitted himself in his prologue to *Aesop* that plays which had no Rape, no Bawdy, no intrigue and no beau would find it

73

hard to achieve more than a run of a night or two. While Sir John Brute remarks in his cups, 'I would not give a Fig for a Song that is not full of Sin and Impudence.'

It is a fair assumption that Sin and Impudence made up the fun and flow of Vanbrugh's ideas of comedy. Playwrights, unlike churchmen, did not have a captive audience; their customers had to pay the box-keepers at the door. Nor could they slip small change or buttons into the collecting bag. If a playwright's audience did not like the entertainment they complained loudly. On the other hand, a congregation which found a parson's ranting distasteful could be charged with a sin against the Holy Ghost.

In Charles II's day the march of the Puritans had been temporarily halted, but by the time of Collier's attack on the stage they had revived and re-mustered their forces. Although Vanbrugh had answered the attack, it was not a convincing answer, and Collier returned to his barricades of piety and purity. But his answer was not the soft answer which turneth away wrath; he was in as good a voice as ever about smuttiness, profaneness, coarseness and bawdy. Those who paint Debauchery, he thundered, should have the Fucus pull'd off, and the Coarseness underneath discovered. One thing Collier regretted, that he did not begin his attacks sooner—presumably before the audience foundy bawdy to their taste.

It was about the time of the production of *The Provok'd Wife* that Collier's attacks began to bear some small windfalls for the Puritans. Tonson, Vanbrugh's close friend and publisher of some of his work, was prosecuted for printing *The Double Dealer* and *Don Quixote*. Some of the leading actors in Vanbrugh's plays, including Betterton, Mrs Barry and the virtuous Mrs Bracegirdle, were summoned for using indecent expressions 'in some late plays particularly *The Provok'd Wife*'. There were obviously people in England who shared Voltaire's views on le Chevalier Vanbrouck.

Some of Collier's harshest strictures were made on the score of the salacity of the prologues and epilogues. There can be little doubt that they were hardly fragrant. But much of the writing of the pamphleteers, like the Tory Ned Ward, was on an even lower level. If Dryden's prologues abounded in references to ladies without noses, Ward went one stage further and invented a 'No Nose' Club which he alleged was started by a gentleman going round Covent Garden and asking all these afflicted people to dinner on the same night. Vanbrugh's age was not delicate in its humour.

The cleaning up of the stage was not a sudden thing which Collier's pamphlet achieved with one blast of the trumpet against a monstrous regiment of lewd jokes. It was a gradual process which began with the attempts to ban vizards in the reign of Queen Anne, which led in its turn to prostitutes finding it more difficult to occupy the stage boxes. It was also linked with the rise of the bourgeois and puritan ethic.

It has been suggested that Collier was the seventeenth century equivalent of those who are seeking to reform some of the abuses which have appeared on the modern stage. The analogy is hardly valid, for Collier was writing against a stage which was small and urban. In London itself there were only two patent theatres. He was also writing against a background of a largely Christian, and very often Puritan, people who lived in the country and abhorred urban goings-on as corrupting and alien to the general tenor of their thought. Nudity was not part of the entertainment; a well-turned leg in a breeches part was as far as the ladies on the stage dared to go. Although the theatre itself was used for meeting available ladies, the ladies who made themselves available kept the goods under the wraps until they had been paid for.

But Collier's pamphlet was a harbinger. As the number of theatres grew and increased over the century, so the bourgeois concept of morality gained a hold over them until, by Jane Austen's day, nothing was left in comedy which could bring a blush to a virgin cheek. Restoration comedy, of which Vanbrugh and Farquhar were the last witty exponents, expired slowly over the eighteenth century.

But Collier's criticisms did not stop the theatrical success of Vanbrugh's plays. London took *The Relapse* for the good witty joke it was and still is, and the comedy held the stage for more than sixty years.

Most of the good actors of the eighteenth-century played in the comedy. After Mrs Verbruggen, Berinthia was played by Mrs Oldfield and by Mrs Pritchard. Kitty Clive played Miss Hoyden for many years, and Foppington was acted by Macklin and Garrick, although Garrick does not seem to have liked the play; possibly Garrick's short stature and quirky humour was not suited to the Foppington drawl. But Sir John Brute was one of Garrick's most famous and favourite parts.

The Relapse was still being acted towards the end of the eighteenth century, but in 1776 Sheridan, bowing to the 'nice' feelings of the audience of his day, bowdlerised it as *A Trip to Scarborough*. This adaptation killed the original for many years. It had taken Collier and his followers more than eighty years, but finally they had achieved their objective, and the ladies in the boxes in Sheridan's day could no longer burst their stays by laughing at a smutty jest.

Even in Vanbrugh's own time he was eventually forced to re-write the scene where Sir John Brute is dressed up as a clergyman. In the second version he dressed up as a lady of fashion and, although the scene remains funny, it is more a comment on the manners of the day than the rip-roaring farcical episode in the fresh original version. Colley Cibber said that this scene was written for a revival of the play in 1725, but this seems to have been a lack of memory on his part. A contemporary news report announced performances of *The Provok'd Wife with Alterations* at the Hay Market Theatre in 1706. These alterations seem to have remained; the picture of Garrick playing Sir John Brute by Zoffany shows him lifting his pink taffeta petticoats to show his cloth breeches underneath.

Cibber himself was less uncompromising in the plays he wrote, being much 'nicer' and more sentimental in his ideas, which could be said to presage a moralistic future. But morals do not always cause a smile on the face of the box-keepers who count the takings. If Vanbrugh had been condemned for his cheerful bawdiness, his fellow writer and friend, Sir Richard Steele, fell into the opposite trap. He attempted to write a play which would fall in with the rising tide of virtue called *The Tender Husband, or the Accomplished Fools*. Unfortunately, the play lived up to its secondary title. It was a failure. Steele later remarked that he had been martyred in the cause of the Church, for the play had been damned for its piety. Possibly the clamour against the plays did not come from the paying customers, but only from the careful searchers after sin in the library.

The next play with which Vanbrugh was associated was an adaptation of *The Pilgrim, originally by Mr Fletcher and now very much Alter'd with several additions*. On 11 April 1700 Dryden wrote 'within this moneth there will be play'd for my profit an old play of Fletcher call'd *The Pilgrim* corrected by my good friend Mr Vanbrook: and to which I have added a new masque; and am to write a new prologue and epilogue.'

The play seems to have been freshened, though not improved, by the reforming spirit, though here and there the spirit of bawdy comedy peeps through.

The Prologue and Epilogue make it clear that the stage and its writers had now to keep their eyes on the reformers.

> 'How wretched is the fate of those who write
> Brought muzzled to the Stage for fear they bite'

begins the Prologue. The Epilogue reinforced the point:

> 'Perhaps the Parson stretched a point too far,
> When with our Theatres he wag'd a War.
> He tells you That this very Moral Age
> Received the first Infection from the Stage.

But sure, a banisht Court, with Lewdness fraught,
The seeds of Open Vice returning brought.'

But even Dryden does not hold out much hope for the Parson's efforts: 'In short, we'll grow as Moral as we can—Save here and there a Woman—or a Man.'

The Pilgrim is thought to have been written for New Year's Day 1700 (25 March in the Old Style Calendar until its reform in 1752), but the actual date of the first performance is uncertain.

Dryden's masque is redolent with historical references, Diana representing the reign of James I, Mars representing the late Civil Wars, and Venus representing the courtly debauchery of the Restoration. The music was said to have been written by Daniel Purcell. But the prologue, epilogue and Masque were not for Dryden's benefit, 'he dying on the third night of its Representation, his son attended the run of it, and the Advantages accrued to his family.'

Vanbrugh's additions shortened and quickened the speeches to appeal to the audience of his day, who were not as inclined as earlier generations of playgoers to give actors time for mouthing long speeches. He added many lively passages which could rouse laughs in pit and gallery.

The play had a historical significance, so far as the theatre is concerned, for the ingenue part of Alinda was played by Mrs Oldfield. Mrs Ann (or Nance) Oldfield was afterwards to become one of the outstanding actresses of the early eighteenth century. According to some sources she is supposed to have been heard reading aloud by Farquhar at the Mitre Tavern in St James, which was kept by her aunt. But Cibber gives the credit of discovering and promoting Mrs Oldfield's talent to Vanbrugh. He wrote that she was first taken into the King's Company in 1699 where 'she remained about a twelvemonth mute', until Sir John Vanbrugh, who first recommended her, gave her the part of Alinda in *The Pilgrim*.

Mrs Oldfield's biographer, William Egerton, also wrote that she was introduced to Mr Christopher Rich and to Drury Lane by Sir John Vanbrugh in the year 1699. While Egerton could be unreliable, the story is lent credence by the fact that Arthur Maynwaring was a close friend of Vanbrugh, who became the protector of Mrs Oldfield. Or as is so delicately put in her biography, 'It is well known that about this time a strict Alliance of Friendship had commenced between Arthur Maynwaring Esq and Mrs Oldfield.'

Cibber does not seem to have been convinced of Mrs Oldfield's talents at the outset, and is quite frank about his reaction to the young actress brought to the fore by his good friend Mr Vanbrugh. But he admitted that the part of Alinda suited her as 'her diffidence kept her too despondingly down to a formal (not to say) *flat* manner of speaking. Nor could the silver tone of her voice incline my ear to any hope in her favour.' In other words as the swooning nervous virgin, dressed in boy's clothes, her failings could be turned to advantage, and were unlikely to harm the play.

Vanbrugh's perception and encouragement made the part of Alinda the first step in Mrs Oldfield's brilliant career. Fielding wrote of her: 'The ravishing perfections of this lady are so much the admiration of every eye and every ear, that they will remain in the memory.' She was said to be tallish in stature, beautiful in action and always looked like one of those principle figures in the finest painting 'that first seize and longest delight the eye of the spectator'. 'Her voice was sweet, strong piercing and melodious: her pronunciation voluble, distinct, and musical.' These were all high compliments paid to a fellow artist by Mr Cibber. He did add, 'If She delighted more in the Higher Comick than in the Tragick Strain 'twas because the last is too often written in a lofty disregard of Nature.' This was certainly true in the theatre of Vanbrugh's day, for the costumes worn for tragedy were so elaborate and heavy that the actress playing the principal part had to have a page to carry her train about, and 'while she raved in madness' the only concern of her lackey was to see she did not disorder the expensive silks of her dress. Mrs Oldfield took a down to earth view of tragedy and said: 'Why do they not give Porter these parts? She can put on a better Tragedy face than I can.' Mary Ann Porter was first the understudy of Mrs Barry and afterwards succeeded her in high tragedy.

Mrs Oldfield seems to have quickly lost her original timidity as she gained more experience, and when a beau in the pit dared to hiss her, merely drew herself up and remarked pityingly, 'Poor creature!'

From her humble beginnings at the inn in St James's she gravitated to being a great lady. It was said she went to the theatre wearing the same clothes she wore to dine at the houses of the nobility. When Arthur Maynwaring died, leaving her a son, the fruit of that 'strict Alliance of Friendship', she was taken under the protection of General Charles Churchill, the son of Marlborough's elder brother. Nothing but the best was suitable for Mrs Oldfield, and when she went from Churchill's house to the playhouse she was attended by two footmen. By this time she had become so aristocratic that she seldom spoke to the other actors. Her taste and the refined way she wore her clothes were appreciated by theatre and audience alike, and she was given an allowance by the management to buy her own clothes. Vanbrugh had obviously noted that Ann Oldfield had instinctive style, and in his day style was a quality which was held in high esteem.

Easy and confident in all he did himself, Vanbrugh seems to have been able to inspire other artists with the confidence in themselves which is so necessary to achievement. He not only encouraged Mrs Oldfield, but Cibber himself. The actor manager gives fulsome praise to Sir John in his autobiography, saying that while his first play *Love's Last Shift* had been approved, Mr Southern had reservations about him as an actor. Vanbrugh took the opposite point of view. He not only complimented the author by writing *The Relapse* as a sequel, but wrote the part of Foppington for him. 'This play had a great success and gave me as a comedian a second flight of reputation along with it.'

Cibber was writing his reminiscences after a career of forty years in the theatre. He was, perhaps, a man of modest talents, and attracted a great deal of satire from Pope and others when he was made Poet Laureate. He had good reasons for disliking many of the literary fraternity, but always in his book refers to Vanbrugh with affection and liking, mentioning his agreeable wit and easy manners.

Mostly, in his life of himself, Cibber was at no pains to whitewash his fellow labourers in the theatrical vineyard. Actors are castigated for being drunken and lecherous, actresses are not spared for being untalented on-stage and given to venery off-stage. Managers starve their actors while pocketing the profits of the productions themselves. But for Vanbrugh he always had a warm word of praise.

In *The Pilgrim* Cibber was offered any part he chose, and being an instinctive actor he chose those of the Stuttering Cook and the Mad Englishman 'in which homely Characters I saw more matter for delight than those that might have a better pretence to be Aimable.' He had picked small vignette parts full of good material for laughs. 'To make up his mess' as he calls it, he was offered the epilogue. When Dryden heard him speak this he was rewarded by being asked to speak the Prologue as well, an unheard of honour. These verses were regarded as acting plums, and in them the actors had occasion to address their audiences directly and they must have had much of the instant appeal of a review number to their contemporary audiences.

On the printed page *The Pilgrim* seems a strange and curious melange of *As You Like It* combined with the Malvolio scene from *Twelfth Night*. But the revivals of the play were numerous, and it was played again and again throughout the eighteenth century. The last revival which is recorded was in 1788, when

Drury Lane was under Sheridan's management and Kemble played Pedro, still in Vanbrugh's version. There must have been a quality in the play which had an appeal for the actors and audience of the period.

Some time in January or early February 1702 *The False Friend*, another adaptation of Vanbrugh's, was produced. This showed his work to have been affected by the Puritan revival. For Vanbrugh, while he scoffed in private, and was half-hearted in his vindication of his plays, had not been entirely unaffected by the trend of opinion. He tried to temper his humour to the winds of prudery blowing about the stage, and with little effect, for the play does not seem to have succeeded.

The False Friend was originally a Spanish play translated into French. Vanbrugh worked from the French version, *Le Traitre Puni*, by Le Sage, which had been published at The Hague in 1700. Tonson, Vanbrugh's publisher friend, forerunner of many modern publishers, was constantly travelling in France and Holland in search of new publishing material, and it is presumed that it was through his recommendation that Vanbrugh adapted the play. Unfortunately plays which move from country to country, and from writer to writer, very often finish by having a used-up look about them. Like the local *vins du pays*, many of them do not travel well. The Spanish original obviously hinged on love, jealousy, and Spanish honour, but the plot, with its noble or traitorous gallants, sits uneasily in its English adaptation like a piece of carved Spanish furniture in a simple English cottage.

The prologue, which was spoken by Captain Griffin, an army officer turned actor, sets out the reasons why Vanbrugh attempted it.

> 'You dread Reformers of an Impious Age,
> You awful Catta-nine-Tales to the Stage,
> This once be Just, and in our Cause engage,
> To gain your Favour we your Rules Obey,

And treat you with a *Moral* Piece today;
So Moral, we're afraid 'twill damn the *Play*.'

This, of course, it did. This attempt of Vanbrugh's to temper his
humour to the prudes did not succeed. It is hard not to feel that
Vanbrugh did not take either the virtuous heroine, or any of her
assorted lovers very seriously. The play only comes to life, and
humour, when the various servants speak. Lopez, having failed
in his attempt to seduce the maid, rounds on her saying: 'Your
Maidenhead may chance to grow mouldy with your airs.'

The maid Jacinta gives some lusty advice to the timid lover.
'Your mistriss is now Marry'd Sir, consider that—she has
chang'd her Situation, and so must you your battery. Attack a
Maid Gently, a Wife Warmly, and be as Rugged with a
Widdow as you can.' This was a reflection of Vanbrugh's own
robust attitude. Equally well observed was the drunken servant
Galindo. 'I have been drinking, sir, tis true, but I am not *drunk*.
Every man that is *Drunk* has been *drinking*, but every Man that
has been drinking is not *Drunk*.' This point of view is marred by
his next reply. On being told to fetch lights, he answers 'I will—
if I can find the Door—'tis grown too little for me—shrunk this
wet weather I presume.'

In the first production Cibber played one of the lovers, Don
Guzman; Penkethman played the servant Lopez, and Bullock
played the drunken Galindo. Mrs Oldfield, in her first comedy
role, played Jacinta, maid to Leonora, the heroine, played by
the chaste Mrs Rogers.

The play seems to have run for only four performances, and,
unlike Vanbrugh's other plays, was not revived again for another eight years. All through the eighteenth century it seems
to have been revived from time to time for short runs. At the
end of the century Kemble adapted it and played in it with Miss
Farren and Miss Pope. It took cold with this adaptation and
finally perished. The play does seem never to have been performed again.

Virtue was only Vanbrugh's strong point when it was in danger.

After these brief excursions into nobility, Vanbrugh's next play was an altogether jollier affair. He left virtuous heroines behind to suffer, quite rightly, on their own, and adapted a play of Florent-Carton Dancourt called *La Maison de Campagne*.

Dancourt wrote over sixty plays, of which this was the fourth. It was shown in Paris for the first time in January 1688, and it is conjectured that Vanbrugh may have seen it on the French stage. It is always easier to judge a play for its comic effect from seeing it acted, than it is to weigh it up from cold print, and much simpler to adapt the action with confidence when it is known to work theatrically.

This time, although Vanbrugh left the setting as in France, the characters are firmly rooted in English soil. The father, Bernard the Paris lawyer, fits as incongruously into a hunting and shooting setting as he did in the French original. His swarms of monstrous relations and pretentious guests who batten on him and arrive at every point in the plot, are easily turned into their English equivalents. Although the plot has not been altered, and in many cases the dialogue has been followed closely, Vanbrugh added his own cheerful earthy humour to give the characters a human quality which sometimes they lack in the French version. He added other little touches. The lovers —about to be torn asunder—are told briskly by the maid: 'Lovers I can allow you but a short bout on't—one whisper, two Sighs, and a Kiss; Make haste I say.' The speech could well have been conceived from Vanbrugh's boredom with his previous virtuous heroines.

When Vanbrugh's version is compared with the French, the true and vivid feeling in his descriptions is brought out. In the French play the stag, which has broken into the garden to create misery and mayhem, is simply described as being out of breath. Vanbrugh's servant says the animal is 'puffing and blow-ing like a cow in labour'.

M. Bernard, plotting his revenge, says in the French version he may serve his tormentors a bad turn. Vanbrugh's Mr Barn-ard, on being asked what he is doing, remarks darkly: 'I'm conceiving, I shall bring forth presently.'

A cousin in the French play becomes in Vanbrugh's version, Charly, a country oaf with a simple, if earthy approach to the ladies. He remarks to the heroine that the handsome gentleman he had seen ogling her at church 'talk'd to me of you, and said you had the charmingest Bubbies, and every time he named 'em—Ha! says he, as if he had been supping hot Milk Tea' and adds 'Cousin, I swear you look very handsome today and *have* the prettiest Bubbies. There—do let me touch 'em.'

When comparing this version with the flat sentences in the French play, it is clear that Voltaire hardly exaggerated when he wrote that expressions and situations were used in English plays which remained veiled on the French stage. If the English version is vulgar, it has a vigorous life which it lacks in the French, and with deft descriptive touches Vanbrugh not only makes the characters come to life, but the landscape in which they move is painted in. These are people in a real country house, not characters in the plot of a play which happens to be set in the country. Charly was a stage forerunner of Tony Lumpkin.

Vanbrugh was the first playwright of his time to take comedy out of its metropolitan setting and see the humour to be gained from adding a Sir Tunbelly Clumsy and Miss Hoyden to the sophistications of Loveless and Berinthia. In the same way, there is no doubt that the characters in *The Country House* have mud on their boots, that the hounds are baying in their kennels, and the midden is not far away—although possibly Voltaire might have remarked that it was on the stage itself.

The Country House is a cheerful, lively farce, and it was acted for the first time at Drury Lane on the 23 January 1703 'at the desire of Several Persons of Quality'. The cast of *The Country House* is not known in detail, but it was played by the Drury Lane company. Possibly Cibber played Barnard, Dogget his brother, and Mrs Oldfield the young lady with the beautiful bubbies. Some two years later, when the play was given at the same theatre, the playbill stated 'The part of Madame Barnard in the Country House, which was originally performed by Mrs Verbruggen to be performed by her daughter Mrs Mountfort.' The latter was the daughter of the actor Mountfort, who had been murdered. The play, being short, did not fill out an evening's entertainment, and the first performance was advertised as being given with 'A Consort [sic] of Musick by the Best Masters with several entertainments of Dancing by Monsieur Ruel—lately arrived from the Opera in Paris.' The notice added that none were to be admitted but with printed Tickets, the total number being four hundred at five shillings a ticket. For the convenience of the Quality who supported the play, these tickets could be purchased in advance at various chocolate houses—White's, Tom's and Will's. But there was a final warning—no persons were to be admitted in Masks.

The warning was a reference to the new tightening up of the regulations governing the theatre. The daughters of the game and their followers, it was hoped, would melt away with the banning of masks.

It was obviously a difficult ban to enforce, for in the following year 1704 there was another decree from Queen Anne: 'Her Majesty has given particular orders that no plays be acted contrary to religion and good manners on pain of being silenced and that no woman wear a vizard in either of the theatres.'

Some contemporary writers regretted this ban. What interest was there in a woman who sat bare-faced in her box? Most theatregoers approved the banning of the vizards and it was welcomed by the actors, who had suffered many affronts and brawls because of a practice which had attracted the dregs of the town.

A Debauch in Piety

Vanbrugh's next new play was to be produced at a brand new theatre, built by himself and his friends at the Kit Cat Club. It was in this Club that all the threads of Vanbrugh's life were drawn together.

CHAPTER VI

Clubbable Fellows

Vanbrugh's was the age of the rise of the club. At the beginning of the reign of Queen Anne, clubs and societies began to form, sometimes with political backgrounds and sometimes for purely social reasons. They were, in their beginnings, places where men who were not necessarily social equals could meet on easy terms and discuss everything from politics to literature, art, architecture, or the fine points of the current toast of the town.

Vanbrugh's club, the Kit Cat, was one of the most famous of all, and is supposed to have grown up in a political context before the Glorious Revolution of 1688, and was formed of men of Whig principles who opposed both regal and papal interference with the affairs of Britain. Horace Walpole spoke of the Kit Cats as 'the patriots who saved Britain'. But other equally stout and patriotic gentlemen on the Tory side were inclined to see the Kit Cats as a posse of Whig noblemen bent on hobnobbing with authors in order to have at hand a number of hired brains who could be relied on to write propaganda pamphlets, or news sheets to put abroad their Whig principles. Though the Tories were to benefit exceedingly from their hired brains at a later date, for they included that incisive clergyman Dean Swift, and the scurrilous, if not pornographic pamphleteer Ned Ward.

John Oldmixon, a Whig historian, remarked that the club 'grew up from a private meeting of Mr Somers, afterwards Lord Chancellor, and another now in a very high station in the Law, and Mr Tonson, sen. the Bookseller, who, before the Revolution, met frequently in an evening at a Tavern, near Temple-Bar to unbend themselves after Business, and have a little free and chearful Conversation in those dangerous times.'

The club's name is variously attributed, but it seemed to have been named after an obscure pastry cook called Christopher Cat, who had a tavern in Shire Lane near Temple Bar. Cat's *spécialité de la maison* was mutton pies, and his skill in making them attracted the Whig gentlemen to his tavern. His pies were nicknamed kit-cats and the club took its name both from the pies and from the man. With the prospering of the pies, and the politics they represented, the Club transferred to Pall Mall, and in its latter days often met at Jacob Tonson's country house at Barn Elms, afterwards Ranelagh.

It was at Barn Elms that Tonson collected the forty-eight famous portraits of the members of the Club, building a room especially to receive them. Most of these portraits are now in the National Gallery in London; they were painted by Sir Godfrey Kneller, the German painter who, having studied in Italy, came over to England in the reign of Charles II. Like Marlborough, he managed to survive many changes of sovereign. He early deserted historical painting in the grand manner for portrait painting, saying that historical painters, however miraculous their powers in restoring the dead to life, never begin to live themselves until after their decease, but those who made the living the subjects of their pencils were kept alive by them. Kneller seems to have shared many of the reportedly scandalous traits of the other members of the Kit Cat, being described as having a fund of humour and quickness of repartee, although his views on religious topics were frequently 'gross and revolting'. He had no children by his wife 'so that his daughter, whose surname was Voss, would appear by a very natural conclusion, to have been the fruit of some licentious amour.'

Mr Caulfield, who wrote the history of the Kit Cat Club at the beginning of the nineteenth century, hints that there was

Meat and fruit by agreement 20ll
for the gentlemen that was not at the
great table, the musique, and the servants.. 1.5—

Claret 20 galons 5
Canarie 6 galons . . . . 2—8—
white wine 4 galons . . . . . . —16—
renish . . . . — 2—
champaigne . . . . — 2—6
bottle ale 42 bottles . . . . . . —10—6
fire . . . . — 5—
Coch hired . . . . —15—
Candels pipes and tabaco . . . . — 6—
sucre and lemons . . . . — 1—
glaces brocke . . . . — 4—6

                                    31ll 8—6

received height guinees   8—18—
                                    22—10—6

London ye 11ber 1669.
Received then of mr Barnwell mr Davenant
mr Offly or our Boulton the sume of
twenty pounds eighteen shillings in full of this
Bill and all other accounts due to men
                              Laurens Renaut

Conviviality at the Kit Cat—A wine bill for an evening's entertainment in 1669.

some collusion between the bookseller Tonson and the pie maker Cat, and that between them they managed to make a successful fusion of pies, politics and poetry.

There is small doubt that Tonson was one of the prime movers in the origin and development of the club, and by the year 1700 it had already achieved a certain prominence both politically and artistically. Tonson himself had begun humbly as an apprentice to a bookseller, but he speedily achieved financial and social success, first by buying a play of Dryden's, and then by acquiring the rights in *Paradise Lost*. It is not every day that a publisher manages to add both Dryden and Milton to his list. On these two outstandingly lucky strokes Tonson's fame and fortune were founded, and the Kit Cat Club extended his influence because here he was able to meet both authors and their patrons.

Jacob Tonson became Vanbrugh's lifelong friend. The letters from Vanbrugh to Tonson show a genial relationship between two men who enjoy one another's company. They shared a middle class origin and attitude, and in the company of the aristocrats who surrounded them they were able to enjoy a relaxed relationship founded on a common attitude towards business and pleasure.

The bookseller was a shrewd man, and although a good publisher he was considered to drive bargains which more often led to his own enrichment than to the benefit of his authors. Dryden conducted a bitter correspondence with Tonson, accusing him equally of underpaying him, or, when he was paid, of settling the accounts with debased silver. Tonson, on the other hand, seems to have bought Dryden's poems as if they had been so many pounds of sausages. He complained that he had been supplied with only 1,446 lines for fifty guineas when he had been led to expect 1,518 lines for forty guineas. This bourgeois carefulness about short weight angered the poet. A gift of two melons does not seem to have softened his heart for the insult.

The wits, lords, and fellow writers of the Kit Cat formed a perfect background for Vanbrugh. By the opening of the new century he was thirty-six, already had four plays produced and was beginning his architectural career. Fellow writers and architects seeking patrons might scratch out grovelling, subservient letters and prefaces, but Vanbrugh always seems to have been on terms of friendly intimacy with his male patrons. His Kit Cat portrait depicts a man with a clear, cynical but not entirely disillusioned eye. The sensual mouth is controlled. It is not the face of a man who acts without thought or reflection.

His plays mirror a detached and amused attitude towards women, but as no letters to mistresses appear to have survived, it must be supposed that he confined his amatory feelings to the spoken rather than the written word. This was less dangerous, and far less binding. He was obviously not a man who left women out of his life, but those whom he favoured remain enigmas; only the echo of their laughter, their tantrums, and their intrigues survives in his comedies.

Amongst the Kit Cats he had found a number of men who shared both his political views and his attitude to life. As far as women were concerned they were not all as circumspect as Vanbrugh, the second generation Englishman. But no doubt their affaires provided him with much food for thought and comedy. As his character Heartfree had remarked, he came to his knowledge of love 'from other people's expence'.

At the height of its fame, the club had forty-eight members, who were amongst the most illustrious men of the age. The writers, apart from Vanbrugh, included Richard Steele, Joseph Addison, and William Congreve. There were eight Dukes, a sitting of Earls, a clutch of Barons, and a few humble esquires. The members included famous soldiers like the Duke of Marlborough, politicians like Robert Walpole, as well as amateurs of art and architecture who were represented by the Earl of Burlington. The fine gentlemen of the Kit Cat Club often married the sisters and daughters of their fellow members, thus prudently keeping money and patronage in the hands of the right Whig families. Francis, Earl of Godolphin, married the Duke of Marlborough's daughter Henrietta and Mary Churchill married the Duke of Montagu. Both men were Kit-Catters.

Although the Kit Cats may have seen themselves as 'chearful' clubbable fellows, their opponents took a different view of the club's activities. It was said that 'if the Tories desired to blacklist the enemies of the Church and the Queen, the Kit Cat Club in the Pall Mall might furnish them with sufficient Heads for such an undertaking.'

The Kit Cats were suspected of subversion, drunkenness, blasphemy, dark political intrigue, and for good measure, atheism. Vanbrugh's reputation for satirising clergymen did nothing to help the club's reputation. His lighthearted view of the cloth was hardly the way contemporary clergy preferred to view themselves, in an age which was not far removed from Cromwell's. Their fulminations were serious, and they expected them to be taken seriously.

The anti-God and anti-Saints reputation of the Club was augmented by the 'open atheism' of Dr Samuel Garth which did nothing to dampen down the fires of suspicion towards the subversive ideas of the club's members. It is difficult not to sense the hypocrisy of the Tory attack on Dr Garth. He was a man in advance of his times, for he began a 'dispensary for the express purpose of affording relief to the indigent sick by giving them advice—gratis, and administering to them proper medecines at the lowest possible rates.' He was, in fact, a bright harbinger of the Health Service. For the free advice he incurred the fury of his fellow doctors, and the low rates of his medicines roused the ire of the Society of Apothecaries. There is no pleasing some sections of closed shops.

The free and easy atmosphere of the Kit Cat Club in which Vanbrugh's wit and friendliness flourished attracted the sharp eyes of envy. Ned Ward, a scurrilous, if not scatological Tory journalist wrote about the Kit Cats in his *Secret History of Clubs*.

In this he suggested that Tonson, having fed poor poets on wine and pies, was able to add their effusions to his publishing list at a low rate.

'He had,' said Ward, 'now nothing else to do, but to lay fresh Foundations for his young Artificers to build upon, and never to come empty, without some project in his Head that might have a probable tendency to his own Profit.' The idea of more successful writers hobnobbing with the nobility and gentry on terms of easy intimacy did not appeal to Ned Ward and the Grub Street fraternity.

But the Kit Cat was not all grandeur, glitter and wit, it was a microcosm of its age, for it included the notorious Lord Mohun. He could be said to represent the dark and violent streak which lay beneath the carving and gilding of the age. He was tried no less than three times for murder. Indicted with Lord Warwick for assassinating Captain Richard Coote, he was allowed to go free. Later, with a Captain Hill, he killed Mr Mountfort, husband of the actress Mrs Verbruggen who appeared in many of Vanbrugh's plays. The biographer of the Kit Cat Club remarked that 'it is certain that a less useful member of society or a more profligate and licentious character has never disgraced the peerage of England than this nobleman.'

Mohun on one occasion acted as a second in delivering a challenge for the Duke of Marlborough.

Sir Winston Churchill takes a less harsh view of the gentleman. Like many bad hats, he came to a violent end, being killed in a duel in Hyde Park in which seconds as well as principals fought. When the fight was over the Duke of Hamilton, elected Ambassador to France, lay dead on the ground and both seconds fled the country. Mohun's body was taken to his house in Soho, where it was said 'the only sensation his Lady is said to have felt on this occasion was the extreme displeasure that the bloody corpse of her husband should have been flung upon her best bed to the great detriment of its splendid counterpane.'

The Kit Cat Club, apart from a leaning towards Whig principles, does not seem to have had any particular rules, but aside from its addiction to mutton pies, another of its customs was the drinking of toasts to the beauties of the day.

When a belle was regularly chosen her name was written with a diamond on one of the Club's drinking glasses. 'The hieroglyphic of the diamond is to shew her that her value is imaginary; and that of the glass, to acquaint her that her condition is frail, and depends on the hand which holds her.' Vanbrugh's was an age when women depended for their power on the men they manipulated. Their frailty was both enjoyed and condemned.

Many of the Kit Cat's couplets must have seemed more brilliant after the first two bottles than they do in cold print. Like the verse written by the Earl of Halifax on Lady Mary Churchill, Marlborough's daughter:

'Fairest, latest of a beauteous race,
Blest with your parents' wit and her first blooming face;
Born with our liberties in William's reign,
Your eyes alone that liberty restrain.'

In spite of the indifference of some of their rhyming couplets, the custom of celebrating the beauties of the *beau monde* is redolent of Pope's Belinda in *The Rape of the Lock*: 'Fairest of mortals, thou distinguished care of thousand bright inhabitants of air!' The assembled gallants could have been toasting those 'eyes which must eclipse the day'.

In *The Tatler* it was recorded that the fortunate toast of the Kit Cats was chosen for a year by ballot 'much like the choice of a Doge in Venice'. When the year of her beauty and toasting had run its course, then she had to be re-elected. This custom of toasting is chronicled in the well-known rhyme about the Kit Cats:

'When deathless Kit-Cat took its name,
Few critics can unriddle;

Some say from pastry-cook it came,
And some from Cat and Fiddle.

From no trim beaus its name it boasts
Gray statesmen or green wits;
But from its pell-mell pack of toasts
Of old Cats and Young Kits.'

The youngest Kit of all who was toasted was Lady Mary
(later Wortley Montagu), daughter of Lord Kingston. Her
name being proposed by her father, it was objected by the
members that they could not elect a lady unless they had seen
her.

'"Then you shall see her" cried he, and in the gaiety of the
moment sent orders home to have her finely dressed and
brought to him at the Tavern . . . where her health was
drunk by everyone present and her name engraved upon a
drinking glass. She went from the lap of one poet, patriot or
statesman to the arms of another, was feasted with sweet-
meats, overwhelmed with caresses, and what pleased her
better than either heard her wit and beauty loudly extolled on
every side.'

A curious evening's entertainment for a child of eight.

Ned Ward, the Tory, takes a less cheerful view of these
goings on of old Cats and young Kits.

'Now every week the listening Town was charm'd with some
wonderful off-Spring of their teeming Noddles; and the fame
of the Kit Cat began to extent itself to the utmost limits of our
learned Metropolis; Not a Court Countess could compassion-
ate her love with the tenderest of her Favours; the young
buxom Wife of an old impotent Alderman be beholden to a
Courtier to make her sensible of the Difference between a
strenuous Sportsman and a crazy fumbler, a gouty Lord select
a jilting Mistress from that fruitful Nursery—the theatre, or
a noted Beau be cheated of an hundred guineas for a second-

6a. Colley Cibber (coloured plaster bust attributed to Roubillac, c. 1750; National Portrait Gallery)

b. Jeremy Collier (Mansell Collection)

a. Tonson

b. Congreve

c. Garth

d. Steele

(National Portrait Gallery)

hand maidenhead, but presently that pleasing adventure would be most notably handled by the Kit Cat Bards and sun down to Posterity.'

Ned Ward's views of the Club were naturally biassed, and it is generally thought that he added the Kit Cat and the Beef-steak to his list of so-called Clubs in order to add authenticity to a book which is scatological and seamy without achieving the merit of wit. His descriptive writings do give a view of London which is unique. In his views of London, the people in the streets, the taverns, the clubs, the brothels, the markets and the fairs of seventeenth and eighteenth century London live again. He was the first of the descriptive journalists.

While Vanbrugh moved in the upper ranks of the artistic world, Ned Ward clung to its lower reaches. Both were equally dependent upon patrons. Ward himself remarked:

'The condition of an Author is much like that of a strumpet, and if the Reason be required why we betake ourselves to so scandalous a Profession as Whoring or Pamphleteering, the same excusive answer will servie us both, viz. That the un-happy circumstances of a Narrow Fortune, hath forc'd us to do that for our Subsistence, which we are much ashamed of.'

Ward being a Tory, his financial success or failure was linked to that party, while Vanbrugh's Whig principles brought him, through the Kit Cat Club, into contact with those chosen and rich patriots, and patrons who had sinecures in their gift.

The lowly Ward was not without a certain sarcastic turn of phrase when it came to attacking the abuses of patronage. He dedicates his *Secret History of Clubs* 'To the Emperor of the Moon' and remarks that as far as he is concerned he feels that he will be as well assisted by the Moon, as by anyone else. 'What signifies a great man's bounty to the cringing author of a fulsome dedication if he proves a bad paymaster, or dancing attendance after the Quality who have nothing to be proud of but their ill-got Estates.'

Vanbrugh never wrote cringing dedications and was always on terms of familiarity with high, low and middling people. His relations with Tonson, unlike Dryden's, always remained cordial. Through his letters to publisher and patron alike his character is drawn in bold, easy strokes, like the dialogue in his plays.

There was, of course, good reason for the jealousy of lesser men for the authors and patrons who drank the toasts to the beauties and chatted politics over their mutton pies. In the age of patronage the Kit Cat was a venue where patrons could meet on easy terms of friendship with those good fellows of sound Whig principles whom they were prepar'd to help. Kissing went by favour as Vanbrugh remarked in *The Provok'd Wife*, publishing and emoluments for fellow Whigs were in the gift of the grandees. The authors and playwrights who joined the Kit Cat Club were not neglected and if a few sinecures could back up the meagre returns for writing books and plays, then the Whig patrons were happy to hand them to their friends. Nor did writers consider it incongruous to collect places like court cards from the pack, so long as they provided the necessary income. Congreve became in succession Commissioner for Hackney Coaches, Customer at Poole, Wine Licenser, Undersearcher of Customs at the Port of London, and Secretary to Jamaica. Richard Steele held, amongst other appointments, the Editorship of the Official Gazette, Commissioner of Stamps, Governor of the Royal Comedians, and Surveyor of the Royal Stables. Authors were not over nice in their acceptance of favours; they were prepared to survey or oversee anything from comedians to horses or pipes of port.

Vanbrugh did not collect as many sinecures as some Whigs, but through the patronage of Charles Howard, Earl of Carlisle, he was launched on another career, that of architect.

This new flowering of his talents began about the year 1699, as is apparent in the letter full of news and gossip which Vanbrugh wrote to the Earl of Manchester on Christmas Day 1699, when the plans for Castle Howard were already under discussion:

'I have been this Summer, at my Ld. Carlisle's and Seen most of the great houses in the North, as Ld Nottings: Duke of Leeds Chattesworth. I stay'd at Chattesworth four or five days the Duke being there. I shew'd him all my Ld. Carlisle's designs, which he said was quite another thing, than what he imagin'd from the Character yr. Ldship gave him on't. He absolutely aproved the whole design particularly the low Wings, which he said wou'd have an admirable effect without doors as well as within, being adorn'd with those Ornaments of Pillasters and Urns, wch. he never thought of, but concluded 'twas to be a plain low building like an orange house. There has been a great many Critics consulted upon its since, and no objection being made to't, the Stone is raising, and the Foundations will be laid in the Spring. The Modell is preparing in wood, wch. when done, is to travel to Kensington where the King's thoughts upon't are to be had.'

In an age of furious rebuilding after the fire of London, and furious re-planning of Elizabethan houses all over the country, as recorded by Celia Fiennes in her journeys. Continental influences were being brought to bear on English architecture, both from France and from Holland. Rich men took a minute interest not only in new design, but in the artistic theory behind it.

It has been stressed by some writers that Vanbrugh had had no training in architecture. Yet it is difficult to believe that he was able, as a first essay in building, to design a palace almost as large as St Paul's with no training or understanding of the principles of architecture. Colley Cibber, who was Vanbrugh's close collaborator in his theatrical projects, states quite firmly that Vanbrugh had studied architecture in France. It is reasonable to assume that Cibber had some evidence from Vanbrugh himself of his interest in, or training for architecture. Apart from his imprisonment in the Bastille, which would hardly have enlarged his architectural horizons, he had travelled for two years in France. It might be reasonable to suppose that he had studied the great hotels of the aristocracy in Paris, and the châteaux in the vicinity of Paris, or in the Loire valley. The grandiosity and size of Vanbrugh's designs have much in common with the huge masses of the Loire châteaux. At some angles the silhouettes of his complicated roofs have much in common with Chambord.

French culture was in the ascendant with the rise of Louis XIV to power and glory, and as Vanbrugh's plays were influenced by the writers of Gallic comedy, so his building ideas fell under the glittering spell of the Gallic age. Unlike other architects, and surprisingly perhaps in view of his Flemish blood, once he had decided to turn his hand to designing houses, they grew into palaces as backgrounds for the Whig grandees for whom he designed them. It might have been thought that the cosy *gemütlichkeit* of Dutch domestic architecture might have had the same appeal for him as it had for William and his Queen Mary. But Vanbrugh had the theatrical instinct, as had the grandees who patronised him. In his mind's eye he saw them sweeping along in their carriages into courtyards with a clatter of hooves, and a swift glimpse of gilded coronets on the panels of coaches. His houses were settings for grandeur and backcloths for sumptuous receptions.

Vanbrugh's versatility has in some senses diminished his reputation. Because he wrote good comedies his architectural ideas have been characterised as theatrical. Because he designed buildings his comedies were considered derivative.

Much of the architecture of the period was theatrical. Inigo Jones, the first of the English architects to study and adapt Italian ideas to an English landscape, began as a designer of Court Masques for James I and Charles I. These showed the operative influence of the Italians. It seemed as if the complications of the scene designers in Italy and subsequently in

England spilled over into real life. Very often it is difficult to differentiate between a design for a tragedy, a set for a comedy, a serious town plan or a design for a projected building. The airy fantasies of the stage designer had taken over from the sober practicalities of the builder, and literary taste was governing the look of houses, streets, and even cities. Each age cherishes some picture of itself and architects arise to give shape to their dreams, and form to their ideas of how life is to be seen.

Although 'Van's genius' was now turning to architecture in a big way, it was turning slowly. His other interests were still in play. In January 1701 *The False Friend* was acted at Drury Lane, and in the same year the foundation stone of Castle Howard was laid.

Talman was Lord Carlisle's first choice as a designer for Castle Howard. The plans were drawn, but later these led to disputes over payment and soon Talman's projected palace merely degenerated into a lawsuit. It was perhaps strange that Vanbrugh, a man with no architectural experience and no reputation, should have been chosen to replace him. But Vanbrugh's was, above all, an age of men with ideas and imagination, and the practical details were worked out as the building progressed. The clue to this change of architect and plan might lie in the fact that Talman was a difficult man. Sometime during 1689, when Wren was pressing ahead with Queen Mary's alterations to Hampton Court, part of the building collapsed, killing two of the workmen. Talman had given evidence against Wren, accusing him of negligence, presumably in an effort to exonerate himself. It was not a course of conduct likely to enhance William Talman's reputation, nor did it add to the ease of his collaboration with Wren, and he gave the great architect much trouble over the years in the re-building of Hampton Court.

Talman was the architect for the Duke of Devonshire at Chatsworth. When Sir Christopher Wren was His Majesty's Surveyor, Talman worked under him as Controller of the

Works. He was considered in his day to be the architectural equal of Wren, though obviously not his equal in equability of temperament.

In June 1702, a mere three months after he had been gazetted Captain in the Earl of Huntington's Regiment, Vanbrugh, through the good offices of his patron Lord Carlisle, then head of the Treasury, was made Controller of the Works in succession to Talman. Gradually through the friends and confrères at the Kit Cat the various threads of Vanbrugh's talents were drawn together.

No doubt Vanbrugh's appointment caused some jealousies. Appointments which are made from political moves invariably do, but in this case the appointment was fully justified by the artistic and practical work afterwards carried out by the great triumvirate of Wren, Vanbrugh and Hawksmoor, and their long continuing and friendly collaboration.

Although on paper Vanbrugh's appointment as Controller of Works may have seemed to be a piece of political jobbery brought about by his friendship with Lord Carlisle and his friends in the Kit Cat Club, Vanbrugh brought his many talents to bear on the problems in hand in a very down-to-earth way. It is perhaps relevant at this point in his career to sketch in Vanbrugh's character as an administrator, or what would today be called a business man.

With Sir Christopher Wren and Hawksmoor, Vanbrugh not only designed new buildings and restored and altered old ones, but he superintended all the practical details of building. They were concerned with drainage, water supplies, planning and altering the Royal gardens, designing and erecting scaffolds for royal weddings, coronations and funerals. Wren even designed a collapsible house for King William's Irish campaign, and '4 funnels on top of the House of Commons to lett out the heat', an amenity which might still prove useful.

The joint interests of the Board of Works were not solely concerned with fanciful designs, or with the imaginative use of façades, Corinthian orders and Italianate cupolas. They sat on boards and attended meetings in which every detail of public expenditure was considered from all angles, architectural, practical and monetary. There were no petty affairs, connected with the building or alteration of the public buildings, or houses with which Vanbrugh was connected in which he did not take an active and professional interest. The details of these meetings of the Board of Works read like the minutes of present day board meetings. The minutest practicalities were considered— sash windows, basso relievos, embossments, plant pots, and the elimination of box hedges, because Queen Anne, successor to King William, disliked the smell. Notes were made as to whether Mr Hawksmoor can see 'where he can have better bricks than those now served'. These men were not living in clouds of baroque magnificence; they made sure that if dreams were realised they were carried out at a reasonable price.

Vanbrugh may have given the impression that he was a wit, a boon companion, playwright, club man and gossip about town. He was all these, but he was also a serious and practical business man. The details of his dedicated work as Controller prove this, and give a very different impression of his character. These are the records of a man who took seriously any job he was given to do. It could be said that it takes a serious and intelligent man to make a witty joke.

But in spite of having three careers he remained the most cheerful and clubbable of fellows. In the same letter describing his designs for Castle Howard he was ever ready to amuse and to gossip. He concludes his letter to the Earl of Manchester, then Ambassador in Paris, by recounting that the Duchess of Leeds had been overturned in her coach. Some thought she was at the brink of death, but Vanbrugh adds that, unfortunately, she had recovered 'beyond expectation, to plague her husband, her son—and many others for some time longer.'

Van could turn from design to wit as easily as he had turned from soldiering to comedy.

CHAPTER VII

The Gilded Arches of
the Hay Market

The Kit Catters, as their unkind opponents called them, were not only staunch Whigs; they were also staunch supporters of the theatre, and of its leading lights. 'Tomorrow night [20 January 1700] Betterton acts Falstaff and to encourage that poor house the Kit Katters have taken one side box, and the Knights of the Toast the other.'

The 'Knights of the Toast' was another club which had connections with the Kit Cat. The club seems to have attended the theatre *en masse*. A contemporary description of a playhouse described some of the fashionable characters to be seen: 'The Lord Dorset is known by his Ribbon, and Tom D'Urfey, or some other Impertinent Poet, talking nonsense to him, the Lord Halifax by sitting on the Kit Cat Side, and Jacob Tonson standing doorkeeper for him.' From this passage it seems as if the Kit Katters had their regular boxes at the theatre.

The club had always included writers and playwrights, and in Vanbrugh's day 'club' had no specialised meaning, nor did it have a purely class background. As late as 1755 Dr Johnson defined the word as 'An assembly of good fellows meeting under certain conditions.' The club was a descendant of the coffee house, which had always been a very democratic mixture of trades, professions, fops, men of good sense, and men about town of no sense at all.

The good fellows of the Kit Cat Club decided to help Vanbrugh in a project which would combine his twin talents of writing and building. The building of a new theatre had become necessary for several reasons. When Vanbrugh began to write plays there were two companies acting under Royal Licence, the King's Company at Drury Lane, the patentees of which were Sir Thomas Skipwith (Vanbrugh's patron, and the original begetter of his plays) and Christopher Rich. The other company, the Duke's under Betterton's rule was at Lincoln's Inn Fields. In 1682 the competition between the two companies was in a fair way to ruin both. They then joined together in an uneasy partnership. Theatrical temperament and theatrical finances being what they were, and are, this fusion did not work. In 1685 the companies split up again.

Colley Cibber gives long and involved accounts of theatrical quarrels which descended to such details as to who should have the best of the new clothes in the plays. Powell, the gentleman who had become so drunk on the first night of *The Relapse* that he had nearly raped Mrs Rogers in full view of the audience, took particular objection to Cibber's fine clothes as Lord Foppington, remarking that he had not nearly such a fine suit—not even when he was playing Caesar Borgia. Cibber remarked acidly, and with pride in his own drawing power. 'He knew at the same time that Lord Foppington filled the house, when his bouncing Borgia would do little more than pay fiddles and candles to it.'

A further complication at the Theatre Royal, Drury Lane, was the attitude of Christopher Rich, who was not concerned with what appeared on the stage so long as the money fell happily into the box-keeper's and management's pockets. The theatre had taken to using turns which would not have disgraced a fair ground, knock about comics, high kicking ladies, and even performing animals of various sorts. He had even been drawn to the idea of a performing elephant as an extra attraction until his builder mentioned that it might possibly bring the house down in a more unpleasant way than the manager fondly anticipated.

Rich was also extraordinarily mean, and Cibber gives a sharp and well observ'd picture of his methods:

'Our good master was as sly a tyrant as ever was at the head of a theatre; for he gave the actors more liberty, and fewer days pay, than any of his predecessors. He would laugh with them over a bottle, and bite them in their bargains. He kept them poor, that they might not be able to rebel; and sometimes merry that they might not think of it. All their articles of agreement had a clause in them, that he was sure to creep out at.'

The reading of the fine print has always been a necessary exercise for the artist. Rich's general plan, according to Cibber was that when there were profits they went into the management's pocket, and the actors were kept on their fixed salaries, but when there were losses they came out of the actors' earnings.

There were other abuses in connection with money. Some sparks about town ran accounts with the box-keepers. 'What do gentlemen run on tick for plays?' one character asks in a play. The answer comes pat: 'As familiarly as with their tailors.'

With this system box-keepers, who were responsible for collecting the money, waxed fat on cheating both the customers and the actors. The extent of their depredations on the exchequer was made clear by an incident which concerned Cibber. He had given offence to some powerful political figures, and his theatre had been shut down as a result of this. Subsequently he was arrested and the damages put at £10,000, an immense fortune at a time when a girl with £5,000 was considered a good catch.

Two of the actors at the theatre, Booth and Wilks, were chatting over the misfortune, when Mr King, the box-keeper offered to stand bail for Cibber. 'Why you blockhead,' said Wilks, 'it is for ten thousand pounds.' 'I should be sorry,' said the box keeper smoothly, 'if I could not be answerable for twice that sum.'

The two actors were dumbfounded. Finally Booth said, with pardonable emotion, to Wilks, 'What have you and I been doing Bob all this time—a box keeper can buy us both!'

It is a heartfelt sentiment which has echoed down the centuries by actors, artists, writers and painters when speaking of their sponsors.

Between Christopher Rich charging the actors for losses, and the box-keeper's depredations, the actors occasionally became mutinous. Rich countered this either by lending them money or by threatening to sue them. 'No wonder we were dupes,' remarked Cibber bitterly about Rich, 'while our master was a lawyer.'

None of these mercenary accusations could have been applied to Vanbrugh, who on one occasion gave the profits of the third night to the actors. When the profits of a play at this time are considered, the salient point is that, although a run of a week or a fortnight was considered an outstanding success, the play was kept 'in stock' and revived again and again. It became in modern terms a 'standard', like a well played tune. Plays were changed daily. New plays were added to the old repertory, and authors would hope that their new and hopeful productions would achieve a run of three nights so that they would be entitled to a benefit. Runs of six or nine performances brought them greater profits, as well as the sale of the published play. It was in this sphere that Tonson was of the greatest financial help to Vanbrugh.

Although the actors at Drury Lane had manifestly suffered at the hands of Rich, Vanbrugh does not seem to have been entirely on their side, for when he came to write the second part of *Aesop*, which he added to the original play, which was acted at Drury Lane, the scene began with the entrance of Aesop and a number of players. Aesop asks them 'Good people who are all you?' They answer: 'We are all players, stage

Players, that's our calling. Tho' we play upon other things too; some of us play upon the Fiddle; some Play upon the Flute; we play upon one another, we play upon the Town, and we play upon the Patentees.' Aesop remarks that he was of the opinion that the patentees had lawful authority over the players. They reply: 'We are free born Englishmen, we care not for law, nor for Authority neither, when we are out of humour.'

It was perhaps natural that Vanbrugh should have been on the side of the sleeping partner, Sir Thomas Skipwith, his patron, who had lent him money and given him his first chance. But it could also be possible that he was tired of the petty backstage squabbles about fine coats and perriwigs. The surprising thing is that he managed, in his good-humoured way, to persuade the players to speak such words against themselves.

But when Vanbrugh had written *The Provok'd Wife*, in spite of his fair words in support of the Drury Lane Management, he had given the play to Betterton at Lincoln's Inn Fields.

There was no doubt that Drury Lane was descending in the artistic scale. Ned Ward in *The London Spy* remarked that there was no difference between a King's House Player, and a Country Stroller, and that Drury Lane had been turned into Bartholomew Fair. Nor did some of its players scorn to pick up a few shillings at the Fair itself. Tom Doggett, who acted in several of Vanbrugh's comedies, when his London reputation as a comedian was at its height, had a booth of his own at the Fair, and would come from Drury Lane to superintend its construction, and then appear among the swings, stalls and sideshows, and bellowing showmen in an old woman's petticoats and a red waistcoat.

This was the background to the idea for a new theatre. It was felt necessary to cut loose from the old traditions.

Cibber outlines the high hopes behind the new theatre.

'To recover them (the actors) their due Estimation a New

Project was form'd of building them a Stateley Theatre in the Hay-Market by Sir John Vanbrugh for which he raised a Subscription of thirty persons of Quality at one hundred Pounds each in Consideration wherefore every Subscriber for his own life was to be admitted to whatever Entertainment should be publickly perform'd there without farther payments for his entrance. Of this Theatre I saw the first Stone laid on which was inscribed "The Little Whig" in honour to a Lady of extraordinary beauty, then the celebrated Toast and Pride of that Party.'

At the time of the laying of the Foundation Stone the membership of the Kit Cat Club was about thirty members, and it would seem likely that the whole project had originated among the good fellows of the club. The little Whig mentioned by Cibber was the Countess of Sunderland, the daughter of the Duke of Marlborough.

The project went ahead. In July 1703 Vanbrugh wrote to his friend Tonson, then at the Stadthouse, Amsterdam, outlining his plans. He began by saying that there had been some warm weather at last and 'we remember'd you when we were sopping our Arses in the Fountain at Hampton Court'.

But he proceeded to more businesslike matters, saying that Williams (presumably the lawyer) had all the documents for the ground of the Playhouse engrossed.

'The ground is in the second Stable Yard going up the Hay-market. I give £2000 for it, but have lay'd such a Scheme of matters, that I shall be reimburs'd every penny of it, by the Spare Ground; but this is a secret lest they shou'd lay hold on't, to lower the Rent. I have drawn a design for the whole disposition of the inside, very different from any other House in being, but I have the good fortune to have it absolutely approved by all that have seen it.'

The nobility and gentry who were putting up the hundred

guineas, in return for the right of free entry, had to be consulted. The age of patronage had its priorities, the first of which was the patron.

The opponents of the Whigs took a more satiric view of this theatre which was to be larger, more grandiose and better run than the old theatres, and under the direction of those two brilliant playwrights, Congreve and Vanbrugh:
'New Hospital in the Hay-Market for the Cure of Folly. Subscriptions will be taken till Lady-day next at the Sign of the two left Legs, near Gray's Inn, Back Gate.' This was a reference to Tonson, who ran his publishing business from Gray's Inn.

In 1704 Royal patronage had been assured, and the Queen announced:

'Whereas, we have thought Fitt for the better reforming of the Abuses and Immorality of the stage That a New Company of Comedians should be Established for our Service, under Stricter Governmt. and Regulations than have been formerly. We therefore reposing especial Trust and confidence in our Trusty and Welbeloved John Vanbrugh & Willm. Congreve Esqs. for the due execution of this our Will and Pleasure, do give and grant power to Collect a company of players.'

There was to be a variation of the patent. In the new theatre, players were to be allowed to present any kind of play whatsoever, whether with music or without, which was a relaxation of warrants granted to the other two houses.

The Reformers, the awful cat-of-nine tails of the stage, were not pleased at the Queen's choice of these trusty and well-beloved esquires. In fact, they had been hunting them both down for some time. The Bishop of Gloucester orated in the House of Lords and demanded categorically that Vanbrugh should be punished for his lewd comedies. It was said that he had been saved from the Bishop's wrath by some 'agility' on the part of his friends. The friendly Vanbrugh could always rely on the good offices of others. As he said himself 'Good manners and soft words have brought many a difficult thing to pass.'

Having failing in their first attempt, the Reformers now turned their eyes higher in the ecclesiastical sphere. They decided to approach the Queen, as head of the Church of England by law established, through the medium of the Archbishop of Canterbury. The projected building of the theatre in the Hay Market gave their activities and their indignation added impetus. They had become outraged. It was astonishing, they said, that the management should be vested in 'Mr Vanbrook—the known character of which has very much alarm'd us.'

It was surely impossible, they went on, that the Queen whose virtue was so shining, and who had campaigned against immorality and profanity should act in so contrary a manner as to give the management of a stage—above all things—to 'that very Man who debauch'd it to a degree beyond the Looseness of all former Times. Tho' there be not one of his Comedies (as he calls them) but is more remarkable for Irreligion than for Wit and Humour, yet the Provok'd Wife is his masterpiece in both.' The scene of Sir John Brute dressed up as a clergyman mouthing foul oaths and improper suggestions still stuck in their clerical throats.

The churchmen were so delicate in their objections that they could not bring themselves to repeat any of Vanbrugh's jokes for the delectation of the Archbishop. They contented themselves with large sweeping generalisations

'The Most Abominable Obscene Expressions which so frequently occur in his Plays (as if the principal Design of which was to gratify the lewd and vicious part of the Audience and to corrupt the virtuously disposed) are in this black Collection wholly omitted. We are asham'd to disgust Your Grace's eyes with such Stuff that is not fit to Read.'

They concluded that Vanbrugh's plays were likely to be

prejudicial to Christianity, as well as to the morality of the whole nation, and that if the Queen knew the men she was recommending for this post her virtue and piety, they felt sure, would soon put a stop to their fears and apprehensions.

The Lord Archbishop of Canterbury, Tenison, who had pronounced a glowing funeral oration at the burial of Nell Gwynn, was hardly in a steady position on her catafalque to adopt a high moral tone on this point.

It was presumably about this time that Vanbrugh decided to shear his Provok'd Wife and temper its fleece to the cold winds of prudery blowing about the stage. He re-wrote the scene with Sir John Brute and made him dress up as a Lady of Quality, instead of a clergyman.

Congreve and Vanbrugh opened their brand new theatre in the Hay Market on Easter Monday, 9 April 1705, with Giacomo Greber's *The Loves of Ergasto*. The two playwrights had called their theatre The Queen's or the New Opera House, and it was here they proposed to foster the new and fashionable singers from Italy. They were amongst the first to sponsor Italian opera in England. Congreve wrote the epilogue to the opera, but 'the new set of singers arriv'd from Italy proved to be the worst that ever came from thence, and after three days being indifferently liked by the gentry—they in a little time marched back to their own country.'

The opponents of the Whigs were delighted at the debâcle:

'The Kit-Cat Club is now grown Famous and Notorious all over the Kingdom. And they have Built a Temple for their Dagon, the new Play-House in the Hay-Market. The Foundation was laid with great Solemnity by a Noble Babe of Grace, and over or under the Foundation stone is a plate of Silver on which is Graven *Kit Cat* on one side and *Little Whigg* on the other . . . There was such Zeal shew'd and all Purses open to carry on this Work, that it was almost as soon Finish'd as Begun.'

The prologue appears to have been written by Dr Garth, 'Chaplain to the Kit-Kat an Open and profess'd Enemy to all Religion.' One couplet ran:

> 'More sure Presages from these walls we find
> By Beauty founded and by Witt Designed.'

A note on a contemporary broadsheet identifies the 'beauty' as Lady Harriet Godolphin, the daughter of the Duke of Marlborough, who married Francis Godolphin. The 'witt' was presumably Vanbrugh.

That the failure was not entirely the fault of the Italian singers was perhaps proved by the fact that it seemed impossible to achieve a success in this theatre. It was much too large. Vanbrugh's grandiose ideas of vast triumphal pieces of architecture as a venue for singers and actors, and a splendid setting for the Quality watching them, had ignored the small details of theatre planning. 'What could their vast columns, their gilded cornices, their immoderate high roofs avail?' asked Cibber rhetorically, 'when scarce one word in ten could be distinctly heard in it?'

He went on to describe the interior of the theatre. A huge semi-oval arch sprang high over the orchestra, and the ceiling of the pit was too high. 'This extraordinary and superfluous space occasioned such an undulation from the voice of every actor, that generally what they said sounded like the gabbling of so many people in the lofty aisles of a cathedral. The tone of a trumpet, or the swell of an Eunuch's holding note, 'tis true might be sweetened by it.'

This mention of eunuchs was a reference to the seventeenth and eighteenth-century custom of using Italian castrati in opera.

Cibber was not the only bluff islander to take a denigratory view of the Italians. Betterton had equally harsh, John Bullish words to say on the same subject.

Defending the actors and the theatre against the Italians and their opera he said:

'But in our times the people of Figure who in Reason might have been expected to be the Guardians and Supporters of the noblest and most rational Diversion That Wit of Man can invent [the theatre] which at once instructs and transports the Soul—were the first, nay, I may say, the only people who conspir'd its Ruin, by prodigal Subscriptions for Squeaking Italians and Capring Monsieurs.'

Whether he held his good friend, Mr Vanbrook, responsible for this disastrous result is not clear. The audience was easily bored, and demanded more and more variety. Opera was only a part of this trend. Betterton despised the new medium; it might charm and flatter the ear, 'but if the Mind remain unsatisfy'd' the soul has nothing to feed on.

He went on with a further knock-down argument:

'There is another thing in Opera so contrary to Nature that it always shocks my Imagination and that is the *singing* the whole from one End to the other . . . Can any man persuade his imagination that a Master calls his Servant or sends him on an Errand *singing*? That politicians deliberate in Council *singing*? That orders in time of battle are given *singing*? And that men are melodiously kill'd with Sword, Pike or Musket.'

Opera, said the old actor, was 'a very odd medley of poetry and music in which the Poet and Master of Music take a great deal of pains to compose a very scurvy piece.' Betterton ended by roundly declaiming that if critics could distinguish between good and bad, they would soon have 'Plays more Worthy of the English genius and Operas would retire beyond the Alps.'

On the occasion of the opening of Vanbrugh's Opera House, Betterton's fond destructive hopes were realised. The Italians, like Hannibal's elephants, crossed the Alps. The echoes had silenced their voices.

John Downes, prompter at Lincoln's Inn Fields, who followed the company to the Hay Market, recorded the facts starkly:

'Upon the 9th April Captain Vantbrugg open'd his new Theatre in the Haymarket with a Foreign Opera perform'd by a new set of Singers, Arriv'd from Italy; (the worst that e're came from thence) for it lasted but 5 days, and they being lik'd indifferently by the Gentry; they in a little time marcht back to their own Country.'

Another difficulty was that, in choosing the Hay Market as a site for his splendid opera house, Vanbrugh was in advance of his time. The great squares of splendid town houses of the nobility, like Grosvenor Square, Cavendish Square and Hanover Square, had not yet been built. The theatre was surrounded by farms. 'So many green fields of pasture,' as Cibber sarcastically remarked, 'from whence they could draw little or no sustenance unless it were that of a milk diet.' Most people lived in the City and around the Strand, and the residents of these districts were no longer within walking distance of their entertainment. Coach hire affected the attendance of pit and gallery—for then, as always, the theatre could not rely for its bread and butter on the coach trade. Later, with the building development, the fashionable part of the town grew up around the theatre, and the Queen's Theatre in the Hay Market was in an excellent way to draw the town. But in both his fostering of the Italian Opera and his choice of a site for a theatre, Vanbrugh was imaginative but premature.

It was clear that neither the comedies of Congreve nor Vanbrugh had much chance in a theatre where the sounds of the actors speaking their lines were drowned by echoes and reverberations.

Undeterred by the disadvantages of his grandiose theatre, or the initial failure of the singing Italians, Vanbrugh produced his next play *The Confederacy*—sometimes billed as *The Confederacy of City Wives*—at his own theatre in the Hay Market. Even John Downes the prompter, disillusioned as he was by any play which did not fall into the category of being up to the standard of becoming a 'stock piece' approved of this play. He described it as 'an Excellent Witty Play, and all Parts very well acted: But the Nice Criticks Censure was, it wanted just Decorum which made it flag at last.'

This is a sparkling comedy which Vanbrugh, in his usual way, adapted, changed and re-shaped until it became as intrinsic a part of London as the cockneys of Covent Garden. The original by Dancourt was *Les Bourgeoises à la Mode*, played for the first time in Paris in November 1692. As this was the very month in which Vanbrugh was released from the Bastille, it is thought very probable that he saw it before leaving France. *Les Bourgeoises à la Mode* has no more theatrical merit than any of the dozens of comedies written by Dancourt, but if Vanbrugh had seen it, its visual appeal would have appealed to him as a comedy writer.

At the Queen's Theatre in the Hay Market on Tuesday, 30 October 1705,

'was presented a New Comedy call'd The Confederacy with several entertainments of dancing by the famous Monsieur Desbarques and others newly arriv'd from Paris. Boxes five Shillings. Pit three shillings. First Gallery. Two Shillings.

No money to be returned after the Curtain is drawn up. Beginning exactly at Five of the Clock.

By Her Majesty's Servants.
Vivat Regina.'

Vanbrugh followed Dancourt's plot, and in many cases, when it fitted into his plan, he translated the dialogue, but in his usual way he downgraded the social status of the characters. When the play is read, Gripe and Moneytrap, who were played by Dogget and Leigh, have the right feel of moneygrubbing scriveners, whereas M. Griffard (le Commissaire) and M. Simon, (le Notaire) seem to have less the smell of fusty offices and locked coffers about them. Doggett, who played Money-trap, adopted a grim humour for the part, wearing an old, threadbare, black coat on which he had put new cuffs, pockets and buttons to make it appear even more rusty. The neck of the coat was stuffed to make him appear round-shouldered from crouching over his accounts and to throw his head into great prominence, and his square plod shoes were enormous, to make his legs appear skinny by contrast. So large were these stage shoes that he could easily slip them on over his own walking shoes.

Dick Amlet, the scheming suitor to Gripe's daughter, Corinna, was played by Barton Booth. This was the beginning of Booth's success in the theatre, although he did not achieve the peak of his fame until he played Addison's Cato in 1713. Madame Amelin (*la Marchande de Modes*) becomes, under Vanbrugh's racy pen, Dick's mother, Mrs Amlet, 'a woman who sells paint and patches, iron bodices, false teeth and all sorts of things to the ladies.' Where the modiste says merely that she sold three pairs of hips to a Countess, Mrs Amlet is more specific in mentioning that she has a bill for 'bolstering up the Countess of Crump's left hip' and, in an aside, remarks of a letter she has been shown: 'A mighty civil letter—not one smutty word in it.'

It is strange to see that the old stage joke of the debtor paying the creditor by borrowing more money from him comes from Dancourt, via Vanbrugh, and is found later in Sheridan.

The plot hinges on the pretensions of two middle class wives who, in order to appear fashionable gamble away their husbands' money, and cuckold them in attempt to emulate the Quality. By a complicated intrigue the City wives encourage their husbands into mutual infidelity and the cross intrigue being discovered the scheming ladies end by being financially the better.

The original play is much enlivened by the characters of Dick and his mother, Mrs Amlet, the vendor of false hips and teeth. Vanbrugh not only adds new scenes, but amplifies mere suggestions. A chance remark about the boredom of a husband becomes: 'Husbands—little peeking, creeping, sneaking, stingy, covetous, cowardly, dirty cuckoldy things, mere dogs in the manger to starve gentlemen with good stomachs.' Underneath the good humour there are many sharp touches of Vanbrugh's observation of people: 'A usurer that parts with his purse gives sufficient proof of his sincerity.' Or 'Some folks we mistrust because we *don't* know them—others we mistrust because we *do* know them.' And the wife, Clarissa's classic observation: 'The want of a thing is perplexing enough—the possession of it is *intolerable.*'

When Dick threatens to run himself through, should his beloved Corinna reject him, the young lady is quick to see the social possibilities: 'Perhaps I mayn't always be in a *saving* humour—I'm sure if I'd let him stick himself, I shou'd have been envy'd by all the Great Ladies in the Town.' Then she remarks, maybe with Vanbrugh himself, 'A foolish girl may make a wise man's heart ache.'

In one exchange between the young men, Brass, who is pretending to be Dick's valet, complains bitterly that he has always played second fiddle to him all his life: 'In our sins too, I must own you still kept me under; you *soar'd* up to Adultery with our Mistress—while I was at Humble Fornication with the maid.'

Mrs Barry played Gripe's wife, Clarissa, and the dark eyed Mrs Bracegirdle played the pert maid Flippanta.

Although the large echoing theatre and the carping of the addicts for decorum had not achieved for *The Confederacy* the success it deserved, the play subsequently had a long history. It was played again and again at different theatres in Vanbrugh's day and continued to be played throughout the eighteenth century. Peg Woffington played Clarissa in the 1740s, Macklin played Brass, and later in the century, in Sheridan's day, Miss Pope (his Mrs Candour) played Flippanta, and Mrs Abington (his first Lady Teazle) played the ingenue Corinna. It continued to be played in Hazlitt's time and at different times throughout the nineteenth century. It is to be revived at the Chichester Festival, Sussex in May this year (1974). A good comedy, like a well tailored coat, has an enduring quality.

The echoing vaults of the opera house in the Hay Market appear to have discouraged Congreve. His discouragement was augmented by the fact that finances were not in a healthy state. Perhaps the Quality were not continuing to support their enthusiasm for the squawking Italians with drafts on their banks. Congreve discreetly withdrew, leaving the echoes and the lack of profits under the sole direction of Vanbrugh.

Congreve, who wrote slowly, and unlike Vanbrugh did not write one play 'fast upon the heels of another', was perhaps reluctant to have his wit wasted on the echoing vaults. Added to which he had always been inclined to overstress his status as a gentleman rather than a writer. He had astonished Voltaire by remarking that he hoped he was being visited as one gentleman visits another. Voltaire, who had a continental respect for literary fame, replied that if Congreve had had the misfortune to be *only* a gentleman, 'I would not have troubled to visit him,' and he added, 'I was shocked at such misplaced vanity.'

After Congreve's withdrawal it became apparent that the theatre had cost a great deal more than had been estimated. Vanbrugh had mistakenly added some of his own money to the project, on which he does not seem to have had any return. Defoe suggested that some of Vanbrugh's patrons had not in fact paid their promised subscriptions. There are few ventures into which money disappears so quickly as theatres, and where grand projects and optimistic ventures are not always matched by the receipts at the box office. Intellectually the English may have wished for opera, but it was no match for a good comedy, or a pantomime when it came to the money received by the box-keepers.

Possibly as a result of his other interests, Vanbrugh wrote no more original plays for his theatre. He contented himself with adaptations. 'He had,' commented Cibber, 'a happier talent of throwing the English spirit into his translation of French plays than any former author who had borrowed from them.' Swift, with less knowledge of the theatre and a talent for wit without good humour, accused Vanbrugh of plagiarism.

> 'So Van resolv'd to write a farce:
> And well perceiving wit was scarce
> With cunning that defect supplies
> Takes a French play as lawful prize
> Steals thence his plot and every joke.'

Careful comparison between the French play which Vanbrugh adapted and his cheerful transformation reveal a great deal about his temperament and his observation of contemporary characters of all classes. Swift's comments did less than justice to Vanbrugh's happy knack with a French play which was commended by Cibber.

Following *The Confederacy*, Vanbrugh adapted three of Molière's plays, *The Cuckold in Conceit* from *Le Cocu Imaginaire*, *Squire Trelooby* in which he collaborated with Congreve to adapt *Monsieur de Pourceaugnac*, and *The Mistake* from *Le Dépit Amoureux*. Even the prompter Downes approved of the last two. He referred to 'Trelooby wrote by Captain Vantbrugg, Mr Congreve and Mr Walsh, Mr Dogget acting Trelooby so well, the whole was highly Applauded. The Mistake also wrote by Captain Vantbrugg; a very diverting comedy, Witty and Good Humour in't.' But Downes added a warning note about the last play: 'will scarce be Enroll'd a Stock-play'.

The Mistake (*Le Depit Amoureux*) was the first play of Molière's to achieve fame for him when he was but a touring actor. It was produced at Béziers in 1656, and was the first of his plays to be seen in Paris in 1658.

Vanbrugh kept to the plot, but added his own racy dialogue, and even superimposed farcial touches of knockabout comedy which are not in the original play. The action, presumably for political reasons, was transferred from France to Spain, and

although the characters are tricked out with names such as Don
Lorenzo and Don Carlos, and the servants called Sancho and
Lopez, they could as easily be called Tom and Dick.

Where Molière's play begins with nicely turned Alexan-
drines Vanbrugh immediately plunges into a conversation
between the jealous lover and his cheerful, impudent servant
Sancho, a typical Vanbrugh creation.

The Mistake was acted under Vanbrugh's management at the
Queen's Theatre in the Hay Market on 27 December 1705,
Betterton playing the father Don Alvarez, and Barton Booth,
who had achieved his first success as Dick in *The Confederacy*
playing Don Carlos.

Booth was obviously a forerunner of the latter day matinée
idols, for he is described as:

'of a Form altogether graceful, accompanied with an Air that
gave the highest Dignity to all his Gestures. His face had a
manly Sweetness; and his features were so happily turned, as
to be able to express the roughest Passions, without losing any
thing of the Agreeableness of his Countenance. His voice had
a great Strength in it, and a tone uncommonly musical, his
articulation was so exceedingly distinct and clear, that he
could be heard to the farthest Part of the Theatre—even in a
whisper.'

No doubt he needed this clarity of diction at the Queen's
Theatre in the Hay Market.

The impudent servant was played by Dogget, that inspired
comedy actor who 'particularly delighted in catching the
manners of low life'. He seems to have carried a macabre humour into life, for when his landlady's maid cut her throat with
his razor, 'the news being brought to him behind the scenes,
Doggett with great concern and emotion cried out "Zounds I
hope it was not my best razor"!'

The prologue, written by Richard Steele, loosed satirical

shafts against the contemporary theatrical fashion for extravagant clothes:

> 'With Audiences compos'd of Belles and Beaux
> The first dramatick Rule is—have good Cloathes.'

In *The Mistake* Vanbrugh's dialogue seems more at home in the down-to-earth wit and comedy of the servants than with the sighing lovers with whom he seems to have had little patience. It was remarked that in French comedies the lovers were characters of a single dimension—they had little to do but sigh. The subtleties of different categories of sighing lovers needed to be speeded up, and a few kicks, cuffs and knockabout touches had to be added to liven up the pit. When the hero leaves his ring, watch and purse as mementoes to be given to his lady, the servant warns 'Pray leave a *little* something for our board wages.'

There are other typical comedy touches of the period when one of the ladies (dressed as a man) is forced into a duel with her secret husband. The impersonation is discovered, according to custom, by the falling of her periwig.

The Mistake was a moderate success and was not taken into the permanent repertory of the company. It was played throughout the eighteenth century on different occasions, Garrick acting Don Felix in 1772. In the 1790s Tom King (the original Sir Peter Teazle in *The School for Scandal*) adapted the play as *Lover's Quarrels*, and the last recorded acting of this adaptation was in 1794.

But both he and his fellow Kit Catters remained passionately interested in the theatre and the club's patronage was eagerly sought. D'Urfey dedicated one of his musical entertainments 'Wonders in the Sun or the Kingdom of the Birds', which was produced in 1706, to 'The Right Noble, Honourable and Ingenious Patrons of Poetry, Music & C. The Celebrated Society of the Kit Cat Club.'

The Mistake was the last full length play which Vanbrugh

either wrote or adapted. His multiplicity of talents, and the numerous patrons who supported them, aided by his generous witty and accommodating nature, were all gradually to draw him away from the theatre. As Steele wrote in his prologue to *The Mistake*:

'Thus all must own, our Author has done more
For your Delight, than ever Bard before.
His thoughts are still to raise your Pleasures fill'd
To write, Translate, to Blazon or to Build.'

Building was to occupy most of his time, although heraldry provided a pleasant sinecure.

CHAPTER VIII

Heralds Rampant

In 1703 *The Country House*, Vanbrugh's cheerful adaptation from Dancourt's *Maison de Campagne*, was acted at Drury Lane, and six months later Vanbrugh acquired the fourth of his many careers. He was made Carlisle Herald on 21 June. It was absolutely clear that this was a sinecure which had been engineered for Vanbrugh by his friend the third Earl of Carlisle. Nor does Vanbrugh himself make any great pretence that it was otherwise.

When writing to Jacob Tonson, then on one of his foreign book-buying journeys in Amsterdam, he says:

'Lord Carlisle went homeward yesterday, with wife and children, and made Lord Essex, Deputy Earl Marshall; to crown that, Harry St. George Garter, and me Herald Extra-ordinary (if the Queen pleases) in order to be Clarencieux at his return to towne; but whether we shall carry either point at Court, is not yet sure, tho' it stands home prest at this moment, and will I believe be known tonight.'

Clarenceux King of Arms was a much coveted place, and Vanbrugh's projected appointment to this office was very badly regarded at the College of Arms. His attitude towards heraldry had a touch of *légèreté*. He was thought to know little about arms-bearing families and to care even less. In fact, in his play *Aesop* he had satirised the so-called profession of geneaology. His geneaologist, Jacob Quaint, was a grovelling flatterer who comes to the hero Aesop and offers to do him some service for his forthcoming marriage. Would he perhaps like 'some good blood' put into his veins, if so Quaint was quite prepared to 'trundle' him back to Shem, Ham and Japhet, or if he preferred to Solomon, the Wise King of Judea.

These jokes against the truth, beauty and value of heraldry were not calculated to appeal to the College of Heralds. Nor did the heralds remain couchant. They attacked the appointment to the utmost of their powers, and to their last supporter.

Gregory King was Vanbrugh's main rival, and was at that time Lancaster Herald. He had begun as a humble clerk to Sir Thomas Dugdale, then Norroy King of Arms, and had learned to draw and paint coats of arms, hatchments, and to set out pedigrees. He was also genuinely learned and versed in the intricacies of tracing families and understanding pedigrees. King was at this time fifty-five and had passed thirty years in mastering the art of heraldry. His work had value, as at that time there were no public records, and most of the statistics of the period were based on the work of heralds, and the records of noble, or at the least landed, families.

King had been well trained to do much of the work about the Earl Marshal's Office, and had first obtained an official post when he had become Rouge Dragon in 1677. Unfortunately for King, although the title had an ancient and noble sound, the fees for the office were so small that he had to eke out his emoluments with the drawing, painting and engraving of coats of arms. He was, fortunately, 'a curious penman and well versed in politic arithmetic'.

Unfortunately for Vanbrugh, it was the custom that the appointment of a King of Arms must be given to a man who was already a herald, but this was easily overcome. Lord Carlisle decided to revive the ancient office of Carlisle Herald solely for the benefit of his friend and architect Vanbrugh.

The Heralds were duly incensed at this piece of political jobbery. King drew up a list of objections which he then presented to Queen Anne as 'a memorable petition'. This stated 'the just remonstrances and protests of the injured, superseded heralds'.

The protests of the superseded heralds were duly considered —and rejected. In March 1703 the Earl of Carlisle's influence prevailed, and Vanbrugh was installed on 29 March as Carlisle Herald Extraordinary. Noble, recording the History of the College, remarked that the heralds remained resentful at 'the slight put upon them in having a total Stranger made King-at-Arms; the more, because though Sir John had great abilities, yet he was totally ignorant of the profession of heraldry'.

In March 1704, though Vanbrugh had been made Carlisle Herald, the confirmation of the senior post had not yet been made, and the battle amongst the Dragons Rouge and Bluemantle was still raging. Right up to the time of final decision on the appointment of John Vanbrugh to the office, the Heralds were fighting a rearguard action. In some senses they objected to the appointment because it was a senior post, and also because it had been made by the Earl of Carlisle, who was only Earl Marshal because the Duke of Norfolk, hereditary holder of that office even today, was disqualified for the honour on two counts, firstly because he was under age, a fact which time would overcome, and secondly because he was a Roman Catholic, which only apostasy could remedy.

Another of Vanbrugh's opponents was John Anstis. Anstis had been born in Cornwall, and although suspected of Jacobite leanings (a heinous offence after the Glorious Revolution of 1688) was a man of learning and industry. He had, besides publishing papers on heraldry, also amassed a large and unique collection of manuscripts concerned with this subject. Stephen Leake, a Garter King of Arms writing later in the century, remarked that Anstis had married Elizabeth 'only daughter and heir of Richard Cudlip, of Tavistock a noted smugler [*sic*].' Although even Leake was compelled to admit that Anstis was a scholar in spite of his smuggling connections.

Incensed by the proposed appointment, Anstis decided to

attack on the distaff side. In March 1703 he wrote to the mother of the Duke of Norfolk about Vanbrugh in bitter terms:

'The Earl of Carlisle (having no pretence of other right than during my Lord Duke of Norfolk's minority) ought in justice as well as honour to promote such a person as is recommended by or at least may be acceptable to his Grace.

'The common discourse, or rather ridicule of the Town which may, I presume not only, surprise but justly displease you, 'tis generally talkt that one Vanborough, the designer and surveyor of the house his Lordship (Carlisle) is building has for some time had the promise of the place of Garter; his name speaks his Dutch Extraction whereby he is (if I am not mistaken) incapacitated by the Statutes.'

This was a piece of pious hope on Anstis' part. Vanbrugh's foreign extraction was not the only grievance; his religion, which is designated as that of a 'Quaker', is touched upon. Even his plays are dragged into the letter and on terms which would not have done discredit to his opponent Jeremy Collier. Possibly Anstis thought that a pious Roman Catholic lady would regard the combination of the Quaker religion and a penchant for bawdy jokes as being an unholy combination for a King of Arms.

'He (Vanbrugh), "went on Anstis," is the person who wrote that *Godly* play called The Provok'd Wife.' After complaining that Vanbrugh had no training for, or knowledge of geneaology he underlined the point by saying that heralds may not be born with the qualifications of a King of Arms, though playwrights may be, 'and therefore when the Court of Honour hath such opponents as were never known before, it cannot certainly be good policy to turn it into a Farce.'

He added that 'Vanborough' may possibly not be acceptable 'to the Government, or the College of Arms'. In this he was to be disappointed, and a great many dragons' scales were to be rubbed up the wrong way.

The point was carried. Patrons had a very powerful way with them in Vanbrugh's day.

In the month of July 1703 Vanbrugh wrote airily to his friend 'Mr Tonson at Mr Vatcks near the Stadthouse, Amsterdam' saying that the Lord Carlisle had stayed in town:

> 'a good while about our Heralds business. There was a good deal of Saucy Opposition, but my Lord Treasurer set the Queen right, and I have accordingly been Souc'd a Herald Extraordinary, in order to be a King at Winter (i.e. Claren-ceux King at Arms). Lord Essex was left Deputy to do the feat which he did with a whole Bowle of wine about my ears instead of half a Spoonful. He at the same time crown'd old Sir Harry, Garter, and King was on the Spot Suspended which the rest seeing, renounc'd him. Own'd he drew 'em into Rebellion and declar'd him a Son of a Whore.'

Sir Harry St George, whom Vanbrugh mentions in this letter as being Garter King of Arms, had been promoted over the head of Anstis. The latter's attempts to influence the Duchess of Norfolk in his own favour had not succeeded. He had insinuated himself into the confidence of the young Duke of Norfolk, and had foiled any suspicions of Jacobite tendencies by burning all his papers. Although he did admit that he had accepted a diamond ring from the Pretender 'as a mark of his esteem'.

Anstis does not appear to have been a very attractive personality in spite of his erudition. But he had time on his side and was less disappointed than he might have been at his failure to become Garter at this point. Sir Harry was old, being already seventy-seven at the time of his appointment to the office. Unfortunately for Anstis, old Sir Harry lived to enjoy the fruits of his appointment for a number of years and did not die until he was ninety. The longevity of the Garter Kings of Arms became a source of irritation to Anstis who thought it 'a very hard fate' that the last three holders of the office should be promoted in the 'dregs of their age'.

8a. Third Earl of Carlisle
(National Portrait Gallery)

b. *M. de Pourceaugnac*, Act I, Scene 8

It is not difficult to sympathise with the well-trained Gregory King, or with Anstis, when they saw Vanbrugh promoted to Clarenceux Herald. On the other hand Vanbrugh's attitude towards heraldry had a great deal of common sense at the back of it. Although heraldry was, and still is, a good way of tracing family and county histories, in Vanbrugh's day it had become intermingled with snobbery, chicanery and remunerative side lines for the heralds over the years.

After the Restoration, between 1661 and 1664, the College of Arms tried to get a bill passed 'for recording the matches and descents of the Nobility and Gentry of England, and for preventing usurpations of their armorial achievements.'

This bill was thrown out by the House of Lords, but the Heralds, who always displayed patience where their own influence and financial gain were concerned, continued on various occasions to try year after year to get the bill passed.

The Member of Parliament for Derbyshire wrote in his Journal in 1667 that the Heralds tried to get their bill passed in that year. It seemed, he remarked, merely a way of getting extra fees for their King of Arms, which it most certainly was.

They had developed various ways of making their offices pay. It had been the custom, after the Civil War, for the Heralds to make 'visitations' round the country to find out which families were genuinely entitled to bear arms, but as the number of families using coats of arms without any right was now so large it was proving 'a great task'.

Most of the gentlemen who wished to prove their undoubted gentility had to pay for the privilege of proving themselves 'armigerous' or entitled to use their coats of arms. But, as a gesture to the aftermath and devastation of the Civil War 'those who were ruined were not charged, and if any gentleman be decayed in his Estate so that he is not worth a Thousand pounds, it has been used to enter his descent and armes gratis.'

No doubt, were the gentlemen in question sufficiently decayed, they were probably not over-concerned with armorial bearings, a roof on one's house is always of more current value than a crest over the front door. Nor did all the country gentlemen take their armorial bearings as seriously as did the Kings of Arms, who were making money out of them.

An account of the visitation of Sir Edward Bysshe, a former holder of Vanbrugh's office of Clarenceux King of Arms, described how Sir Edward had arrived at the Crown Inn, near Carfax in Oxford.

'Few gentlemen appeared because at that time there was a horse race at Brackley. Such that came to him he entered if they pleased, if they did not enter, he was indifferent. Many looked on this as a trick to get money.' Others went so far as to suggest that he was selling pedigrees, as pardoners once sold indulgences. Later he admitted that he had fallen 'into some errours', but the only fraudulent pedigree which was proved against him seems to have been his own, a pardonable vanity. If a King of Arms cannot give himself a good set of ancestors there would appear to be little benefit in the office.

These visitations of the provinces to search for armigerous families gradually declined. The ruin of many families and fortunes had been caused by the Civil War, and the fabric of society had been split. But, as always in England, new people were making money and seeking gentility to set it off. Defoe wrote, 'the tradesmen of England, as they grow wealthy, come every day to the Herald's Office to search for coats-of-arms of their ancestors in order to paint them upon their coaches and engrave them upon their plate, embroider them on their furniture, or carve them on the pediments of their new houses.'

There were other benefits to which the College of Arms laid claim, such as the right to direct funerals and have the sole privilege of causing coats of arms to be painted on hatchments. Unfortunately for the Heralds, under James II the coffin makers had found a way of extending their business by arranging funerals and 'copying arms'. The Heralds took various of these tradesmen to court, including 'two painter stainers for painting false arms and marshalling a funeral'. The painting of arms appears to have been the sole monopoly of the College of Arms. Painter stainers were supposed to work under their licence. These two unfortunate men had obviously been slipping in a few illicit hatchments to pander to the snobberies of the rising city knights or their ladies, as Vanbrugh portrayed them in *The Confederacy of City Wives*.

These abuses were not easily put down. When there is a demand it is supplied. In 1707 a paper signed by Henry St George (Garter) and John Vanbrugh (Clarenceux) mentions amongst other irregularities the 'use of incorrect arms and the marshalling of funerals by painters and undertakers. The City of London and parts adjacent continually swarm with Hatchments publickly set over Houses upon the deaths of ignoble Persons.' Pandering to snobbery would always be profitable, but when it was not profitable to the College of Arms the Kings were against it.

Despite the grand and noble attitude which the Kings of Arms took towards their office, they were not above using it, not only as a means of income, but also of selling the office when they had no further use for it. Old Sir Harry St George was said to have bought the office of Garter from Lord Carlisle for £1,000. The wronged Gregory King had bought his place as Lancaster Herald for a mere £220. In view of these various abuses it is hard not to agree with Vanbrugh and his character Jacob Quaint 'that there's ne'er a Herald in all Asia shall put better Blood in your Veins than your Humble Servant.'

In spite of the ruffling of the Tabards, Vanbrugh's appointment was confirmed and he did become 'a King at Winter'.

He had from the beginning had a very off-hand attitude towards heraldry, and in a letter to Tonson said 'The coat of arms you mention—I'll send it to you.' Whether this was a coat of arms for Tonson or for some friend is difficult to know. But this casual mention of a coat-of-arms, as if it were a draft on a bank or a casual enclosure in the letter, gives a good idea of his general attitude towards his office and explains much about current patronage.

In spite of the Heralds' anger, Vanbrugh seems to have managed his office in a reasonable way, and once he had obtained his tabard there was no attempt to strip him of it, and he continued to enjoy the fruits of the office for many years.

While it is quite understandable that the Heralds should have been incensed by Vanbrugh's appointment to the office, it is equally hard not to be aware that many of the transactions of the Heralds did fall over into the farcical as well as the venal. Vanbrugh's airy attitude towards his noble office would seem to have had a certain justification.

Heraldry at its inception was merely a recognition signal, a way of distinguishing one baron's peasants from another's. In the days when men could neither read nor write, it was a way of demonstrating to opposing peasants that green dragons were on their side, while red bears were not. Crests were equally a recognition signal when knights were entirely cased in metal from head to foot. These emblems, which were of practical use at the beginning, later became a means of distinguishing noble families, and so they have come down to our own day as a charming and archaic decoration to life.

Unfortunately for the aggrandisement of the Heralds' influence as well as the successful lining of their pockets, during Vanbrugh's time at the College of Arms, there was a general decline in interest in the idea of nobility. Between December 1704 and December 1706 no solitary coat-of-arms was registered. The Glorious Revolution had instituted an era of social change and ended the visitations of the counties by the Heralds. The great Whig Lords found little of use to them in coats-of-arms. A decayed squire might possibly have a more ancient lineage than a recent earl. Supporters and escutcheons, however carefully recorded, did not interest them. The nobility of England in the early eighteenth century was strictly practical. Their power was vested in land and wealth not in quarterings.

There seems to be little doubt that the heralds took their office more seriously than 'the Town'. Swift, in a reference to Vanbrugh's securing the sinecure of his office at the College of Arms, merely remarked 'Now Van can build houses.'

If Gregory King had lost his chance of Office, Anstis was to continue his subterranean intrigues.

Vanbrugh was installed as Clarenceux King of Arms on 29 March 1704. Some two years later, in April 1706, it was decided to confer the Order of the Garter on George Augustus, Prince Electoral of Brunswick-Luneberg, afterwards to be George II. It had become more and more obvious that Queen Anne was unlikely to bear healthy children. Her only surviving son was a weakly child who was to die two years later. It had been decided to honour the son of the heir apparent to the British throne.

Old Sir Harry St George, who was over eighty at this time, was judged to be too infirm to withstand jolting across the continent in an uncomfortable travelling coach. Or, if he were to arrive in reasonable health, to be too frail to undertake the long and arduous ceremonies connected with the conferring of the order on the Prince. As Clarenceux, Vanbrugh was chosen to deputise for Sir Harry. His fluent French, then the language of the European courts, his easy manners as well as his knowledge and liking for foreign life, made him an excellent choice for a diplomatic mission.

It was perhaps just as well that the intriguant Anstis had not achieved his ambition to be Garter at this juncture. His appearance would hardly have made him an attractive envoy.

'Mr Anstis was of a just proportion and middle size, but of a swarthy complexion, a great sloven and so begrimed with snuff that he was often taken for a Jew; a down look hardly ever looking at any person in the face, tripping along with little steps in a very particular manner; and of a fawning sheepish address, for want of the Accomplishments of a gentleman which were as necessary in his station as the greater qualifications.'

The Court of Hanover had had a lucky escape.

Vanbrugh had his instructions from Queen Anne who, writing under her sign Manual at Kensington the 23th [*sic*] of April 1706, instructed 'her trusty and well beloved John Vanbrugh Esq one of our Kings at Arms that the investiture is to be made in some room of state in that Prince's Court. It is left to you whether to make the presenting and putting on the George and Garter a distinct particular act, or whether to do it on the same day and the same time as the putting on the surcoat, but it must precede it.'

The descriptions of the ceremonies, and comings and goings which preceded them, were given by one Samuel Stebbing writing from Hanover on 10 June (New Style). It paints a neat picture of the stiff etiquette of the small German electoral court. The Elector was not anxious that his son should be over-honoured during the ceremonies. He also refused to conduct the ceremonies himself which, as a Knight of the Garter, he would have been entitled to do. Kings and Princes are not normally over-fond of their heirs, who seem living proofs of their own mortality.

If the Elector of Hanover and his Court were anxious to meet and to honour these envoys of the Kingdom over which he was to rule, the envoys, Lord Halifax and Vanbrugh, were equally anxious that the Whig faction should be able to initiate their influence with a future king.

As described by Mr Stebbing the 'curtailed' ceremonies seem to modern ears to be protracted. They stretched out over several days. On the evening of 6 June John Vanbrugh arrived from England bearing with him a large trunk which contained the habit, ensigns, and the diamond George and collar of the Garter. The following day 'my Lord Halifax and the said Mr Vanbrugh, who were appointed the Sovereign's Commissioners

for this solemnity delivered a copy of their credential letter to
the Baron de Goertz.'

The Baron was the Elector's President of the Council, and
Minister of State, and at this solemn presentation of their
credentials, the Lord Halifax and the well-beloved John Vanbrugh, Esq. humbly asked an audience. At which point the
Elector sent a message to say that he did not propose to undertake the ceremonies and the envoys could carry them out. This
was only a preliminary skirmish. There were then various pieces
of protocol to be decided. The number of coaches to be used
while coming and going from town to palace had great significance. It was decided that the English envoys merited the
highest number. Mr Stebbing records, with pride, that two
coaches with six horses each, and six coaches, with two horses
each, were used to conduct the Commissioners to their audience.
This took place on 11 June, three days after Vanbrugh's arrival.
The great decisions about who was to receive whom, and in
how many coaches, and in what manner, had taken three days
to conclude. These were weighty matters.

Once the Commissioners and their followers were in their
coaches they were conducted with due ceremony by Baron de
Grooten, the Prince's Chamberlain and several other digni-
taries of the Electoral Court to the Elector's Palace at Herrenhausen in Hanover. The grandeur of the baroque palace of
Herrenhausen, with its complicated formal 'parc', fountains,
rotundas, garden 'theatre', and parterres laid out in the geo-
metrical French style must have appealed to Vanbrugh's sense
of the theatrical. Old pictures of Herrenhausen show it with an
entrance gateway of great magnificence, much like the design
given in *Vitruvius Britannicus* for Castle Howard. But Vanbrugh's formal entrance and courtyard to Castle Howard were
never built and that of Herrenhausen was destroyed with the
rest of the château in the last war.

Mr Stebbing's account continued: 'Being arrived within the
inner court of the Castle the Commissioners alighted and were

received at the foot of the great stairs by Mons. de Hardenburgh.' De Hardenburgh is designated as *Schloss Hausman* (or
Housekeeper of the Court, officiating as Hoff Marshall). He
was presumably a sort of Court Chamberlain, for he seemed to
have a number of officers of the Court under him. The picture
presented of the petty officers of the German court in their stiff
brocaded clothes and wigs, the bows—carefully regulated according to the rank of the court official—and the rigid etiquette
to be followed on pain of social solecism, gives the idea of a
strange minuet, the steps of which have been pre-ordained by
a gentleman dancing master.

Several days had elapsed, and the English envoys had only
advanced as far as the Grand Staircase.

'At the head of the stairs they were saluted by Baron Goertz
from whence they proceeded through the Gallery to the
Prince Electoral's Apartment, at the entrance whereof they
were received by his Highness's Principal Officers and conducted to the Ante-Chamber where the company falling off
on each hand made a lane for the Commissioners to pass
through the chamber where his Highness staid to receive
them.'

They had achieved the Presence.

Alone with the Prince Electoral at last, Lord Halifax made
a short speech, and presented his letter from Queen Anne. Vanbrugh likewise said a very few well chosen words and gave the
Prince the Book of the Statutes of the Order. At this point there
were further pieces of ceremonial to be observed. Vanbrugh
withdrew to the ante-chamber, put on his mantle, and came
back into the Presence, carrying the 'blew Ribbon Garter and
George', which the Prince then was graciously pleased to
accept, in token of which he was equally graciously pleased
to place his plump leg on a footstool. The Lord Halifax and
John Vanbrugh Esq. both then tied the Garter round the Royal
Leg, Mr Vanbrugh reading the 'proper admonition'. How he

managed to read the admonition while tying on the Garter is
not quite clear. The Prince then signalled that he would receive
the diamond George, which was duly put into his hand while
another admonition was read. The Diamond George was 'put
about his Neck. viz. over his left shoulder and under his right
Arm, which done, they took leave of His Hs.'

At this point they were able to meet Madame the Electrice,
the two Princesses, Duke Ernest August, younger brother to
the Elector, and as a final and glittering climax to this their
first visit, they were ushered into the presence of the Elector
himself, the future George I. He had apparently been adopting the attitude that the investing of his son was beneath his
dignity as Elector, but all in a day's work for the English
envoys.

Mr Stebbing does record that the day ended with hospitality
for the Commissioners 'dind [*sic*] with the Electoral family and
about five in the afternoon were re-conducted to My Lord
Halifax lodgings in the same manner as they were carried to
court.' This meant that they were allotted the same number of
carriages, horses, and court officials to accompany them. The
eighteenth century obviously paid great attention to these
dignities which added lustre to the status of their country, and
paid due honour not only to their office but to themselves.

This was only, as it were, a preliminary canter. His Royal
Highness had merely signified that he was graciously pleased
to run an Electoral eye over the Commissioners' credentials,
and to signify that he would be pleased to accept the honours
of the order at a later date. According to Mr Stebbing, Sunday
13 June was appointed for the 'solemn ceremony', and six
o'clock in the evening was the appointed hour. Baron de
Grooten set out again (with the same number of horses and the
required number of coaches), arrived at Lord Halifax's lodging
to escort Vanbrugh and Lord Halifax once more to the Castle.
Here Vanbrugh put on his official mantle, and the two Englishmen were immediately conducted to his Highness' ante-

chamber. Here they found the great gentlemen. A great deal of dressing and undressing then followed. Firstly, Vanbrugh and Lord Halifax took off the 'Blew Ribbon and George' which they had put on previously. He was then divested of his Upper-coat and finally of his sword and belt. The newer and more splendid surcoat and sword of the order having been previously arranged on a table, Vanbrugh handed the surcoat to Lord Halifax, and the two men solemnly put it on for the Prince. They once again buckled on his sword and belt, and finally put on the 'Blew' Ribbon and Diamond George again. During all this divesting and re-divesting various admonitions were read, and finally his gracious Highness signed the certificate which was duly sealed.

That was the first stage. Vanbrugh had apparently arranged the rest of the insignia in the Prince's room on a velvet cushion the three men then proceeded in solemn procession towards this insignia. Here Mr Stebbing himself seems to have taken a part in the proceedings, because in his account he added that when the cushion was 'taken up' by Vanbrugh 'myself bearing one part thereof'.

The whole party then made their way to the Great Room where the actual ceremony was to be performed. Here the whole Electoral family, who were listed as before—Madame the Electrice, the two Electoral princesses, and Prince Ernest August—had seated themselves. They were attended by a great number of persons of Quality of both sexes, not to mention Foreign Ministers, as well as Ministers and Officers of the Court. Only the Elector himself was missing.

The procession filed between the bowing courtiers to the upper end of the room, where a large 'armed' chair was placed for his Highness. Vanbrugh and Lord Halifax were also hon-oured by two similar 'armed' chairs. The account continued 'His Highness and the Commissioners having a while exposed themselves in their chairs' the ceremonies began.

The three men then stood up and more reading and passing

of documents took place. Lord Halifax made a speech and Vanbrugh presented Halifax with the document which enrolled the Prince in the Order. Lord Halifax gave the document to the Prince, who immediately passed it to his secretary to read out. The Prince then sat down and put his Royal Leg on a 'couple of high Cusheons placed for that purpose'. Vanbrugh and Halifax then began undressing the Prince again, taking off his Blew Ribbon Garter, and in its place buckling the diamond garter about the Royal Left Leg. Once he was on his feet again the Blew Ribbon George was taken off, and he was dressed again with the mantle, hood and afterwards with the Great Collar and George.

Vanbrugh, during all this dressing and buckling, was reading out various admonitions appropriate to each piece of equipment. The Prince was again given the Book of Statutes, and finally he was handed the Cap and Feathers. It need hardly be said that all this gracious acceptance and preliminary nodding and bowing was window dressing. The Prince had already had his cap and feather 'enricht with diamonds'.

Once the Prince had his rich diamond cap on his head, Vanbrugh made a speech suitable to the occasion, supposedly in French, the language of polite court circles. The ceremonies were concluded by Vanbrugh presenting the Prince with the two Glories or Stars and two pieces of Ribbon of the Order. At this point his Highness was graciously pleased to sit down, and the two Commissioners were relieved to be able to do the same. All the company bowed, and the Prince and the Englishmen processed solemnly from the Great Room back to the Ante-Chamber. 'His Highness—en passant—receiving the compliments of the whole Court upon his Investiture.' The ceremonies were then concluded. The Prince thanked the Commissioners saying 'how highly sensible he was of the great Honour Her Majesty had done him in sending him the Order and that he should make it his Endeavour on all occasion to Improve himself in Her Majesty's favour and esteem.'

As Queen Anne disapproved of Germans succeeding to the British throne this was a pious hope. The Germans were Protestant, and that was their only claim to favour in the Queen's eyes. She had on several occasions refused to let them visit her in England.

The Commissioners were then allowed to be conducted to their lodgings for an hour's respite. The coaches waited at their door and re-conveyed them to the Elector's ball.

Mr Stebbing, a practical gentleman, added that they had been eating at the Elector's table since their first audience, and even more important, their retinue were likewise 'treated at the Elector's charge'. They had, added Stebbing, been treated as Ambassadors which would seem to indicate that Ambassadors in our own day have been lacking in certain honours due to their status.

Various other Englishmen seem to have taken this opportunity to participate in the Garter celebrations. The Earl of Dorset had travelled with Lord Halifax, and the usual gentlemen of quality were 'also being honourbly treated'. My Lord Dorset was lodged in the same house as Lord Halifax. The Whigs were taking advantage of the junkettings to ingratiate themselves with the future Royal family. Political capital can always be made out of social occasions.

It is difficult not to imagine that Vanbrugh himself, while enjoying the comings and goings by Royal coach, the bright eyes of the ladies around the Electoral table, must have found the divesting and investing of the Royal Leg a subject for comedy. On the other hand, he had achieved a certain status for himself, and in a continental setting his best qualities were of practical use.

The whole incident ended like a comedy of Shakespeare's with a fanfare of trumpets for the betrothal of the Elector's daughter Dorothy Sophie to the Prince Royal of Prussia. Salutes of guns announced the news, and a grand ball was given in honour of the union. The King of Prussia arrived, and because of this illustrious visitor the English party were not received for their official audience of leave. This did not seem to have dismayed them, for the whole party, and the other gentlemen of quality stayed another three weeks in Hanover enjoying the festivities. In Vanbrugh's day there was always time for social occasions, and if the English contingent were anxious to make the acquaintance and foster the friendship of the Elector's family, the Germans were equally anxious to penetrate the higher echelons of the English aristocracy.

There was no doubt that as things had developed with the College of Heralds, the social flair and panache of Vanbrugh, with his fluent knowledge of the French language, were of far more use at the German Court than a sound knowledge of geneaology. Whether the third Earl of Carlisle had envisaged such a royal occasion is doubtful. It had merely been a simple way of awarding his architect an extra income. There was little difference between Vanbrugh being a King of Arms, and Congreve sole director of Hackney Carriages.

CHAPTER IX

The Palaces Begin to Rise

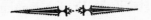

Vanbrugh ran his careers like a team of mettlesome horses. He had been made Clarenceux King of Arms on 29 March 1704. The following day *Squire Trelooby* was acted at the theatre in Lincoln's Inn Fields. This was the adaptation by Congreve and Vanbrugh of *Monsieur de Pourceaugnac* by Molière. The cast of the play is not known, nor does this joint effort of the two playwrights appear to have been published or to have survived.

But already architecture was gaining in favour on Vanbrugh's other careers, which he used as a means of supporting his main interest. Through the Kit Cat Club he was at the centre of Whig influences, and possibly the complications of theatre finance, and the inflated egos of theatrical personalities had palled.

It is very difficult to get an idea of how playwrights made money out of the theatre in Vanbrugh's day. In some cases, when impoverished, they sold their plays outright, which meant that they either had to get a very good price for them or rely on the sale of copies of the printed play for their reward. There does seem to have been some suggestion that as a participator in the theatre revenue Vanbrugh had some other financial stake in his plays, although as far as the theatre in the Hay Market was concerned this had turned to his disadvantage. In view of the currently depressed state of the theatres in London, and the internecine warfare which rumbled on between them, it was not surprising that he was attracted to a career which seemed on the surface to present grander and easier possibilities.

As Sir Thomas Skipwith had helped to foster Vanbrugh's career in the theatre, the Earl of Carlisle was instrumental in promoting his architectural talents. In June 1702, when Vanbrugh was appointed Controller at the Board of Works, his patron, Lord Carlisle, was at the Treasury. It was not surprising if the family had a 'whiggish' tendency, for Lord Carlisle's grandfather had been of Cromwell's faction during the Civil War and had sat in the House of Lords under the Commonwealth. Somehow he managed to sail over his past misdemeanours and was restored to favour at the Restoration, being made Earl of Carlisle in 1661. The Kit-Cat portrait of him shows a young man of plumply arrogant demeanour, but how far this was an artist's view of the ideal aristocrat and how much it depicts the real man is hard to discern.

Vanbrugh's patron, Charles Howard, became third Earl of Carlisle in 1692 at the age of twenty-three. In this same year Vanbrugh was 'clapt up' in the Bastille by le Roi Soleil. Lord Carlisle was said to be a gentleman of great interest in the country 'very zealous for its welfare; hath a fine estate and a very good understanding; with very grand department, is of a middle stature and fair complexion.'

The Earl was thirty years old when he engaged Vanbrugh to build his palace for him. The original house was Henderskelfe Castle, a name of Saxon or Viking origin, and had stood on a tableland surrounded by its church and dependencies. There had been a new house built on this ground in 1683, but it had burned down. The outcome of this unlucky accident was that the Earl decided to build himself a new and splendid palace as a setting for his own grandeur, and for this project he had chosen Vanbrugh's design.

The plans for the castle obviously ante-dated Lord Carlisle's appointing his architect as Controller of Works, for Vanbrugh was already writing about the practical details of the building plans to his patron sometime in 1700 or 1701.

'My Lord,

'I am got no farther than Tadcaster yet. My Lord Burlington carrying me away with him to Lanesborough. I wish't I cou'd possibly have stay'd there till Tuesday, that I might have seen your Lordship and known whether you are come to an agreement with the Mason and Carpenter. I talk'd a great deal to 'em both, the morning I came away; but found 'em very unwilling to come to any abatement. They made a world of protestations of its being impossible without letting the work pay for't: they say'd they believ'd your Ldship might expect some abatement from their proposal as a matter of course; but Mr. Hawksmoor had persuaded 'em to make no provision for that, but to make the lowest offer they cou'd possibly work for—and do it well.'

Builders were ever free with fair promises which they decline to put down on fair paper.

Vanbrugh, practical and always willing to choose the *via media*, had discussed the matter with Hawksmoor, and the two men had come to the conclusion that if the builders were compelled to reduce their prices still further it might give them 'a loophole to play the Rogue'. In other words, it was better to pay them their full price and to be in a position to insist on work of the utmost excellence. In the same letter he dots the i's and crosses the t's of the financial arrangements for Hawksmoor. He suggested 'forty pound a year Sallary and fifty each journey which amounts to £100 clear' and adds that he hopes that Hawksmoor will deserve it, and that 'all will go to yr. Lordships Sattisfaction, for I shou'd be very sorry to have meddled in anything which shou'd do otherwise.' He ended by saying that he would be at Chester for at least a week where he could be reached at Mr Samuell Taylor's. Possibly Vanbrugh was visiting old friends or his family in the town where he had been brought up.

This is the first mention of Vanbrugh's collaboration with

Hawksmoor. A great deal has been written about this partnership, some of it calculated to destroy Vanbrugh's reputation. All architectural projects, like all theatrical projects are the result of collaboration. The playwright needs his actors, his producers, and his scene designers, and an architect similarly needs his team of practical men. In modern times the architect needs numerous technical assistants. In Vanbrugh's day, although the engineering problems were less complicated, for their buildings were conceived (fortunately for their inheritors) more in artistic than in practical terms. But they still needed their technical assistants to translate the airy dreams into the practical realities of brick and stone.

Hawksmoor was a good choice as a collaborator, for he had been working under Wren since 1679. In age which did not concern itself with specialisation, Hawksmoor seems to have fulfilled many of the duties of a quantity surveyor as well as amplifying or altering his collaborators' designs, or designing himself. Hawksmoor chronicled his own beginnings: 'I had the favour to serve under Sir Christopher Wren in the rebuilding of the churches, the Cathedral Church of St Pauls, London and many other fabricks both Private and Publick, for which service Sir Christopher Wren appointed me Clerk of the Works at the King's House at Kensington.' In much the same way, Vanbrugh had appointed him clerk of the works at Castle Howard.

Hawksmoor and Vanbrugh worked in close association for more than twenty years, and although some architectural critics have put forward the theory that Hawksmoor could do without Vanbrugh a great deal more easily than Vanbrugh could do without Hawksmoor, this leaves out the vital spark of imagination which conceived the plans. Architecture had not yet become a combination of science, engineering, and design. It was a subject for learned dilettantes who could study foreign books and foreign designs. Another Sir John, Sir John Denham, who was appointed Surveyor General by Charles II, had been in turn playwright, poet, law student and diplomat. Careers were interchangeable in Vanbrugh's day. A man of many parts could be chosen to play any part. There was no hard and fast line between one profession and another. Wren could turn from mathematics and astronomy to architecture, and Newton from science to theology. Inigo Jones began with stage designs as Vanbrugh had begun with stage plays. The playwright often sees in his mind's eye the set for hit comedy or tragedy, and at a double birth he hears the actors speaking his imagined lines in his imagined setting. So Vanbrugh conceived his grand palaces as settings for his gentlemen of quality.

The modern tourist often surveys with wonder the immense distances of Vanbrugh's interiors. The huge halls, the grand staircases, the vast galleries, and the dramatic vistas. These were not designed as cosy little homes, they were backgrounds to splendour, or if architecture is the expression of the soul, as challenges to kingly authority. When the Norman barons dominated the Saxon peasant they built castles to intimidate. When the Church was dominant it built monasteries and Cathedrals to prove the point. In the eighteenth century the Whig noblemen built their palaces as a proof of their power.

Castle Howard was the first of Vanbrugh's palaces. But although it was the first of his buildings, he continued to help its progress towards the ideal till the very end of his life. It spanned and encompassed the whole of his architectural career. It was, perhaps, the ideal to which he gave the most time and its owner and only begetter was the patron whom he served for the longest time.

Lord Carlisle and Vanbrugh became close friends and correspondents, and they always remained so, which is a tribute to their good nature and to their parallel views on art and architecture. It is not often that architect and patron remain in harmony over a period of more than twenty years. Nearly every summer Vanbrugh was to travel up to Yorkshire for refreshment, repose and friendly discussion of the progress of his palace.

146

By the spring of 1701 Hawksmoor was well at work and writing from Yorkshire: 'I find the work at Henderscelf to go on with vigour and great industry although there is not so much done as I expected by this time, but the impediment has been by the backward season which has much obstructed it. I am come in time enough to regulate some errours and difficultys the workmen were going into.' Over the centuries the delays in building are always the same, nor do the excuses vary. Hawksmoor goes on to say that they have had other difficulties with the site chosen by his Lordship, which has entailed levelling, and 'makeing our access to ye great facade and principall Courts'.

It is easy, when looking at a finished work of architecture to forget, in the wonder and glory of its site, the troubles entailed by its choice. Vanbrugh's sites were always chosen to take advantage of some distant view, or stretch of landscape which would enhance the massive baroque of his palaces.

There are different interpretations of the baroque style (the word comes from *barrocco*, a term for a misshapen pearl used by Portuguese fishermen). The men who lived during the Baroque age did not use the word, and the age of the baroque was felt to be merely a decadent manifestation of Renaissance art. Architecture has always been a fluid art; one idea suggests another, and it is only long after the creators and the builders are dead that art historians are able to trace the influences on their work. Artists, who work instinctively, are often unaware of the strands from which their art is woven.

The influences which pressed on architecture in Vanbrugh's day were the large scale grandeur of the French and the triumphant building of successive Popes who became rich patrons of the arts, culminating in the work of Gian Lorenzo Bernini, the dominating exponent of the dramatic in church building. Every kind of art was called in to emphasise the glory of the church— painting, sculpture, and the carved masses of the façades of the churches, made them seem like operatic arias in stone.

The grey shades of the Reformation had been forgotten. Perhaps in the same sense the English baroque sprang out of the mists of puritanism. Many of the country houses planned by Vanbrugh and his followers used carvings, frescoes, bas reliefs, and dramatic interiors. To walk into a Vanbrugh hall gives much the same impression as walking into an Italian church, except that Vanbrugh's art has a strength and virility of feeling which is sometimes obscured by over-decoration in the Italian manifestations.

In Europe baroque art lasted for nearly a hundred years until about 1780, when it was elaborated into decorative rococo. In England, where architecture has always been simpler and more masculine, the patrons turned first to the strict rules of the Palladian under the influence of Burlington, Kent and the Adam brothers. Then finally, towards the end of the eighteenth century, the modish taste was for the 'Gothick', which lingered on into the Victorian age. Some art historians find a foreshadowing of the gothic fancy in some of Vanbrugh's work.

During Vanbrugh's lifetime his ideas of building were gradually superseded by the strict followers of Lord Burlington, who were inclined to denigrate the baroque as being out of line with strict classicism. Yet Vanbrugh himself was writing to his friend Tonson, who was as usual travelling abroad in Holland: 'The book you mention wch. I wanted, you'll oblige me to get. Tis Palladio in French, with the Plans of most of the Houses he built, there is one without the Plans, but' tis that with 'em I could have.'

Whatever the strict followers of Lord Burlington may have had to say about Vanbrugh's designs, he was obviously not averse to being influenced by the classicism of their god. Palladio (Andrea di Pietro della Gondola) was given this classical name by his patron, the Count Trissino. He lived and worked in Italy in the sixteenth century, yet his ideas eddied into England, and because they fitted in with the feelings of the classicists of eighteenth century England, Palladio's was one of the most potent and enduring influences on art forms of that century. Many of the close adherents of Palladio's classical forms had, like Vanbrugh, never visited Italy. Yet through books and the cross pollination of ideas the forms spread from Europe, much as, later in the eighteenth century, the pattern books for furniture spread the ideas of Hepplewhite and Chippendale across England.

In 1703 Vanbrugh was writing cheerfully to Tonson that he had nearly 200 men at work, that a new quarry had been discovered 'much better than the old one, so all go's on smooth'.

All the stone for the house was quarried on the estate from pits within the boundary of the park, while the limestone used for paving and courtyards came from another quarry in the vicinity. It was, perhaps, because of this use of local stone and the dramatic choice of their settings, that the country houses of the period, even those on a grandiose scale harmonised in colour with their surroundings.

It was in this same year that Vanbrugh had begun his grand Opera house in the Hay Market. In the summer of the year his careers were running neck and neck, and he himself was verging on forty years old and in the full vigour of his ideas. His gusto for life comes over most vividly in his letters to Tonson about the rebuilding of Tonson's house at Barn Elms:

'Every room is chips up to your chin. They han't been at work you must know this fortnight: There's a great deal done however—one week's sticking to't will fit it for the reception of a King: my room is finish'd and a bed in it. The compass window below and above is made, but the shashes [sic] are not yet up; both rooms are ten times the better for't.'

Even the vegetable garden causes his enthusiasm to spill over, like a cornucopia for a harvest festival:

'Neighbour Burgess has been too honest; the pease and beans ly all languishing upon the earth; not a cod had been gathered.

There will be a hundred thousand apricocks ripe in ten days; they are now fairer and forwarder than what I saw at the Queen's table at Windsor on Sunday—and such strawberrys as never were tasted: currants red as blood too; and gooseberrys, peaches, pairs, apples and plumbs to gripe the gutts of a nation.'

He complains in genial terms about Sir Godfrey Kneller, who was commissioned to paint the portraits of all the members of the Kit Cat Club. 'The fool has got a country house near Hampton Court and is so busy about fitting it up (to receive nobody) that there is no getting him to work.'

A month later he again refers to Sir Godfrey's house, and remarks that he is 'eternally there; he has reduc'd that in Towne to a lodging to save Charges. We shall get nothing finish'd there till you come; The Kit Catt too, will never meet without you, so you see here's a general Stagnation for want of you.'

He writes all the current gossip to his travelling friend. Lord Essex is at Cashiobury with his friend Jack Dormer, who has kept him company 'by the help of Di Kirk who has been there as long'. There may be a possibility of marriage, 'what if he should but into the Candle too at last.'

That old prig Sir Stephen Fox 'has tack'd himself to a young Wench of Twenty. She was a Parson's Daughter and a Parson managed the match, a young dog, a Smirk, who I suppose has agreed with her how matters are to be—when Widdowhood comes.' This letter is the essence of a comedy, with the old duped husband and the smirking lecherous parson ready to claim both bride and heritage. There may be something afoot between Lord Hartford and Lady Mary Churchill (daughter of Marlborough).

There follows a cheerfully cynical account of Lord Wharton's illness. How he had prepared himself to die, acted the hero, 'took formal leave of them all', charg'd his son to respect his mother, showed tenderness and regard to Madam, explaining that he had left the guardianship of his son to her 'only during her Widdowhood, he being fearfull that if she marry'd again— it might prove to his prejudice.' Even on his death bed Lord Wharton did not forget his politics, or his voters. All the principal burgesses of Aylesbury were shaken by the hand 'by his usual Treatment of honest Tom, Dick and so forth bid 'em farewell— and Stick firm to their Principles.' After this, thanks to the ministrations of the ubiquitous Dr Garth, he recovered. The letter ended with a commission from a Mrs Roach, who hoped that Tonson will not forget her Flanders lace.

Every letter draws a picture of a man who is interested in everything. Politics, how the carpenters are getting on at Barn Elms, whether Mrs Roach will get her lace for collars. Yet he was a man of strict practicality and took his post as Controller of the Works with down to earth good sense.

The first official building with which Vanbrugh is believed to be associated after he had been appointed to the Board of Works was Greenwich Hospital. The Hospital had, like many state or royal projects, a long and protracted history. Charles II built a small country palace there, when that other Sir John, Sir John Denham, was Royal Surveyor. As he knew nothing about either surveying in particular or architecture in general, he needed professional help, and employed Inigo Jones' pupil, John Webb, to do the actual work. When Dutch William came to the throne, he and Queen Mary were more interested in enlarging Hampton Court and building Kensington Palace, so the work lapsed.

After the battle of La Hogue in 1692, the seamen wounded in the fight were sent home and inhumanly lodged in insanitary hulks on the Thames. Queen Mary (Anne's elder sister) heard about this and proposed to build a hospital for seamen in much the same manner as Charles II had built Chelsea Hospital for old soldiers. Little was done in Queen Mary's lifetime, but after her early death from smallpox at the age of thirty-four King William began to think again of her charitable project. He

reproached himself that nothing had been planned for the seamen's retreat. Wren submitted the designs and the work commenced. Sir Christopher gained nothing from his effort, as he
gave his work freely to this charity.

The funds were raised in most curious and exotic ways.
There was a duty of sixpence on every marine, which could
perhaps be said to be a social insurance against being disabled.
A state lottery produced another £600. The King himself subscribed £2,000 a year and a grant of land. But the most curious
subscriber of all was the pirate Captain Kidd.

Captain Kidd seems, like many characters of the seventeenth
century, to have had a certain ambivalence about his career.
He had been given instructions to suppress piracy and was
supplied with a small ship of war. He had a special 'letter of
marque' which enabled him to seize pirates whom he should
meet sailing about the seas near the coast of America, or elsewhere. He set sail from Plymouth in a ship called the *Adventure*
and picked up a crew in New York. Immediately he sailed for
Madagascar and was gone for some three years. Reports
filtered back that, so far from capturing pirates, he had decided
that commercial prospects were far better in the piracy business
than in helping the Admiralty. Orders were sent out that he was
to be apprehended if he returned to America, which he did in
July 1699 and was immediately thrown into gaol.

There is no doubt that, whatever Kidd may or may not have
done in the form of piracy, he did not receive a fair trial. The
evidence was insufficient. Kidd himself alleged that the ships
he had taken had been French ships and therefore lawful prize
according to the articles of war. Two of Kidd's crew turned
King's Evidence, and Kidd was hanged in the Execution Dock
in 1701. His effects were declared forfeit to the Crown and sold
for £6,472 and one shilling, a small fortune at that date. It was
perhaps only poetic justice that mayhem on the high seas should
have helped to pay for a refuge for aged and infirm seamen.

Once the building project was decided on, the hospital then

proceeded at a rapid rate and with constantly changing architects. Wren, who was now very old, was succeeded by Hawksmoor, and he in his turn was followed by Vanbrugh, and
Vanbrugh was followed by Colin Campbell, the author of *Vitruvius Britannicus*. When the different hands and brains which had
planned and built Greenwich Hospital are considered, it says
much for the taste of the seventeenth and eighteenth centuries
that building carried on over so many years should have
achieved a pleasing artistic harmony of thought and feeling.

Greenwich Hospital, although it had been the idea of Queen
Mary, was carried on by Queen Anne, who in spite of her dis-
agreements with her sister Mary in her lifetime was quite prepared to foster her charitable intentions after her death. Anne,
who had always suffered from bad health herself, may perhaps
have had a tender thought for others reduced in health. Or the
start of a new war may have pushed the plans for wounded
seamen forward.

It has been thought probable that the plan for completing the
hospital which was produced in 1702 shows the influence of
Vanbrugh on the designs. A new and grandiose feeling entered
the plan, for he never thought on a small scale.

The year when Vanbrugh joined the Board of Works, 1702,
was also the year of the accession of Queen Anne, who although
a Stuart was a pious Protestant. She favoured the Tory or, as
she called it, 'the Church' party.

In Queen Anne's day, kissing hands at court produced substantial favours, and these favours descended all down the line,
so that even architectural projects could be affected by a
change of ministry. Sir Christopher Wren was generally con-
ceded to be a moderate Tory. Sidney Lord Godolphin, also a
moderate, was Treasurer, equivalent to Prime Minister.

The Duke of Marlborough had been made Captain-General
of the Army; his politics were ambiguous. But the Duke's lady,
Sarah, was a dedicated Whig and had most of the Court
appointments under her hand.

Although the Ministry was moderately Tory, there was no opposition to Vanbrugh's appointment, although he was a well-known Whig. Wren probably thought him a pleasant change from the ever-intriguing Talman. To an old man there would be nothing sweeter than a man of easy temperament as a working partner.

Sir Christopher had, in the increasing weight of his years, become lax when dealing with his masons. The Board of Works was engaged in the building of what was called the 'greenhouse' at Kensington Palace. This was the orangery, and in the usual way of many royal or government contracts at the time, a certain amount of money was sticking to various fingers. Vanbrugh, perhaps because of his Puritan upbringing, was taking this seriously.

The trouble stemmed from one Benjamin Jackson, the Master Mason, who was employed merely to oversee the work, but not to act as a contractor or use his own workman.

Laurence Whistler, who found new evidence of Vanbrugh's rivalry with Talman, has suggested that his stern views of Jackson stemmed from the fact that Jackson was Talman's 'creature'. On the other hand, Vanbrugh was later to write equal strictures about a workman at Blenheim.

Vanbrugh wrote about 'those very officers doing the Work themselves, who rec'd Sallarys from the Queen to prevent her being imposed on by others.' Sir Christopher was quite prepared to admit that this was an abuse; there was only one slight difficulty. While the building was going on the workmen were not paid, and Jackson, presumably by reason of the abuses, was able to finance himself and keep the job going. He was a formidable watchdog to his own interests, for he had managed to dissuade anyone else from working on the site.

Vanbrugh had an official letter from Lord Godolphin stating in express terms that 'for the future no such thing should be suffered directly or indirectly'.

'Upon this I desir'd Sr. Chr. there might immediately be

another mason got to work at Kensington upon the New Greenhouse; but recommend none to him, leaving that entirely to himself.'

Jackson recommended one Hill, but after a few days this Hill was not to be seen about his stone mason's business. Vanbrugh enquired the reason for this and it turned out that he 'had been frightened with some hints of what shou'd befall him if he durst meddle with the Master Mason's business.'

The Trade Union idea of seeing that strange craftsmen leave the site is not a new practice.

Vanbrugh then went back to Sir Christopher to enquire why 'one Hill' had not started work, and the old man replied that this Hill was a strange whimsical man who would not start work 'until he had consulted the Starrs, which probably he had not found favourably enclin'd upon this occasion.'

An old man's quiet joke is to be suspected. Vanbrugh was not disposed to see the funny side on this occasion, and suggested that someone less superstitious should be employed, and having set down his view, Vanbrugh left for Yorkshire to stay with his friend Lord Carlisle.

When he came back he found that Jackson still had his men at work, although the bills were being presented in the name of the new mason Palmer.

'I ask'd him' wrote Vanbrugh, 'if he had forgot your Lordship's letter, and all that had past on this subject. He said no; but Jackson wou'd not be quiet without he let him do the work.' It was one way of staying in business.

Vanbrugh puts the record straight by writing that Sir Christopher had not the least financial interest in the business:

'But your Lordship will see by this decisive proof the power that those Fellows have over him wch. they never made so effectual a use of as when they prevail'd with him to let 'em have a clerk of the Works of Whitehall, whom he himself own'd but a week before he cou'd put no trust in; one who by nature is a very poor Wretch; and by a many years regular Course of morning Drunckennesses had made himself a dos'd Sott. Yet this man, My Lord, is by his place entrusted with the whole measurements; and he is our Sole Voucher for the Quantity of all Works done at St James's, Whitehall and Westminster so that 'tis very probable the Workmen put in their Bills what Quantitys they pleased, for he's One that (by all appearances) they can either perswade or deceive.'

Jackson and his workmen obviously had managed to make a little niche for themselves in the building world of Westminster, Kensington and St James's, and, like Rich at Drury Lane, were adepts at the art of nook building.

While asking His Lordship's pardon for the freedom of his expression Vanbrugh concludes by an incisive thumb-nail sketch of the Master Mason.

'As for Jackson, my Lord, besides this Crime the highest nature of his Office will admit of, I must acquaint your L'dship He is so Villainous a Fellow and so scandalous in every part of his Character: and that in the unanimous opinion of all Sorts of People he is known to; that he is indeed a disgrace to the Queen's Service and to everybody that is oblig'd to be concern'd with him.'

Unfortunately the schemes of controllers and architects are in the hands of masons and carpenters. Fifteen years later the villainous Jackson was still using his own workmen, and presumably still had a 'creature' to survey his accounts. There are some people who, like the ivy, cling to buildings and are not easily detached.

CHAPTER X

It Was a Famous Victory

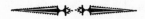

Vanbrugh's fortunes were to be closely linked with the fortunes of the Marlboroughs. For good—and ill. In the summer of 1704, on 2 August (Old Style), Marlborough had shattered the glory of the French King by defeating his armies at Blenheim and preventing the fall of Vienna.

The victory created a state of euphoria at home and abroad. Marlborough's enemies, who had been cavilling and carping at foreign adventures, were silenced by the brilliance of the victory.

It is presumed that it was through the Kit Cat that Vanbrugh met the Duke of Marlborough before he had achieved world fame. As Blenheim was afterwards to become the crowning achievement of Vanbrugh's ideas on architecture, the relationship between these two men is interesting and important.

The pictures of the Duke of Marlborough whether they are on the staircase at Marlborough House, in stately homes or museums, invariably portray him at the height of his career as a famous general, immaculately clad, pointing out some distant objective to his interested and admiring followers. It all seems so easy when history has already been written by achievement. But Marlborough's career had its less tasteful sides.

Living in a dangerous age, and relying as he had to do on royal favours, he was, like others of his time, not above turning his coat with reasonable regularity.

Sir Winston Chruchill skates delicately over the murkier sides of his illustrious ancestor's early career, but it is often instructive to turn to writers of the opposition who do not burn candles to his memory.

The splendidly sarcastic Mr Caulfield, who at the beginning of the nineteenth century wrote the history of the Kit Cat Club, takes a less noble view of the great Marlbrouck. His book commences with an elegant piece of purple prose:

> 'There is no object in the natural world so picturesque as a lofty mountain seen from an imposing distance; its summit bright with the purest rays, and soaring above all the neighbouring hills in the majesty of inaccessible grandeur. Clouds, indeed, may envelop its might base, storms, and tempest rage around it, but still "Eternal sunshine settles on its head."'

This, says Mr Caulfield, is the manner in which John Churchill, Duke of Marlborough, had been contemplated.

It did not take the writer more than a couple of paragraphs to gallop through Marlborough's splendour before taking up the 'torch of history' so that it shed its penetrating light upon less creditable parts of Marlborough's private life. 'We shall,' says Mr Caulfield, find our admiration of his unrivalled talents is chequered 'with surprise and indignation.'

He then launched into a peroration which obviously gave him much pleasure:

> 'We shall behold him rising into prosperity through the medium of his sister's dishonour and accepting offices and emoluments from the prince by whom she had been avowedly so degraded; as a friend, faithless to his first and greatest benefactor in the hour of his extreme adversity; and a traitor to the sovereign who dethroned that benefactor. We shall see him intriguing for the restoration of the exiled monarch. And lastly sullying the brightness of his laurels as a conqueror by sharing in the inordinate gains of the contractor for the supply of the confederate army, and descending from his dignity as a man by the most revolting and rapacious avarice.'

In a final burst of what Mr Caulfield considered to be impartiality he added, 'Such and so various and inconsistent an admixture of light and shade is the character of the great Duke of Marlborough.'

The facts, which even Sir Winston does not gloss over, were that Churchill was appointed page to the Duke of York, later James II. His sister Arabella fulfilled the double role of Maid of Honour to the Duchess of York and mistress of the Duke of York, a convenient if somewhat unorthodox arrangement. John Churchill, who was extremely good looking as well as having irresistible manners, became the lover of Charles II's mistress, Barbara, Duchess of Cleveland. Or as Caulfield put it:

'The Duchess, whose constitutional warmth of temperament is well known, became enamoured of the embryo hero, and zealously promoted his interests. The freshness of youth in the object beloved, and the luxury of inspiring a passion ardent with all the glow and concentration of juvenile feeling, and intoxicating in proportion to its novelty, is, perhaps, the most precious tribute which can be offered at the altar of sensuality.'

Several historians also recount the manner in which the Duchess rewarded her lover. She gave him £5,000, which he then immediately, and prudently, invested in an annuity, which according to Lord Chesterfield, he bought 'of my grandfather, Halifax'. This last fact seems to be undisputed.

While prudence in the young lovers of Duchesses is not an admirable quality, it must be said in mitigation that he came from a family which had been impoverished by the Civil War. Not all the families who had poured out their blood and treasure in the cause of the Martyr King had been rewarded by his son. John Churchill had also made over his small prospects to help his parents. It cannot be denied that both the Churchills, sister and brother, had used their attractions in the promotion of their interests, but in times of stress and political upheavals impoverished sons and daughters cannot be over-particular in their methods of advancement.

Every generation of historians is biassed. The nineteenth-century writers were shocked by sexual aberrations and financial corruption, and historians in our own day are over 'nice' and puritanical in the parade of their snowy social consciences, at the same time peering through keyholes for possible sexual deviation. It is difficult to think back into a past when the bed of a duchess could lead to the promotion of what would be termed today a four-star general. Every age must use the weapons at its disposal.

Marlborough rose to prominence at the Court of Charles II; he had defeated the Duke of Monmouth, Charles II's bastard, when he tried to oust James II. When William III landed at Torbay, the General had prudently changed sides and joined the forces of the Glorious Revolution and Dutch William.

Marlborough had married Sarah in 1677 or 1678, and by the time Vanbrugh became friendly with the great General, she was in her late thirties but still as beautiful and dominating as ever. Colley Cibber saw Sarah about the time of the Glorious Revolution, when she had taken flight from London with the future Queen Anne, and had already become her firm favourite. 'We had not been many days at Nottingham before we heard that the Prince of Denmark (Anne's husband) with some other great persons were gone off from the King to the Prince of Orange.' These defectors obviously included the great General Marlborough. 'The Princess Anne, fearing the King, her father's resentment might fall upon her, for her consort's revolt had withdrawn herself in the night from London, and was then within half a day's journey of Nottingham; on which very morning we were suddenly alarmed with the news that two thousand of the King's dragoons were in close pursuit to bring her back to London.'

Rumours and counter-rumours were flying about the country, including one that Irish Catholics were about to cut

10a. The Royal Hospital, Greenwich (Mansell Collection)

b. View of London from Greenwich Park (Mansell Collection)

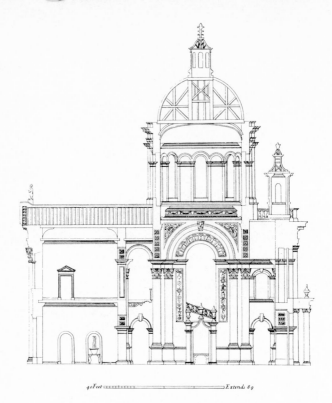

40 Feet ⊏⊐⊏⊐⊏⊐⊏⊐⊏⊐ ⊐ Extends 89

11*a*. The Section of Castle Howard

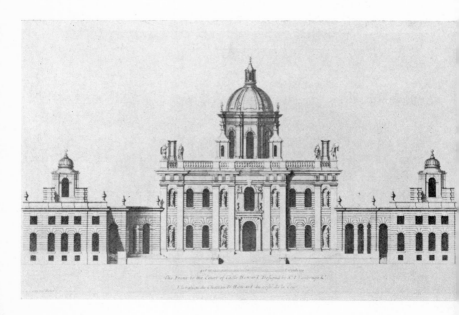

b. The north front of Castle Howard (from *Vitruvius Britannicus*)

off all the Protestant forces. But the troops took their arms and sprang to the defence of their Protestant Princess, whom they met in a coach attended by the Lady Churchill, and the Lady Fitzharding. The three ladies were escorted into Nottingham 'through the acclamations of the people'.

Subsequently all the local grandees and persons of distinction 'then in arms' gave a large dinner for the courtly fugitives. This was apparently provided by the Duke of Devonshire. Cibber, whose family was in the employ of the Duke, was used as an extra serving man at the tables where the 'noble guests at the table happened to be more in number than attendants out of liveries could be found for.' It was the first role Cibber had played. As maitre d'hotel he listened attentively to the conversation of the future Duchess, but was compelled to confess that all he heard her say was 'more wine and water'.

Overcome by Sarah's beauty, he said, 'All my senses were collected into my eyes and the whole entertainment wanted no beter amusement than of stealing now and then the delight of gazing on the fair object so near me.' He went on to say that twenty years later, when the Duchess was already a grandmother, he still found her as beautiful.

'Were I now qualified to say more of this celebrated lady, I should not conclude it thus: That she had liv'd a peculiar favourite of Providence; that few examples can parallel the profusion of blessing which have attended so long a life of felicity. A person so attractive! A husband so memorably great! An offspring so beautiful! A fortune so immense! and a title which she only could receive from the author of nature; a great grandmother without grey hairs.'

Vanbrugh's experience and opinion of the lady was not to endure in so favourable a manner.

But all that was in the future. The morning of victory was still dew pearled. On 7 September 1704 there was a thanksgiving service at St Paul's. Sarah, Duchess of Marlborough, rode in a coach and eight with the Queen. The Duchess, dramatising her beauty and her power over the Queen by dispensing with jewels, while the Queen blazed with them.

John Churchill had been made Duke of Marlborough by Queen Anne, while the Emperor had made him Prince of the Holy Roman Empire and Prince of Mindelheim. There had to be further gifts and expressions of national joy, so it was decided that the Duke must be given an estate on which to build a great house. In the year following the victory of Blenheim, Vanbrugh was appointed to the greatest of all his grand projects: he was made surveyor of Blenheim. This was to seem the crowning jewel of his career as architect, as it was intended to be the crowning jewel and reward of the great Duke.

Grandeur, in 1704, being the outward sign of England's rising power and influence, was appreciated and sought after, and the grandest and noblest house of all was to be built by the grateful Queen and nation for the victorious Duke.

The Queen's magnificent gift was the Royal Manor of Woodstock. This estate had a long and stormy history, and the building of Blenheim Palace did not detract from it.

Defoe, when recording his Tour of Britain, refers to the building of Blenheim, and brings into great clarity the eighteenth century's views on State and Magnificence as the outward expression of the nation's glory:

'The magnificence of the building does not here, as at Canons, at Chatsworth, and at other palaces of the nobility, express the genius and opulence of the possessor, but it represents the bounty, the gratitude, or what else posterity pleases to call it, of the English nation, to the man they delighted to honour. Posterity when they view in this house the trophies of the Duke of Marlborough's fame, and the glories of his great achievements will not celebrate his name only; but will look on Blenheim House, as a monument of the general temper of the English nation; who in so glorious a manner rewarded the services of those who acted for them as he did. Nor can any nation in Europe show the like munificence to any general, no not the greatest in the world.'

The manor had been the home of Henry II's mistress, the fair Rosamund, generally said either to have been poisoned or, as an even worse fate, forced into a nunnery by the jealous queen. Becket was driven from the door of the Manor, King John had treated there after being made to sign the Magna Carta at Runnymede, Queen Elizabeth had been imprisoned in its gatehouse, and James I had used it for hunting, not without complaints from his courtiers. Sir Robert Cecil wrote that 'The place is unwholesome—all the house standing upon springs. It is unsavoury for there is no savour but of cows and pigs.'

During the Civil War the Parliament men had struck back against it. It was then reduced, occupied by the Parliamentarians and taken over as Crown Property—forfeit to Parliament. Thanks to 'Colonel Rainsborough, who had played hard against Woodstocke Manor with his ordnance', by the time Cromwell's men came to make an inventory, it was remarked in the report, 'The said house is much out of repaire, yett most of it fitter to stand than to be demolished.'

In 1660 the Manor was restored to the Crown, and during the reign of James II he was said to have dined there in great state which would seem to show that there was a good deal of the old palace which was still habitable.

When Queen Anne came to reward the Duke with the lands and Manor of Woodstock, it was necessary to pass an Act of Parliament to make this possible. William III had impoverished the Crown with his wars and Parliament had passed an act limiting his grants of leases to thirty-one years. But once Parliament had approved the grant the Queen was able to give the Duke 'All that honour and manor of Woodstock with the rights, members and appurtenances thereof situate, lying and being in the county of Oxon.' These rights included the royalties of hunting, hawking, fishing, fowling and even included, *en passant*, the chattels of felons and fugitives. It was stated that the said Manor House was ruinious and that the meadows and pastures were kept for hay and pasturing for the deer. Old prints of the manor show a romantic building which obviously had some appeal to a man of Vanbrugh's imagination.

Vanbrugh's appointment seemed the obvious choice at the time. He was Controller of Works under Sir Christopher Wren, and although the commission was in some senses an official appointment, Vanbrugh was the personal choice of Marlborough. Castle Howard had obviously been much talked of at the Kit Cat Club and the architect's reputation was in a 'rising way'. The grant of the estate and the land was a clear mandate.

The financial arrangements were more ambiguous. The Right Honourable Sidney Lord Godolphin, Lord High Treasurer of England, sent his greetings to all 'to whom these Presents shall come' and laid down that under his warrant his Grace John Duke of Marlborough 'hath resolv'd to erect a large Fabrick for a Mansion at Woodstock in the County of Oxon.' and that John Vanbrugh Esq. was not only appointed Surveyor of Works and Buildings, but the Lord Godolphin also arranged for him to sign all the contracts for materials, artificers and carriages (transport) and to 'do all other matters and things in order to carry out the said works.'

After which the said John Vanbrugh was empowered to lay before the Lord Godolphin the account of his proceedings.

No mention was made of the sum of money to be expended, no mention was made of the final responsibility for the finances. Everything was to be done in a friendly and happy way. The news of the battle was fresh in everyone's mind, and the Queen had been graciously pleased to approve the design.

As Vanbrugh had, as he wrote,

'The honour of being Comptroller of Her Majesty's Works,

and as such was ordered to frame a Modell of the Designed Building; and a Modell being framed and compleated was Sett in the Gallery at Kensington by the Queen's Order, and left there some time that She might Consider it at her Leisure, both alone, and with other people, and she was pleased to view it thoroughly with the prince, and to ask all the questions Necessary for her understanding it perfectly, and She express'd herself extreamly Satisfied with it, and desired to have it dispatcht with all Application and required no sort of Alteration in it.'

Vanbrugh had his Warrant, but although the warrant was signed by the Chief Officer of the Crown Lord Godolphin and Vanbrugh himself was, as Controller, an appointee of the Crown, the document seemed to say that, although the building was being paid for by the Queen, it was the Duke who, in fact, was building it.

This was a document drawn up on the understanding that the Lord Godolphin would always be Lord Treasurer, that Marlborough would always be Captain-General, and that Sarah, his wife would be the Queen's adviser and friend. And finally that the building would be pressed forward with all convenient speed. Human nature is ever optimistic.

This cat's cradle of contracts was then further confused by the fact that, although another official of the Office of Works, a Mr Joynes, had already been appointed as an overseer of the building works, a 'coadjutator' called Mr Boulter was also appointed. His signature was another necessity before any work could go forward. Joynes and Boulter were not only clerks of works, but their signatures as well as Vanbrugh's were vital to make any contract valid. Boulter, the late comer, was afterwards described as a 'creature' of the Duchess's.

Vanbrugh's warrant was issued in June 1705, ten months after the famous victory, but the site had already been chosen by the Duke and his architect. The Queen had seen and approved the 'modell'. Happy anticipation filled the minds of architect, Queen and General.

Ten days after the signing of the warrant on 18 June 1705, a fête champêtre celebrated the event: 'About six o'clock in the evening was laid the first stone of the Duke of Marlborough's house, by Mr Vanbrugge, and then seven gentlemen gave it a stroke with a hammer and threw down each of them a guinea.' There was dancing on the green of men, maidens and beldames with several sorts of music. These efforts were refreshed with a hundred buckets, bowls and pans of wine, punch, and the inevitable cakes and ale. The gentry and 'those of the better sort' then went from this ceremony to Woodstock Town Hall where they were in their turn revived with sack, claret and cakes. While the common people, who presumably were not to be fobbed off with a mere hundred bowls of refreshment, partook of another eight barrels of ale, and an abundance of cakes.

All was warmth, good fellowship and good cheer. But already there was a crack in the 'fabrick' even before it had been begun. It was the opinion of the Duchess of Marlborough, who does not seem to have joined in the stone-laying ceremonies. Her opinion concisely expressed was that she hated all Grandeur and Architecture. This opinion was shared by neither the Duke nor his architect, who were men of their times. Grandeur appealed to them. But already she had insinuated her creature into the contracts and this was an ill omen for the architect.

It is a curious fact that in the Augustan age, when women had no rights, when they were treated as chattels, and their persons, money and goods were at their husband's disposal, some few women seem to have exercised a more incisive influence on events than in the days of their votes, their rights, or even their liberation. One of the most incisive of all influences was that of Sarah, the wife of Marlborough. She has been desscribed over and over again as a shrew, a viper, a clever woman, and a foolish, sharp-tongued bitch. Many praised her looks, few can praise her disposition or her temper.

Sarah was the daughter of an impoverished Royalist, as was John Churchill. Both of them acquired, and retained, a reputation for avarice born of early poverty.

Sarah's sister, Frances, was given, as a sop to the impoverished family, ruined in the King's cause, the post of lady-in-waiting to Anne Hyde, Duchess of York, King Charles' sister-in-law. The Count de Grammont waxes lyrical in praise of Sarah's sister.

'Miss Jennings, adorned with all the blooming treasures of youth, had the fairest and brightest of complexions that ever was seen; her hair was of a most beauteous flaxen; there was something particularly lively and animated in her countenance, which preserved her from that insipidity which is frequently attendant on a complexion so fair. Her mouth was not the smallest, but it was the handsomest mouth in the world. Nature had endowed her with all those charms which cannot be expressed . . .'

Her hidden charms may not have been expressed, but they had been canvassed, both by the Duke of York and by others. But Miss Jennings remained inviolably virtuous and quite intent on accepting only honourable approaches to her charms.

Sarah Jennings, younger than her sister, was brought to join her at court when she was only twelve years old. Sharper eyed, as well as sharper tongued than her sister, she learned her lessons of worldliness and cynicism from an early age. By the time she was fifteen she had already made sure that her mother, who was acting as her chaperone, was sent away from Court.

'Miss Jennings and her daughter, Maid of Honour to the Dutchesse have had so great a falling out that they fought; the young one complained to the Dutchesse that if her mother was not put out of St James's where she had lodgings to sanctuary her from debt, she would run away; so Sir Alleyn Apsley was sent to bid the mother remove.'

Old Mrs Jennings remarked that she did not want to upset the Duke or Duchess and she would take her daughter away from Court. But this was not at all the idea of little Sarah: 'Mistress Sarah Jennings has got the better of her mother who is commanded to leave the Court—and her daughter in itt, notwithstanding the mother's petition that she might have her girle with her, the girle saying she is a mad woman.' This was her first victory.

Sarah was generally considered to have been less handsome than her sister. Her fair hair had auburn lights. But she was equally fresh complexioned and with a tip-tilted nose. Pictures of her show a young lady well aware of her sexual potentialities, and the blue eyes, though outwardly languishing, would obviously only languish to the young lady's own ends. The happy disarray of her bodice reveals an expanse of creamy inviting flesh.

All these attractions she was to use, to quote the old lines, as a sexual shrimping net in which to entice John Churchill, who had fallen passionately in love with her. His letters to her when she was only fifteen years old mirror a strong, handsome man reduced to a state of grovelling, difficult to understand except in terms of sexual obsession, heightened by Sarah's iron determination to say 'no'.

He begs her to let him see that 'you wish me better than the rest of mankind; and in return I swear to you that I never will love anything but your dear self, which has made so sure a conquest of me that, had I the will, I have not the power ever to break my chains.' He never achieved this desirable result.

Sarah was born four years before Vanbrugh, in 1660, the year of the happy restoration of Good King Charles. She and Churchill married in the winter of 1677–78. Their marriage was secret and financially imprudent owing to the impoverishment of both families. The Churchill family had hoped that their son would dispose of his handsome person to better monetary advantage, and had picked out an heiress for him—Catherine Sedley, daughter of Sir Charles Sedley.

As Sarah had chased her mother from Court, so by her tough tactical moves she managed to eliminate her rich rival. The rival became the mistress of James, Duke of York. Of the Duke, Miss Sedley remarked: 'What he saw in any of us (his mistresses) I cannot tell. We were all plain, and if any of us had had wit, he would not have understood it.'

Sarah was now free to devote her considerable talents and drive to promoting the career of the man she had married. The first of her assets was her dominion over the future Queen Anne. This had begun when they were both children, and little by little the dull, plain princess had come to rely more and more on the opinions, abilities and amusement provided by Sarah Jennings. It would be said that the erstwhile Sarah Jennings was in no way modest about her attractions:

'Indeed her Highness' court was throughout so oddly composed, that I think it would be making myself no great compliment, if I should say, her chusing to spend more of her time with me than with any of her other servants, did no discredit to her taste. And, if from hence I may draw any glory, it is that I both obtained and held the place without the assistance of flattery.'

Throughout her life Sarah prided herself on her 'Mrs Candour' approach, which is a happy way of approving one's own sharp tongue.

When Vanbrugh was a mere Ensign with his way to make, Sarah had already become a powerful influence. She helped the Princess Anne to choose the Protestant side in the 1688 Revolution. She had kept her away from London till the Protestant succession was well established. The Princess Anne's star had been in eclipse during the reign of Queen Mary, who had exercised considerable pressure to try to detach Sarah from the Princess. But she held on to her post as Woman of the Bedchamber. Not only that; she had advised the Princess to good financial effect, and enabled her to get an income settled by

Parliament in order to make her independent of the good—or bad—offices of the King and Queen. For this Sarah was rewarded with a settled income which she was graciously pleased to accept, and the enmity of Queen Mary, which she took in her stride. Further monies and honours had been conferred on the Marlboroughs over the years, and by 1705 Sarah was established and at the peak of her influence and her power.

This was the formidable rival who faced Vanbrugh in his airy and sanguine hopes for the Duke's palace.

Sarah did not approve of palaces and preferred a convenient 'clean house' with a neat garden. But she realised that the Duke was drawn to a seat of great magnificence to commemorate the splendour of his victories and to show to Europe that he was honoured at home as he was feared abroad. It was to be a national monument and an enduring memorial for the Duke's family. He had chosen an architect who understood his views, who could plan splendid rooms of parade and grandiose settings for receptions within and without doors. There were to be triumphal arches, sheets of water spanned with bridges, and gardens as splendid as the costumes for which they were to provide the backcloth.

Vanbrugh was a European by birth and by feeling. He had seen the splendour of France, and the French grandees, and the Duke's conquests merited that his reward should be as glittering as his victories.

Unfortunately the Duchess's opinions were succinct, and diametrically opposed to Vanbrugh's ideas of State, Beauty and Convenience. It was only the latter quality which had any appeal for her: 'I never liked any building so much for the show and vanity of it as for its usefulness and convenience and therefore I was always against the whole designs of Blenheim as too big and unwieldy, whether I considered the pleasure of living in it, or the good of my family who were to enjoy it thereafter.'

The Duchess was not the only one who took the view that it was an expensive toy. Defoe, although he was prepared to admit that it had been built for the glory of the British nation, had his reservations.

'The magnificent work is a national building . . . nothing else can justify the vast designs; a bridge, or ryalto rather, of one arch costing 20,000 l. and this, like the bridge at the Escurial in Spain without a river. Gardens of near 100 acres of ground. Offices for 300 in family. Out-houses fit for the lodgings of a regiment of guards rather than of livery servants. Also the extent of the fabric, the avenues, the salons, galleries and royal apartments; nothing below royalty and a prince, can support an equipage suitable to the living in such a house.'

The Duchess shared Defoe's views but her opinions were brushed aside. She realised that the Queen was as set on presenting her glittering gift as the Duke was to receive it. Neither Queen nor General was in the mood to do anything which Sarah would have considered useful with the money—like saving it.

The Duke was as enchanted with the plans as was Vanbrugh himself. Even when abroad campaigning, the Captain-General's head was full of the designs. The Earl of Ailesbury, writing years later, draws a vignette of the great General in his campaigning days, getting into his chaise, then remembering the great project of Blenheim, which was always so near to his heart:

'He set foot to the ground again and told me he had forgot to show me the plan of his house and gardens at Woodstock, and so went up again and in pointing out the apartments for his and his lady etc. laid his finger on one, and told me "This is for you when you come and see me there". I asked him who was his Architect (although I knew the man that was) and he answered "Sir Jo. Van Brugg" on which I smiled, and said: "I suppose my Lord you made choice of him because he is a professed Whig." I found he did not relish this, but he was too great a Courteor for to seem angry. It was at my tongue's end for to add that he ought as well to have made Sir Christopher Wren, the Architect Poet Laureate. In fine I understand but enough to affirm (by the plan I saw) that the house is like one mass of stone without taste or relish.'

The Earl was remembering, with advantages, what things he said that day, because when Vanbrugh was appointed to design Blenheim he had not been knighted, and for the most part it is as difficult for a layman to form any impression of a building from a plan, as it is for the ordinary reader, without stage knowledge, to see the possibilities of a comedy. Vanbrugh happened to have the imagination to give form to both.

The Duchess, like the Earl, writing years later, said of Vanbrugh and Blenheim: 'At the beginning of those works, I never had spoake to him, but as soon as I knew him and saw the maddnesse of the Whole Designs I opposed it all that was possible for me to doe. Sr. John tho hee was in the Queen's Office of Works would not have been employed in the building if hee had not been recommended.' She had only heard of him as a writer of comedies, and although the Duchess may have had a sharp tongue, she was hardly the kind of woman to appreciate jokes. People who take themselves and their affairs as seriously as the Duchess did, cringe from jokes like the sea anemone at the slightest touch.

At first the Duchess and the architect were friendly. Vanbrugh was trained to amuse people and if Sarah did not appreciate his wit there were few people whom he could not please with his good nature.

'I'm in with Captain Vanbrugh at the present
A most sweet natured gentleman and pleasant;
He writes your comedies, draws schemes and models,
And builds Duke's houses upon very odd hills:
For him, so much I dote on him, that I
If I was sure to go to heaven, would die.'

Swift had satirised Captain Van's varied talents, jingling that he could rebuild a decayed house in his capacity as a herald, 'or by achievement, arms, device; Erect a new one in a trice.' He had amused himself at Vanbrugh's expense in rhyming couplets about Van's Goose Pye House, built on the ruins of Whitehall Palace. This rhyme had been much appreciated by the Duchess. Those with no sense of humour are ever ready to appreciate jokes against others. The Duchess, although brought up in the corrupt court of Charles II, was disposed to be a prude and in later years was known to expurgate harmless plays when they were to be acted by her children and their friends. It is possible that she did not approve of Van's comedies nor of his racy wit.

> 'Van's bawdy, Plotless Plays were once our Boast
> But now the Poet's in the Builder Lost.'

But his turning to architecture had coincided with a feeling in the country of building, and for building in the grand manner. This feeling is brought out most strongly in the notes which Celia Fiennes made on her journeys through England in the 1690s. She constantly speaks most contemptuously of the older type of architecture. In Norwich she remarked: 'All their buildings are of an *old* form mostly in deep poynts and much tileing.' In Shropshire she strikes the same disparaging note. Poor Sir Thomas Patsell's house was unfortunately old and low; he would have rebuilt it but death had carried him off. She hoped that his heir would have the good taste to demolish his Elizabethan inheritance. These old, low, timbered buildings were to be swept away and replaced by country mansions, towns and palaces all built of stone or brick. The men and women of Vanbrugh's day were convinced, like the Victorians, of the validity of their own taste.

Vanbrugh, a man who projected the spirit of his times, gave a clear explanation of his ideas about the Palace at Blenheim:

'When the Queen had declared she would build a house in

Woodstock parke for the Duke of Marlborough and that she Mean't it in Memory of the Great Services he had done her and the Nation, I found it the Opinion of all People and of all partys I convers'd with, that altho the Building was to be calculat'd for, and Adapted to, a Private Habitation, Yet it ought at ye same time, to be consider'd as both a Royall and a National Monument and care taken in the Design and the Execution, that it might have ye Qualitys proper to such a Monument, Viz. Beauty, Magnificence and Duration. I must own I was very glad to find the General Notion so entirely my owne and was encourag'd by it, to do all I cou'd sometimes Obstinately, and sometimes Artifically, to get such a Fabrick Agreed to, as I thought the happy Occasion and the Queen's glory requir'd.'

It was a wonderful opportunity to be seized to give his imagination full rein. A Design for a Great House, the Greatest house in England.

At first all went well. The enormous building was being 'carried up' with despatch. The best quarries, the best stone, the best stonemasons were chosen. The works were, in fact, being carried on much faster than the Treasury were issuing money to pay for them.

Unfortunately, simultaneously with the carrying up of the great house, Sarah's influence with the Queen was slowly declining. Like many dull women, Queen Anne was obstinate and devout. Sarah had been lecturing her about the nobility of the Whig view of life for many years, but the Queen was pious and Tory. She harboured in her mind the view that the word Whig was very little removed from that of atheist, and that should the Whigs seize too much power, they would not only destroy every vestige of the divine rights of the Monarchy but they would attack the Church.

Like Sarah, Vanbrugh did not take the word Church at its face value. She put it forcefully: 'The word CHURCH had never any charm for me, in the mouths of those who made the most noise with it; for I could not perceive that they gave any other distinguishing proof of their regard for the *thing* than the frequent use of the *word* like a spell to enchant weak minds.' Vanbrugh had expressed the same thought in more bawdy comedy terms.

But Queen Anne represented, like Queen Victoria, a pious middle class point of view. Hers was a transitional reign, and the powers of the monarch were to disappear after her death in the pudgy hands of German monarchs, with one feeble attempt to resuscitate them in the reign of George III. Queen Anne had great feelings about her royal powers, and the constant lecturing of Sarah had obviously palled over the years. They were no longer children, and Sarah had misjudged the degree of deference which Anne expected to herself as Queen.

It was Vanbrugh's misfortune that he fell into a nest, not of songbirds, but of pecking hens. Anne had quarrelled with her sister Mary over Sarah, and now Sarah's influence was to be undermined in its turn, and this turning point was gradually being reached.

A year after the junkettings at Woodstock and the solemn burial of the commemorative coins, the Duke was writing from his campaigning tent 'Pray lett Mr Travers know that I shall be glad to hear sometime how the Building goes on at Woodstock, for the Gardening and Plantations I am at ease, being very sure that Mr Wise will be dilligent.'

Simultaneously with the building of the house, the gardens and 'outworks' were being laid out. The idea was that the trees should be planted in as great a maturity as possible so that they should reflect the planner's ideas the sooner. Already in 1705 Vanbrugh was enquiring about the amount of timber which had been used in Mr Wise's 'works'.

George London and Henry Wise were landscape gardeners on a vast scale. From their headquarters at the Brompton Nurseries, which covered many acres in South Kensington where the great Victorian museums now stand, they supplied mature trees and shrubs all over the country.

Although Wise was engaged in carrying out the landscaping, the ideas were partly Vanbrugh's, whose inspiration lay in the grandeurs and formalities of the French *parc*. His influence, and the influence which was felt by many others of his day, was Le Nôtre's, who designed Vaux le Vicomte, the château built by Fouquet for himself. It was splendid—too splendid—for King Louis XIV decided that if any subject could build and decorate on such a costly scale it must have been at the King's expense. He confiscated the château, and this led to Fouquet's arrest and fall.

In France in the seventeenth and eighteenth centuries the garden was seen as an extension of the house and a setting for formal fetes. Le Nôtre's gardens were architectural in feeling and called for statues, urns, gateways and architecture of all kinds. In some cases the terraces near the house were merely designs, like embroidery, carried out in stones and different coloured sands, and without flowers.

Vanbrugh visualised the garden round the house being enhanced with sculpture, and presumably Wise's outworks were the budding beginnings. The architect also planned a military garden or bastion parterre, which may have been based on the 'Castle Garden' of the Duc d'Enghien. But influences and fashions change even in gardens. The English, under Queen Anne, conscious of their rising power, had decided to be English and, disregarding foreigners, to employ their own landscape as a background to their houses. Vanbrugh himself felt this influence, for he is said to have been asked who should design the park at Blenheim, and to have replied, 'Send for a landscape painter.' His ideas for the formal gardens round the house showed a continental influence, but he was sufficiently a man of his age to see the soft English landscape as a setting for his great house.

If the trees and plants were in an easy state of growth the

same could not have been said of the building. At first it had been decided that the stone used for ashlar (which is the expensive facing stone and is most important for the building's final appearance) should be quarried in the park. Unfortunately, although the stone looked promising, when the cold Midlands winter came it was found that it lacked frost resisting qualities. Boulter, the Duchess's creature, was on hand to report these defects to the ever vigilant Duchess.

On 1 January 1706 Vanbrugh was writing to Boulter:

'I had a letter from you in which you mention some things relating to Mr. Bankes's Work. (He was one of the principal and most experienced masons employed in the building.) But you say nothing of the Additional Covering wch. I write to you upon. The flying of the stone has made a great noise amongst People who are glad of any Occasion to discredit the work, and those who are concern'd in it. Now, tho' I am satisfy'd the damage is easily repair'd and what has flown of no Consequence to the Structure in Generall. Yet I shou'd have been glad we had taken such measure as not to give any handle even for a Disadvantageous report, and that I believe had been prevented by a timely covering.'

But Boulter was not there to take preventive action, only to report defects to his employer, the Duchess. Vanbrugh goes on to say that the other mason, Strong, had told him that he was not satisfied with the covering, even at that juncture, and that some parts of the building were not covered at all:

'He [Strong] says you tould him you had not boards enow: But I fancy there must have been some other reason, because boards enow, were to be had, And the River has long been in a Condition to send 'em.'

Travelling and cartage conditions in Vanbrugh's day were appalling, and when these are considered, the extent, variety and magnitude of the architects' and builders' achievements become even more astonishing. Vanbrugh himself complained to the Earl of Carlisle that he had taken three days to get from York to Castle Howard in the snow. Miss Fiennes mentions that she took eleven hours to do twenty-five miles, and that 'a footman could have gone much faster than I could ride'. Goods were carried about on sledges, even in a large town like Bath, and in Devonshire they used only pack horses. The nearness of rivers was of vital importance to the carrying on of building work. Some roads were so narrow that horses could only pass in single file, and roads were inundated in winter with floods or made impassable by the collapse of the banks that flanked them. It was obviously of the utmost importance that building work should be carried on with as much despatch as possible during the fair weather.

Vanbrugh was naturally concerned for the protection of his cherished building:

'I won't pretend to determine any positive Opinion on this matter (the cracking of the stone from the frost) till I have been downe, but as far as I can at present See, It seems as if you thought the Covering Sufficient tho others did not. And therefore I once more make it my Request that you will give such direction, that if any Severe frosts or Rains shou'd happen the remaining part of the Winter the Work may not receive any farther damage by 'em for want of Shelter. 'Tis that I am answerable for these things as far as the Direction go's and you and Mr. Joynes for the Execution. You never had in your Life to do with any body more easy than you'll find me, and I beg nothing may ever happen to make any dispute between us.'

During the same winter Vanbrugh wrote constantly to Boulter and Joynes at Blenheim about obtaining ashlar from Glympton and buying trees from Sir Richard Temple. In another letter he mentions casually that he feels 200 trees more 'will go near to answer our Wants'. Stretches of woodland were being felled to the greater glory of the Duke of Marlborough.

Vanbrugh concerned himself most diligently with all the small details, from asking Hawksmoor to supply further designs for ornaments, chimneys and the cupola, to the choosing of the correct facing stone.

In the spring of 1706 there were administrative troubles with carpenters. These could be solved, Vanbrugh thought, by playing one off against the other. There may have been misdemeanours, but these could be kept in check. 'The Bearer (who accused Simons ye Carpenter of some misdemeanours) is it Seems arrested by him, and forc'd to run away; so is come here to Towne to beg Protection.' Vanbrugh's solution was practical if cynical.

'Now, although 'tis very possible this Accusation against Simons had not been made but for some particular end; and tho' Simons has made some tollerable defence, Yet considering the appearance of the facts laid to his charge were true I think (tis sufficient for him, that we have Allow'd his Defence;) but he shou'd by no means be suffered to prosecute this Man; for 'tis certain he is—we shall never henceforward hear a Word, tho' the Greatest Roguerys in the World shou'd be Committed; whereas if this Man be still employ'd it will keep Simons in awe (who I think there are many reasons to Suspect).'

He added, 'I think we shou'd take advantage of their quarrells for our Instruction and at the Same time suffer neither of them to gain their ends upon the Other.'

During the winter of 1706 the Duke was back in England from his summer campaigning and anxious about the financing of his Palace, which, considering the extensive state of the operations, was not surprising. Vanbrugh wrote to Boulter, the Duchess's creature:

'My Lord Duke has Spoak to me within these two days to prepare a true State of things to lay before him with what I wou'd propose for this Years execution. I believe in Order to do this, and some Other things 'twill be necessary we All meet together here in Towne, and the Sooner the better.'

But by the time the campaigning weather had come again in March and the Duke's return to the Continent was imminent, the bankers' bills were still not forthcoming from the Treasury: 'There's no more money Order'd yet, tho' we are in daily expectation of it. My Lord Duke talks of going about the 20th. And I hope will so Adjust things with my Lord Treasurer before he leaves us, that we may begin our Campaigns at least as soon as he do's his.'

In May the Duke won the battle of Ramillies and, in spite of the slow payments, the Lord Godolphin was reporting to his General on the good progress of the building campaign at Blenheim. 'The building is so far advanced that one may see perfectly how it will be when it is done. The side where you intend to live is the most forward part.'

Vanbrugh had begun work on the private apartments, as he had done at Castle Howard, and in both houses these still remain the apartments of the family. The rooms of state were added later; the rooms of convenience came first.

By the autumn there were more troubles with stone, and Vanbrugh wrote to Boulter: 'I just now hear a report, I am much Alarm'd at, that all the Glimpton Stone in the building flys to peices with the frost.' It was not only the stones which were flying; it was the Duchess's temper, too. As her position with the Queen became less secure she seemed to take a more intimate and detailed interest in the progress at Blenheim. The Duke was far away with his battles and his diplomacy, and in the autumn of 1706 there was no one to restrain her in any of her relationships, either personal, political or architectural. The Duke wrote to her from Grametz in October of that year. 'I am to return my thanks for five of yours, all from Woodstock.'

The Duchess had obviously been extremely active, surveying the work from close proximity to the site and reporting her views at some length in her illegible handwriting to her patient husband. A note of great weariness with campaigning and with her complaints creeps into his letter. 'I could wish with all my heart everything were more to your mind, for I find when you wrote most of them you had very much the spleen, and in one I had my share, for I see I lie under the same misfortune I have ever done, of not behaving myself as I ought to the Queen.' The Duke added that he hoped Mr Hawksmoor would be 'able to mend those faults you find in the house, but the great fault I find is that if the war should happily have ended this next year, I might the next after have lived in it.'

In spite of the Duchess's complaints, the building went on, and in the following year not only stonemasons and bricklayers were employed, but carpenters, joiners and plumbers were at work on the interior. By July 1707 Vanbrugh wrote in his detailed way to Boulter about the prices to be paid for brick-layers, for vaulting and for groins, and compared the prices given to them with those which were paid to the workmen engaged on the Queen's works at Greenwich. He added, 'Our Contract with them is three Shillings pr. Rod lower than the Directors have ever had it at Greenwich in the same kind of Work.' He felt that they should get their price. 'Besides considering the Low Work (as in Garden Walls & c) is now past, I believe we must not refuse them in this point.'

As always in his detailed estimates of the work, and the politics connected with the building, Vanbrugh takes the *via media*. The new kind of sash window required 'more Stuff and Labour' and it is for this that the carpenters were demanding a higher price, which the work warranted. The plumbers were not easy, their price would have to be paid because the contracts had not been met 'in point of payment'. It was obviously difficult to get workmen to reduce their prices if they had not been paid at all.

By July of the same year the architect showed his first hint of impatience and wrote: 'I find Mr Strong despairs of getting up both the East Towers, wch. I am heartily vex'd at; but I am still more Concern'd to hear him even doubt of quite finishing One. Pray follow him hard.' In the postscript to the letter Vanbrugh said that he had seen my Lady Dutchess at Windsor on the previous Sunday. It is to be thought that the stone mason's being 'followed hard' could be connected with the Duchess following her architect hard.

Vanbrugh was on the point of leaving to stay with Lord Carlisle, and also to give a loving eye to his other and less difficult project, Castle Howard. There at least the Duchess would not be following hard. Before he went, however, the lady had had a few words to say about his projected design for the bridge at Blenheim: 'She said she wou'd write to me to York if my Ld. Duke resolv'd to have the Bridge go on; but I told her a Line to you [Mr Boulter] to tell you my Lord Duke's pleasure in it wou'd be Sufficient, there being full instructions left to proceed.' Unfortunately for the building and its architect, my Lady Dutchess's opinions were apt to come between plan, project and execution.

Vanbrugh was eager to be on the road to Yorkshire. He sent instructions for detailed drawings to be made for works both at Blenheim and my Lord Carlisle's, and added a cheerful postscript: 'Pray tell Mr Ryves I had the Venison yesterday, and 'twas very sweet.' The only surprise is that the Duchess was not prosecuting her architect for eating poached venison.

But as always, Vanbrugh took an optimistic extrovert view of his situation for a week or so earlier he had written to the Earl of Manchester giving a cheerful report about Blenheim. He referred to the expenses of the long wars.

'There is so much money requir'd for Publick good this Year, that My Ld Treasurer can't afford us at Blenheim half what we want; however, there will be a great deal done and two Summers more will finish it. My Lady Dutchess was there lately, And return's to Windsor, so entirely pleas'd that she tould me, she shou'd live to Ask my pardon for ever having

Quarrel'd with me, and I find she declares the same to My Lord Treasurer and everybody. So I hope I shall come off in her good graces at last.'

This was a pious hope to which many were to burn tapers to no avail.

CHAPTER XI

Progress of a Palace

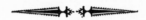

In the summer of 1707 the Duke was away on his summer campaign. The weather being hot and dusty, his thoughts were on the green shade of Woodstock. To his Duchess he wrote:

'I was not more sensible of the heat than I am at this moment. If you have the same weather, it must make all sorts of fruit very good; and as this is the third year of the trees at Woodstock, if possible I should wish that you might, or somebody you can rely on, taste the fruit of every tree, so that what is not good might be changed. On this matter you must advise with Mr. Wise, as also what plan may be proper for the ice house; for that should be built this summer, so that it might have time to dry. The hot weather makes me think of these things, for the most agreeable of all presents is that of ice.'

Ice wells, or 'snowe wells' as they were sometimes called, were one of the new continental ideas which had been brought to England by Charles II and his court when they returned. Ice wells were brick lined pits of great depth into which snow and ice were put during the winter. The 'well' was then boarded up and thatched. Sometimes the snow and ice kept for two or three years, and in certain cases it was possible to put in the bottles to be cooled without opening the well itself. In St James's Park, there were six ice houses, five for the royal household, and one for the Duchess of Cleveland, the lady whose favours had so kindly supplied Marlborough with an independent income. The snow well in Berkshire Garden is listed as being twenty-four feet deep and twenty feet wide.

In the Wren Society's papers there is a note of one of the Board's meetings at which Sir John Vanbrugh was present, when one of the works decided on was 'the ice well in St James was to be thatched'. The great Palace of Blenheim was to have its modern ice house.

At the end of the long dusty summer Tournai fell to the Duke's armies, and by November 1707 the Captain General was back from his campaigning and anxious to review the progress of his palace.

Vanbrugh was quite as anxious as the Duke: 'I waited this morning on my Lord Duke, who is eager to come downe but will however forbear till the scaffolds are struck about the great Pavillion and Quadrant; wch. he wou'd have finish'd preferable to every thing.' Even the Duchess appears to have been well disposed at this point. 'Both my Ld. Duke and Lady Dutchess are in perfect good humour with the Acct. I have given 'em of what we have done and are doing, And I wou'd fain keep 'em so if possible which nothing will contribute to than if I can shortly tell 'em the Work is ready for their Visit.'

A week later Vanbrugh wrote feverishly to Boulter that he was concerned about the difficulties of getting stone. He stated categorically that my Lord Duke, so far from being in perfect good humour, is 'out of patience about it'. Vanbrugh had had to tell him that it would be at least three weeks before the scaffolds 'cou'd be Struck about the Great Tower'. Vanbrugh reinforced the point by adding that the Duke was quite peevish about it, as he had wanted to 'go downe by that time'.

Unfortunately for the Duke, workmen were not as easy to move swiftly across the Oxfordshire countryside as troops were to march across rivers, mountain and continents. A month later Vanbrugh was still writing in great urgency about the Duke's visit, about the striking of the scaffolds and the 'clearing of every place about the building that can be, both within and without to show it to the best Advantage.'

Rich clients have ever been difficult to please and my Lady Dutchess was keeping her watchful eye on everything. Vanbrugh announced his intention of being at Woodstock on Sunday night in preparation 'for the Duke's setting out on Monday'. The anxious architect was eager to see that everything possible had been done for the Duke's inspection.

Although a great deal of building had already been achieved about the house and in the garden, unfortunately nothing was actually finished, not even the family wing. By the following spring work had started again, and although the Duke was leaving for Holland at the end of March he would be back in a fortnight and was quite resolved to see Blenheim before starting on his spring campaign.

This time the work seems to have made a certain amount of progress, for Vanbrugh wrote to Boulter about vaulting the Kitchen and the corridors. A small note of a personal nature creeps into this letter when Vanbrugh says, 'I hear the Roof is up on the old Mannour, Pray Order Schrivens to get it Leaded with Nine Pound to the foot.'

Vanbrugh always had the idea in mind that the Manor, 'Rosamunds Bower', should be preserved both for its historical associations and also because it would provide a romantic focal point in the park like a ruin set in a landscape painting. His concern for its preservation was also in part due to his leaning towards the Gothic.

Many critics and art historians, in fact, date the Gothic revival back to Vanbrugh's ideas, which ante-dated it by many years. The Goose Pie house he had built on the ruins of Whitehall Palace was a little crenellated building much like some of the 'cottages ornés' of the early nineteenth century. The house he was later to build for himself at Greenwich had 'somewhat of a castle air'. He always seemed to make a great distinction between the great set pieces he planned for Dukes and

Grandees and the strange little castles which he built for himself which, in many instances, differ from them not only in size but in style.

It was Vanbrugh's fond feeling for Rosamund's Bower which was to cause him so much trouble in the future.

In the spring of 1708, his idea was to preserve it, not only as a feature in the general plan of Blenheim and its outworks but also as a temporary *pied à terre* for himself. It was difficult to get permanent lodgings in the town of Woodstock, presumably owing to the number of people employed about the palace and its grounds. At one time they numbered over a thousand. Vanbrugh had to visit Blenheim not only in summer but also in winter, and he needed a permanent place of residence near the building works. There were three lodges in the park, but he was later to maintain that they were too far away from the main building projects which were in progress. He therefore combined comfort with convenience, and at the same time added concern with an historical relic of the past, which would later serve to add a charming ruin to his landscape. With all these ends in view, he gave orders for the least ruined part of the Manor to be covered. By the month of June he asked whether 'Mr Bankers had near done at the old Mannour. I hope at least all is ready for the Plumber to cover it which I wish he wou'd do out of hand.'

In the intervening three months my Lady Dutchess had been busy as usual. She had sent an unnecessary man down to be found employment and was threatening a 'progress' to survey the state of the works at Blenheim. Vanbrugh was anxious that everything should be arranged to receive the great lady, and on May Day 1708 he wrote somewhat anxiously:

'I'm obliged to Stay till my Lady Dutchess had determin'd Several things in relation to the Joyner's Work; I hope to get downe in ten days at farthest; My Lady Dutchess Designs to come about that time, but the Covings in her Bedchamber and

My Ld. Duke's Rooms shou'd be lath'd that she may the better Understand them. I therefore desire you'll get Some Laths in; Not only just for that particular but the Business in Generall, for I wou'd set the Plasterer to Work in the Offices, and in the Upper Rooms of the House as soon as might be.'

The activities of masons, plasterers, carpenters and brick-layers were to be speeded up. The Dutchess's visits seem to have had the same effect at Blenheim as the visit of the Queen of Hearts to the garden in *Alice in Wonderland*. White roses were to be painted red and all was to be swept and garnished lest she should misunderstand.

One thing was yet to be determined. During the Duke's winter visit to England there were plans for digging the foundations of the bridge. She had been against the bridge from the beginning, but the Duke and his architect had decided that the bridge must be built. That was one small campaign which the Duchess had lost.

Behind the scenes there were other and more vital political campaigns which she was losing. While Marlborough was winning his victories abroad his position at home was gradually being undermined. His wife, that ardent and hectoring Whig, had been long bored by the Queen's passionate attachment to her. She had spent more and more of her time away from the Court. By 1707 although outwardly her political influence with the Queen seemed to be as strong as ever, the whole nicely balanced team of Captain-General abroad, the Lord Godolphin at home, and the Duchess in the Queen's parlour was in a state of disintegration. The Duchess in her vindication of her own conduct sketched in the outline of the driving of the wedge.

The underlying seeds of the decay of her relationship with the Queen had always been there, the instrument was a poor relation of the Duchess, Miss Abigail Hill.

It is always a mistake for the powerful to patronise and to think that the patronised will feel gratitude. The Duchess's account of the Hill family is as contemptuous as her attitude towards Miss Hill must have been. She gives a brief description of the financial disasters and poor investments which had beset the family, culminating in an account of an acquaintance of hers who 'came to me and said She believed I did not know that I had relations who were in want . . . when she had finished her story I answered that indeed I had never heard before of any such relations'. She remarked that she never knew there *were* such people in the world. It was not an auspicious start.

The Duchess gave herself great credit for everything which she had done for the Hill family, the places she had obtained for them, and the pensions which she was instrumental in arranging. As for Miss Hill, 'I had so much kindness for her and had done so much to oblige her, without having ever done any thing to offend her, that it was too long before I could bring myself to think her other than a true friend'.

The curtain was about to be drawn upon the Duchess's downfall, and although the downfall took several years it was to involve Vanbrugh and his cherished palace. In 1707, when Vanbrugh was busily engaged on his plans for his bridge and getting up the East Towers, the slow fuse had already been lit.

'The first thing which led me into enquiries about her conduct', wrote the Duchess 'was, the being told [in the summer of 1707] that my cousin Hill was privately married to Mr Masham.' The Queen knew of the secret marriage and the Duchess immediately went to confront her with this breach of faith, and indeed quoted Montaigne to her. 'I have,' said the Queen, 'a hundred times bid Masham tell it you, and she would not.' It took only a few days to discover 'that my cousin was become an absolute favourite'. The long reign of Sarah was waning.

But the Duke was not anxious that anyone should know of the favourite's fall. He had always been able to wend a careful diplomatic way between a Catholic King and his Protestant successor, between Tory and Whig, Jacobite Pretenders and possible Hanoverian successors to the throne. 'The wisest thing,' he wrote to his wife, 'is to have to do with as few people as possible. If you are sure that Mrs Masham speaks of business to the Queen, I should think you might with some caution tell her of it, which would do good. For she certainly must be grateful and will mind what you say.'

Most poor relations who have superseded their powerful predecessors are neither grateful nor minded to listen to advice. They have seen how simple it is to deceive, and having profited by deception can see no reason why it should not continue to succeed. For them there is always a certain quiet satisfaction in double dealing.

The campaign of 1708 proved 'very glorious to the Duke of Marlborough by the victory at Oudenarde, the taking of Lille, and the saving of Brussels.' On the home front the Thanksgiving Service for the glorious victory of Oudenarde had been marred by the Queen and the Duchess quarrelling, both before and during their drive to St Paul's, and in the Cathedral itself. The Duke, who in the circumstances might have been spared these broils, was drawn in because the Duchess was passing on his letters to the Queen. 'I cannot help sending your Majesty this letter to shew how exactly Lord Marlborough agrees with me . . . though when I said so in the church on Thursday you were pleased to say it was untrue.'

The Queen had refused to wear the jewels which the Duchess had set out for her, but the Duchess, instead of taking her humiliation quietly, reacted with her usual aggressive tactics.

Sarah had always taken an easy view of her relationship with the Queen and had neglected to realise that, once Anne had become Queen rather than Princess, their whole relationship was on a different and more delicate pivot. The Queen's reply made her resentment on this point quite clear:

'After the *commands* you gave me on the Thanksgiving Day of not answering you, I should not have troubled you with these lines, but to return the Duke of Marlborough's letter safe into your hands, and for the same reason do not say any thing to that, nor to yours which enclosed it.'

Vanbrugh was not unaware of the way matters stood.

'Things are in a very odd way at Court not all the interest of My Lord Treasurer [Godolphin] and Lady Marlborough, backed and pressed warmly by every man of the Cabinet, can prevail with the Queen to admit my Lord Somers into anything. My Lord Chamberlain is in a tottering way. He has in trivial things disobliged my Lady Marlborough in a great degree. She is very much at Court & mighty well there, but the Queen's fondness of t'other lady is not to be expressed.'

With the waning of the Duchess's influence at Court came the quickening of her interference at Blenheim. In June 1708 Vanbrugh was still sanguine about the progress being made. He also made plans for his own little eyrie, and hoped to hear that 'Mr Banks had near done at the Old Manour'. He gave further orders for the plumber to finish the roof.

The first shot from the Duchess came on the grounds of economies on cartage. 'My Lady Duchess' was determined not to raise the price for the carriage of stone. Her orders were explicit: 'rather let the Work stand Still than to give any thing more than Six pence a foot, they must bring in the Great Stones for that Price as well as the Small Ones.'

Vanbrugh merely reported the facts, but he kept his temper. In September he wrote soothingly from Blenheim acknowledging receipt of what he called her 'commission about the carriage of stone'. He went on to say that the difficulty had been the weather. He assured her there was no 'Combination' (i.e. trade union) among the carters. When it came to the 'Great Stones' the carriers had reason on their side, but unfortunately for them my Lady Dutchess was ranged against them.

By the end of the month the Duchess threatened to make her official visit. The alarmed architect sent complicated instructions to put glaziers, carpenters and plasterers to work. 'That the room may look the better, let the Carpenter instead of Rough boards, lay downe Some of those they have plan'd as Likewise in her Dressing Room and Closet.'

The Duchess's temper was not so easily smoothed as the boards, and it was not long before she found a real *casus belli*, and became as disobliged with her architect as she was with the Queen, Abigail Hill, her husband, and the whole political scene. To misquote Pope, 'What dire offence from architecture springs, What mighty contests rise from trivial things.'

On paying her state visit to the site at Blenheim in the autumn of 1708 the Duchess found that Vanbrugh had repaired the old Manor and was living in Fair Rosamund's Bower. It was then her fury broke all bounds. She accused the architect of misappropriating £3,000 of public funds, and of using workmen and materials which could have been put to better purpose. The Duchess, like many others of her age, regarded the old Manor as an eyesore; it was to be pulled down, and the site levelled.

The following spring the Bower still stood, but only in part. Vanbrugh wrote to Lord Godolphin with a request for more money—an immediate advance of £6,000. At the same time he took up his position of defence and hoped that Lord Godolphin would pardon him, but he felt he must mention 'one word of the old manner [*sic*].' Lord Godolphin had, it appeared, been told that £3,000 had been spent on it. Gently Vanbrugh explained that although some of the house had been demolished he would be happy if a little thought could be given to the remainder of the building:

'I much fear the effects of so quick a sentence as has happened to pass Upon the remains of the Manour. I have however taken a good deal of it down, but before tis gone too far I will desire your Lordship will give yourself the trouble of looking upon a picture I have made of it which will at one view explain the whole design, much better than a thousand words.'

12. First Duke of Marlborough (National Portrait Gallery)

13a. The Old Palace in Woodstock Park

b. Blenheim (from *Vitruvius Britannicus*)

This letter does much to explain Vanbrugh's tender attitude towards the preservation of the past. In June of 1709 he wrote a long explanation of his feelings towards the Manor as an historical relic.

'I hope I may be forgiven if I make some Faint Application of what I say of Blenheim to the Small remains of ancient Woodstock Manour. It can't be said, it was erected on so Noble nor on So justifiable an Occasion But it was rais'd by one of the Bravest and most Warlike of the English Kings; and tho' it has not been Fam'd as a Monument of his Arms it has been tenderly regarded as the Scene of his Affections. Now amongst the Multitude of People who come daily to view what is arising to the Memory of the Great Battle of Blenheim, are there any that do not run eagerly to See what Ancient Remains are to be found of Rosamund's Bower. It may perhaps be worth some little reflection upon what may be said, if the Very footsteps of it Are no more to be found.'

Vanbrugh also explained his artistic feelings towards the old building: should it not be preserved 'there would be no variety of objects to soften the view.' He saw the Manor as a romantic landscape painter might have seen it. It was 'rightly dispos'd to supply all the wants of Nature in that Place.' The habitable part and the chapel would make 'one of the most agreeable objects that the best of Landskip painters could invent.' Gradually the old building would be surrounded by a wild thicket of yews and hollies. These were the dreams of a man who sensed the genius of the place and had a subtle feeling for the past and its meaning. The old was to be linked with the new to produce beauty of a particular kind.

It was useless for Vanbrugh to send sketches of his ideas; the Duchess had no tender recollections for the past. The explanation was endorsed: 'something ridiculous in it to preserve the house for himself.' She was not disposed to regard Fair Rosamund's Bower as anything but an eyesore and the sooner it was demolished the better. Accustomed as she was to ride rough shod over the feelings of others, a mere hired architect's views about his work did not merit a second thought.

In the autumn, after the battle of Oudenarde, Prince George, the Queen's husband, died, and she became from that time onwards an even easier prey to the softly insinuating sympathy of Mrs Masham. Of Queen Anne's husband Charles II had said, 'I have tried him drunk and I have tried him sober, and there is nothing in him.' But to the poor Queen his death was an inconsolable loss. Unfortunately, even in this moment of grief, Sarah had remained her usual managing self. She had taken away the Prince's portrait from the Queen's bedroom. She did not approve of dwelling on grief and knew quite well what was best for the Queen. The Duchess had forgotten her own grief at the death of her son, and the Duke's heir, from smallpox at the age of seventeen. Then the Duchess was said to have been seen haunting the cloisters of Westminster and many of her friends had believed she was in danger of going mad. Like many extroverts, the Duchess lived in the present. The past was forgotten and the present was not to her liking.

During the years 1708 and 1709, when the Duchess's position at Court was too nicely balanced to permit of precipitate actions, she was encouraged in her rash letters to the Queen, and her even rasher courses of conduct, by Vanbrugh's friend Arthur Maynwaring.

Maynwaring was the lover and 'protector' of Ann Oldfield, the young actress whom Vanbrugh had promoted from the inn in St James's to leading parts at Drury Lane. Whether he had introduced her to Maynwaring, or whether she was merely one of those recruits to fashion who came from 'that fruitful nursery', the theatre, is unknown. Mrs Oldfield and Maynwaring were a devoted couple. They remained together in spite of the attempts of Maynwaring's friends to separate them, and indeed in spite of Mrs Oldfield's feelings that Maynwaring should marry into a better sphere of life. Both of them remained

firm friends of Vanbrugh's. With one notable exception, he did
not collect enemies.

It is difficult not to form the impression that Maynwaring,
who called himself the Duchess's 'unpaid secretary', was like
many people who court the favours of difficult women, inclined
to be two-faced. Already, when complimenting the Duchess
on the victories of her husband and the capture of Lille, he
wrote: 'And if he brings home a peace next winter it will be as
impossible for his enemies to hurt him as for the wind to blow
down Mr Vanbrugh's thick walls.' There is a slight note of dis-
paragement in the sentence, as if the Duchess had been complaining to Maynwaring about the carriage of stone. Nor were
Maynwaring's fervent expressions of admiration distasteful to
her: 'I cannot help confessing that I believe in the main you
certainly do what is right, I do not think you were ever wrong
in your life.'

This was precisely the Duchess's own opinion, and it must
have been satisfactory to have it so heartily confirmed. Maynwaring could remain cheerfully in the Duchess's confidence,
but the position of Vanbrugh was less secure. He needed money,
money to carry on at Blenheim.

His various projects, including the opera house in the Hay
Market, had left gaps in his finances. Arthur Maynwaring was
ever at the Duchess's elbow and it was conceivable that he
could help. Vanbrugh wrote in July of 1708 asking him to use
his good offices with my Lady Dutchess: 'I thought to have
Seen you again before I came out of Town but coud not. I am
now at Blenheim but under such uneasyness, that I'm scarce
fit for Service now, having only a Short Reprieve from what I
expected would have immediately fallen upon me.'

Presumably he was referring to his possible imprisonment for
debt, which was always an ever present reality in the eighteenth
century.

'I must therefore before it bee too late, make one Application more. Which I hope My Lady Dutchess will think so Moderate, that she will desire My Lord Treasurer to Allow it: Which is: that for the time past, and to come (till something can be had by way of a place, which she has been pleas'd to promise me her Assistance in) My Lord wou'd order me upon the Queens Account, but what he did to Mr. Boulter. Without this, (of which my Expences come to more than half) There is no means left to prevent the Mischiefs that attend me And with it, I must Still go through Extream Difficultys to Spare My Lady Dutchess the trouble of a letter. I beg the favour of you to Speak of this to her. Tis impossible it can be refused me.'

It must have cost Vanbrugh, that most independent and least subservient of men, a great deal to write such a letter. But Maynwaring was a reed bending always to the prevailing wind. 'I cannot advise you,' he told the Duchess, 'to do anything for him out of your own estate.'

As Vanbrugh had remarked in *The Confederacy*: 'Some folks we mistrust because we don't know them—others we mistrust because we *do* know them.' In an age of patronage there were few trimmers who could be trusted.

If the Duchess still had her 'sixpence a foot' mentality, the Duke was no less careful with his well-tended, and well-husbanded fortune. He suggested it was much better for Vanbrugh to have a regular income of £400 a year, which was presumably the stipend of Mr Boulter, the Duchess's creature. It was hardly just or generous in one so immensely wealthy as the Duke to drive a hard bargain with his architect who was faced with severe financial difficulties, if not prison. But this was what he did. Neither at this date, nor later did Vanbrugh imagine that this small pittance, thrown like a bone to a dog, was to be regarded as his sole recompense for building an enduring national monument. The Duchess's promises of 'places' of profit, to be conjured out of the air, remained only in her mind. Arthur Maynwaring had little interest in the affair. He was snugly wrapped up in his sinecure of £3,000 a year as auditor of imprests. Other people's financial worries cannot be shared. This could be socially unrewarding.

Maynwaring may have been a cheerful friend to Vanbrugh at the Kit Cat Club but the impression he produces in his relations with Sarah is that of the White Rabbit who shakes his watch and hurries off to meet his Duchess with all convenient speed.

In the same letter about his financial worries, Vanbrugh goes on to explain that Boulter's job was merely to see that the prices were right, and that the controlling, general planning and expenses of the building should be in the hands of 'the Surveyor', who was himself. 'The Comptroller being only an Assistant to him': 'But in the great article of Management, they have no sort of Concern Which is in so casting things in the Execution of the Building, And disposing the Materialls that nothing may be Superfluous or Improperly Apply'd; But that the Appearance of everything may Exceed the Cost.'

He painted a strange little picture of himself, in his capacity of an artist who, as a practical architect, was chained by realities. He compared the architect's job to that of a frugal housewife.

'I take ten times the Pains to succeed in it, that Others of this kind of Business usually do, the Custome is, to give themselves very little trouble, after they have once found the Generall Scheme, whereas there is not one part of it, that I don't weight and Consider a hundred times before tis put into Execution.'

He went on to say that he 'haunts the Building like a Ghost, from the Time the Workmen leave off at Six a clock, till tis quite Dark and in a Word whereon I am, tis very seldom that I am not earnestly Employ'd in Studdying how to make this the cheapest, as well as (if possibly) the best House in Europe, *which I think my Ld. Duke's Services highly deserve.*'

But the haunting artist who worried and fretted over his

masterpiece only rated £400 a year (including expenses) as far as the frugal Duke was concerned. Patrons, though difficult and hard to please, were not inclined to consider art as something which had to be paid for. Imagination was considered an airy commodity which could be picked up cheaply.

The main difficulty between architect, client and client's wife, was that the Duchess had been against the 'madde' scheme from the beginning. She had only wanted a suitable and sensible house to live in. She had never been concerned with grandiose projects, the carrying up of stones for triumphal arches or the throwing of bridges over non-existent lakes, or even the preserving of love nests of ancient kings, long laid to rest.

The whole building was differently conceived by the Duke and his architect on the one hand, and the Duchess on the other. She was only concerned to make the best use of the estate which had fallen into her hands and to see that the Queen paid for the building which went up on it. A nice plain square house with no frills was more to her taste. This in 1709, she started to build with the help of Wren. She had, in spite of her precarious position at Court, managed to persuade Queen Anne to give her a site near St James's Park, and here she intended to show the world the kind of town house she preferred.

The Duke was full of forebodings about his wife's building project. 'It is not a proper place for a great house, and I am sure that when you have built a little one you will not like it, so that if you have set your heart upon it, I should advise you would think well upon it, for it is certainly more advisable to buy a house than to build one.' A curious maxim for one who was engaged in fostering the building of a palace like Blenheim.

The Duke's warnings to his wife fell, as usual, upon deaf ears. The foundation stone of Marlborough House was laid in May 1709. The news of this stone laying, and the engaging of Sir Christopher Wren as architect to the Duchess, was not a pleasing item of intelligence for Vanbrugh, struggling with his

financial and artistic difficulties at Woodstock. If she was engaged on another building operation this could only fall hardly
upon his beloved Blenheim, and himself, as indeed it did.

Vanbrugh's difficulties with Blenheim, the Duchess's difficulties with the Queen, and the intrigues of Mrs Masham and
Harley to undermine the position of the Whigs, now all ran on
together like a headlong rush of stampeded cattle.

The Marlboroughs suddenly seemed to lose that magic touch
of political timing which they had once possessed. It was perhaps not the most tactful moment for the Duchess to build herself a new and splendid house in St James's Park, when her
influence was in a failing way.

The Queen and the nation were tired of the endless wars.
Anne's remark on hearing of the victory of Oudenarde, 'Oh
Lord, when will all this dreadful bloodshed cease?' underlined
not only her feelings as Queen on the subject of Marlborough's
wars but the feelings of the ordinary people—those ordinary
people who were so far removed in thought or feeling from the
Duke and his Duchess; those ordinary people who were being
press-ganged into foreign wars and expected to die in foreign
adventures.

The Duke himself made the cardinal error of asking to be
made Captain-General—and for life—just at the moment when
his wife was behaving in her most tiresome and tactless way
with the Queen. His reasons for making this demand were quite
simple. He felt his position being undermined at home by the
political intrigues against the Whigs. The solid phalanx which
had supported him in his foreign adventures was no longer
secure. There was no longer any stability and he needed a firm
status symbol when confronting his allies and enemies on the
Continent. His request was refused and for once he forgot his
conduct of a 'courteor' and a diplomat; he wrote an angry letter
to Queen Anne suggesting that his request had been refused
because of Abigail, the new favourite.

The Queen's reply was simple. In October of 1709 she wrote:

'I saw very plainly your uneasiness at my refusing the mark of favour you desired, and believed from another letter I had from you on that subject that advice came from Masham; but I do assure you, you wrong her most extremely, for upon my word she knew nothing of it.'

With this request he had played into his enemies' hands. They were now very free with their insinuations. Marlborough was prolonging the war to his own financial advantage. He was seeking to make himself more powerful than the Queen, and his aim was to impose another army dictatorship, like Cromwell's, on the nation.

During these months of delicate negotiations and difficulties the work at Blenheim continued, and Vanbrugh constantly wrote to the Duchess explaining progress and making clear that he was doing his utmost to use the right stone for the correct type of building. Unfortunately for him and for the building itself, the foundations of this piece of grandeur were not standing on a firm bottom. In June 1709 Vanbrugh wrote to his patroness again at great length on technical matters and ended with a short financial dissertation.

'As to the Main concern of all Madam, which is the Expence of the Whole, I will (as I write your Grace Yesterday) prepare in a very little time a Paper to lay before you, that I hope will give you a great deal of ease on that Subject Notwithstanding there is £134,000 already paid. But I beg leave to Set your Grace right in One thing, which I find you are Missinform'd in.

'The Estimate given in was between Ninety and a Hundred thousand; And it was only for the House and the two Office Wings next the great Court; For the Back Courts, Garden Walls, Court Walls, Bridge, Gardens, Plantations and Avenues were not in it, which I suppose nobody cou'd imagine cou'd come to less than as much more.'

If Marlborough had not chosen the most opportune moment

to ask for his appointment for life, Vanbrugh had equally not chosen the right moment to tell the Duchess that the building was going to cost more than twice as much as the original estimate. Grandeur always costs money. The Duchess neither appreciated the grandeur nor the expense which was needed to support that grandeur. The Duchess hated both architects and architecture; and was only awaiting her opportunity.

CHAPTER XII

Projects and Friendships

Fortunately for Vanbrugh, the Marlboroughs were not his sole clients, and as with Wren his various building projects progressed simultaneously. Nor was Wren better treated with regard to money than Vanbrugh. For his masterpiece, St Paul's Cathedral, his salary was fixed at £200 a year. Even this small amount was not easily come by. For in 1697 the City Fathers, no more delicate with regard to architects' feelings than the Duchess, decided to halve his salary 'until the said Church should be finished; thereby the better to *encourage* him to finish the same work with the utmost diligence and expedition.'

Vanbrugh's interests were more complex than Wren's. For he combined his architecture and his practical meetings with Wren and Hawksmoor at the Board of Works with his theatre business, his post as Clarenceux King of Arms, and his interest in promoting the new Italian operas. His friendships flourished, enriching his life and aiding his reputation as an architect.

Amongst his friends was the Earl (later to be Duke) of Manchester. Lord Manchester was a member of the Kit Cat Club and one of Vanbrugh's earliest letters was to the Earl when he was Ambassador in Paris. It was full of the gossip of the town, giving a curious sidelight on the unchanging nature of human behaviour. He retails a piece of intelligence which reads like a scene in his comedy *The Confederacy*. 'My Lady Ardglass, having been for some time under strong Suspicions for pocketing some small goods—by the by—in shops was tother day catcht stealing four or five fans at Mrs Tooms.' Shoplifting by ladies with money in their reticules is obviously no new phenomenon.

Lord Manchester was not only the recipient of Vanbrugh's amusing town gossip, he was to become a patron and a fellow promoter of Vanbrugh's operas.

It is a truism, often repeated, that in former times 'they knew how to build'. Fortunately for Vanbrugh this was not entirely true, for in 1707 the front of Lord Manchester's house, Kimbolton Castle in Huntingdonshire, fell down. The Earl had consulted Vanbrugh as to how it could be 'carried up again', and had asked him to re-design and re-plan it.

At the time Lord Manchester was abroad on his second embassy to the Venetian Republic, and Vanbrugh had been asked down to Kimbolton by Lady Manchester. He reported back to the Earl that he had visited the house with Hawksmoor, and 'having considered everything, we all agreed on the enclosed design.'

In re-designing Kimbolton there were certain problems. The original building had been mediaeval with massive stone walls. In the central quadrangle the building had been refaced. The warm brick and the carved architraves of stone over the windows and the filigree ironwork of the balusters leading up to the central door have a French air, as if a small château had come to rest inside the stout protecting walls.

Vanbrugh's imagination was immediately fired with the problems presented by the crumbling of the castle walls. He proposed to enclose the house as it stood. A new thick building would envelop the old one. As usual his ideas were grand and splendid. He outlined his difficulties:

'Your Lordship will see something that differs from the Cast of the Rooms, from the Common mode; which is, to go immediately out of the Drawing Room into the Bedchamber. But the Drawing Room here, falling in the beginning of the

Line, had the Bed Chamber been next, there cou'd have been no regular nor propper way out of this Front into the Garden which wou'd have been an Unpardonable want. There was therefore a necessity for some new Contrivance.'

Vanbrugh had immediately conceived the solution.

'I thought, there cou'd nothing in reason be objected to being surpris'd with a large Noble Room of Parade between the Drawing room and Bedchamber.'

The Duke was not at first convinced that he wanted to be surprised by a large noble room of parade. He already had an adequate hall on the east side of the quadrangle. But his architect, once having the picture of a room of parade in his mind, did not easily abandon his fancy. He suggested that, even if there were already one hall in the house, it did not follow that the house might not be the better for a second and nobler room. He added, 'I shall be much deceived if people do not see a manly beauty in it when it is up, that they did not conceive could be produced out of such rough materials.'

His idea quite simply was to leave the remaining parts of the house standing and to add to them. The letter expresses not only the architect's views, but his attitude towards his noble clients, who were also his friends and collaborators.

Architecture was the passion of the age, and every client aspired to a knowledge of the art. Architects had to tread warily. Many clients shared the Duchess of Marlborough's opinion when she wrote, 'I fancy the house may be built up again without the help of an architect, for I know of none that are not mad or ridiculous and I really believe that anybody that has sense with the best workmen of all sorts, could make a better house without an architect than any that has been built these many years.' The part of the house at Kimbolton that had fallen down had been built without the help of an architect. There are always disadvantages.

Lord Manchester had his own views, like most eighteenth-century patrons. Vanbrugh expressed his plans tactfully:

'As to the Outside I thought 'twas absolutely best to give it something of the Castle Air, tho' at the same time to make it regular. And by this means, too, all the Old Stone is Serviceable again; which to have had new wou'd have run to a very great Expence. This method was practic'd at Windsor in King Charles' time, And it has been universally Approv'd, So I hope your Lordship won't be discourag'd if any Italians you may Shew it to, shou'd find fault that 'tis not Roman, for to have built a Front with Pillasters and what the orders require cou'd never have been born with the rest of the Castle: I'm sure this will make a very Noble and Masculine Shew.'

A sentence which could also have been applied to its designer. Lord Manchester agreed with Vanbrugh's ideas. No Italian opinion was presumably sought and Kimbolton keeps its manly castle air to this day.

Running in tandem with Vanbrugh's architectural projects was the Opera House in the Haymarket and here both his artistic interests coincided. But like all theatrical projects, the Opera House had occasioned Vanbrugh great financial losses. These had been partly incurred by over optimism, for he took a sanguine view of all his projects. Another contributing factor had been perhaps that his noble patrons' payments had sifted away into promises which had never materialised. But he hoped that better singers and better financing would bring in the 'Towne'.

By 1708 Vanbrugh's patron, Lord Manchester, became Ambassador in Venice. It was said of him that he made his public entry into Venice 'with a degree of splendor which inspired the Venetians with a lofty idea of the power and magnificence of the British Nation.' He was therefore well placed to help in what Vanbrugh called 'Our Opera Affaire.' He was soliciting his patron's help in seeking better singers for his Opera house to put the project on a more lucrative basis:

'People are now eager to See Operas carry'd to a greater perfection, and in Order to do it the Towne crys for a Man and Woman of the First Rate—to be got against next Winter from Italy.'

At the same time, quite naturally, the 'Towne' did not appear to want to pay for this. Vanbrugh had been at some pains to enquire if he could get any finance from Lord Godolphin.

'I have therefore (with severall to back me) laid before my Ld. Marlborough the Necessity there is for the Queen to be at some Expence.' Godolphin had requested Vanbrugh to write to enquire of Lord Manchester whether Signor Nicolini and Madame Santini would be ready to come to England from Italy.

Presumably he hoped the audience were not as anxious as the actor Betterton to see the Italians driven permanently back over the Alps.

In his letter to Lord Manchester Vanbrugh mentioned that he could offer a thousand pounds between the two singers. This was an immense sum at the time, especially as the performers were only being asked to sing from 10 September until the season ended in July. Vanbrugh underlined this point: 'The Opera is very rarely performed above twice a week, and in the beginning and latter part of the Season not above once, so their labour won't be great.'

The singers were to be paid in 'pistoles or Louis d'or', not in pounds, which would seem to prove that even the eighteenth century had its currency problems. Italian opera singers were not ready to be fobbed off with mere pounds.

In order to encourage the Italians to come over, Vanbrugh added one of his encouraging postscripts. The singer Valentini, already in England, was 'mightely pleas'd with the Civill Treatment he meets with'. Valentini was a well known castrato who was already singing at the Opera House, and one of the few good singers of whom it could boast. But he has not sufficient drawing power to put the Opera House in a rising way.

For a short time Vanbrugh had handed over his control of the Haymarket to a company of young actors. Downes recorded the facts of the theatre's decline:

'The last opera was the Kingdom of Birds made by Mr. Durfey perform'd in July 1706.

'After this Captain Vantbrugg gave leave to Mr. Verbruggen and Mr. Booth and all the Young Company, to act the remainder of the summer what plays they cou'd by their industry get up for their benefit; continuing till Bartholomew Eve 23rd August 1706, ending on that day with the London Cuckolds. But in all that time their profit Amounted not to half the Salaries, they receiv'd in Winter.

'From Bartholomew Day 1706 to the 15th Octoc. there was more acting there.'

Vanbrugh, as sole proprietor, had decided he must attempt to find someone to take some of his obligations from his shoulders and act as a working partner. As both theatres were in the doldrums the old question of uniting the two companies came to the fore again. The actual progress of the complicated negotiations is shrouded in the usual theatrical politics, and overlaid with the cats' cradle of Rich's tricky character and ability to turn everything to his own advantage.

Cibber says, 'Sir John Vanbrugh knew too, that to make the union worth his while, he must not seem too hasty for it; he was therefore himself under a necessity, in the mean time of letting his whole theatrical farm to some industrious tenant that might put it into better condition'.

The theatre being in a parlous way, purchasers of patents, with cash in hand, were hard to come by. It seems that Vanbrugh had working under him a Mr Owen Swiney, Swiny or MacSwiney, as his name is variously given. He was described as a 'sort of premier agent, in his stage affairs, that seemed in appearance as much to govern the master, as the master himself did govern his actors.'

Swiney does not seem to have received any salary, but had managed to put himself into a position of trust under Vanbrugh, helped by his cheerful humour and devotion to Vanbrugh's interests, both traits likely to commend him to the playwright. Cibber, writing many years later, was equally enthusiastic about Swiney's talents and character. He remarked that Swiney was well known in almost every metropolis in Europe and that

'few private men have, with so little reproach, run through more various turns of fortune; that, on the wrong side of three score, he has yet the open spirit of a hale young fellow of five and twenty; that though he still chuses to speak what he thinks to his best friends, with an undisguis'd freedom, he is, notwithstanding acceptable to many persons of the first rank and condition.'

Swiney seems to have had many traits in common with Vanbrugh.

There was some ambiguity in Swiney's position because he appears to have had hidden links with Rich, the owner of Drury Lane. Rich's interests were, as usual, entirely devoted to his own concerns and his lawyer's mind had planned the link between the theatres in such a way that, although both companies should in reality be under Rich's direction, it would be in 'so loose a manner that Rich might declare his arrangement with Swiney good—or null and void—as he might best find his account in either.' The manager was still in a fair way to bite his collaborators in their bargains.

Further ambiguity is lent to this collaboration between the theatres by the fact that Swiney owed Rich £200, a goodly sum at the time. Rich overplayed his hand and perhaps counted a little too heavily on the debt. For Swiney then proceeded to tempt Rich's actors away. The actors so tempted included Cibber, who by this time had become a considerable draw both as playwright and performer.

At first Cibber was disinclined to go over to the other side,

particularly in view of the fact that his witty speeches were
likely to blow about amongst the gilded cornices in the Queen's
Theatre in the Hay Market without being heard. He brooded
darkly on the offer and then went back to interview Rich about
the coming theatre season. At Drury Lane he found that, in the
fallow theatrical period of the summer, the manager had been
at work with bricklayers and carpenters constructing yet more
trap doors and wonderful stage effects. 'And', added Cibber
contemptuously, 'there are so many odd obscure places about
a theatre that his genius in *nook* building was never out of
employment.' Like some giant bird colony, the nooks in Drury
Lane increased yearly.

On being asked the pertinent question, 'Where are your
actors?' Rich countered with descriptions of various exotic
singing and dancing entertainments or circus acts with which
he proposed to astonish audiences. This was more than enough
for Cibber and several of the other actors. They had no fancy
for joining in competition with performing animals and high
wire acts. They left to join the company at the Haymarket.

The prompter, Downes, implied that while the theatre was
dark, the negotiations were swiftly carried on:

'In this Interval Captain Vantbrugg by agreement with Mr
Swinny, and by the concurrence of my Lord Chamberlain
Transferr'd and invested his License and government of the
Theatre to Mr Swinny; who brought with him from Mr Rich,
Mr Wilks, Mr Cyber, Mr Mills, Mr Johnson, Mr Keene, Mr
Norris, Mrs Oldfield and others, united them to the old
Company; Mr Betterton and Mr Underhill, being the only
remains of the Duke of York's servants from 1662 till the
Union in October 1706.'

He ended; 'Now having given an Account of all the Principal
Actors and Plays down to 1706 with the said Union, I conclude
my History.'

It was suggested that Swiney and the actors who left had

behaved in an underhand way, but it is hard not to be sympathetic to actors who had been treated so shabbily and were regarded as walking substitutes for nooks by the manager. The contract they signed with Swiney shows that their salaries were not low. They ranged from Wilks at £200 a year, Doggett and Cibber at £150, down to a Miss Younger who only merited £10. It is devoutly to be hoped that her low salary did not contribute to a moral decline. Even Betterton, who only acted on a few nights in the year, was paid £100.

As a result of being in the right place at the right time, Swiney was able to gain control of the Queen's Theatre in the Hay Market. Cibber was apparently well aware that Vanbrugh's finances were not in a healthy position when he sold his interests to Swiney. He wrote:

'Sir John Vanbrugh, in this exigence of his theatrical affairs made an offer of his actors, under such agreements of sallary as might be made with them; and of his house, cloathes, and scenes with the Queen's licence to employ, upon payment of only the casual rent of five pounds upon every acting day, and not to exceed 700 l. in the year.'

It was not a brilliant conclusion to his dreams of a glittering Opera House which would make his fortune.

By the spring of 1708 the affair was concluded, and Vanbrugh wrote to Lord Manchester:

'I have had two letters from yr. Ldship of ye 16th March & 20th Aprill. And am (as well as the Towne) much oblig'd to you, for the endeavours you use to improve the Opera here. What yr. Ldship says of having one or two of the Top Voices, is most certainly right; As to my Self; I have parted with my whole concern to Mr. Swiney; only reserving my Rent; So that he is entire Possessor of the Opera And Most People think, will manage it better than any body. He has a good deal of money in his pockets and is willing to Venture it upon singers.'

A thousand pounds, which was being offered to Nicolini,

could be calculated, wrote Vanbrugh, at 1,200 pistoles, 'which undoubtedly he may Carry away clear in his pockets.' La Santini would be offered the same amount, but lesser voices would be expected to be bought more cheaply at about 600 pistoles.

'If your Ldship can get any of these People over and on the Terms here Mention'd, Mr Swiney desires me to Assure you of punctuall performance on his part; Nor is there any reason to doubt him; for he has behav'd himself so as to get great credit in his dealings with the Actors.'

Prompt payment in pistoles was to be the added inducement. High salaries were useless if the money was not forthcoming. Vanbrugh went on to say that the Vice Chamberlain was supporting Swiney and he underlined the patronage aspect of all theatrical projects by adding 'Besides he [The Vice Chamberlain] has Power Sufficient to Oblige him to it, the License being only during the Queen's Pleasure.'

My Lady Duchess of Marlborough had not yet been consulted about the Opera project. But Vanbrugh added that he found 'no disposition in other people to promote Manza's coming at any great expence'. Manza was the Duchess's protégé. Manza wanted six hundred guineas a year. This was 'not to be thought of'. Apparently Manza was not considered a voice of sufficient quality to be worth importing.

Again Vanbrugh emphasises that the Opera needs good voices to bring in the customers, besides there are other aspects to be considered in the age of patronage.

'If these Top Voices come over, 'twill facilitate bringing the Queen into a scheme now preparing by my Lord Chamberlain and others to have Concerts of Musick in the Summer at Windsor, twice a Week in the Apartment. There is no doubt, but by some such way as this if the best Singers come, they will tast of the Queen's Bounty'.

It seems as if the Queen and the Nobility were quite prepared to patronise the Italians once their main expenses had been paid. Nothing succeeds with people better than that their amusements should be financed by others.

This policy of paying immense sums to foreigners was not popular with the actors. Cibber remarked bitterly:

'The patentee of Drury Lane went on in his usual method of paying extraordinary prices to singers, dancers and other exotick performers, which were as constantly deducted out out of the sinking salaries of his actors. It seems he had not purchas'd his share of the patent to mend the stage, but to make money out of it.'

It was the age old cry of the dedicated actor. Nor were the opera singers entirely harmonising. Vanbrugh wrote to Lord Manchester. 'Valentini tho' he pretended to wish for Nicolini's coming will underhand do all he can to discourage him for he has link'd himself with Mrs Tofts. And in order to make a great bargain for themselves for next Winter, will certainly play some trick, to hinder both Nicolini and a Woman from Coming over if yr. Ldship don't Apprise 'em ont.'

Then, almost immediately, Vanbrugh dismissed the whole opera affair from his mind and switched immediately to the affair of rebuilding Kimbolton. He was certainly a man who, like a juggler, was able to keep several Indian clubs in the air at the same time.

'Coleman [the builder] is going on at Kimbolton. I shall send him this Post the Design for the Upper Story in which there will be four Bedchambers, and good Accommodations to 'em with a Corridore that runs the Whole Length behind 'em and will be very pretty & very well lighted. I hope yr. Ldship will see what we have done by Sept. wch. if it pleased you, will much rejoyce,

yr. Lordships,
Most Obedient humble Servant,
J. Vanbrugh.'

He added his usual postscript perhaps as much to raise his own hopes as to inform the Earl of Manchester:

'My Lady Marlborough go's now very often to Court, and is in perfect good humour. I hope all will keep right.'

Although the note was cheerful, the doubts about Blenheim remained. Kimbolton was another matter and he wrote constantly to Lord Manchester reporting his progress with the Castle's replanning, and setting out how he had consulted with Lady Manchester about the details of the rebuilding.

In the spring of the year, he wrote with great enthusiasm to his patron about the perfection of the espalier hedges, and how the fruit trees were 'strong enough to produce in abundance'. The old stone of the Priory had been turned to good account and 'without one foot of freestone Kimbolton will be made handsomer than any Gentleman's house in Huntingdonshire.'

A well balanced character, Vanbrugh was sure of his own talents and not afraid to give credit to others. Coleman, the builder, was praised. He had managed the old materials to admirable advantage and executed the directions he had had extremely well. There is a freshness and frankness in Vanbrugh's letters to his friendly patrons which is entirely lacking from his correspondence with the Duke and the Duchess. When he wrote to them he always seemed to be aware of the burden of the palace and of the watching housewifely eyes of the Duchess. There always appeared to be something to explain or to explain away.

With Lord Manchester he was on easy terms whether he wrote about the opera and the necessity of bolstering up the season with more expensive singers, or carrying up Kimbolton Castle to a new design with old stone.

When the building had been satisfactorily completed, the eyes of architect and patron turned to the embellishment of the interior. The Earl brought back from his Embassy at Venice two Venetian painters, Giovanni Antonio Pellegrini and Marco Ricci.

It was not yet the high noon of the Italian influence on English decoration and architecture, but Vanbrugh being a man of his age he liked dramatic effects. His massive stone hallways, hidden staircases, arches and columns demanded the richness of tapestry and painting to complement them. In his liking for the splendour of the Italian interior Vanbrugh was in some senses the precursor of the intricate Italianate interior which made the later Palladian houses into intricate jewel boxes.

When the Venetian painters arrived in England their first commission seems to have been the settings for the opera 'Pyrrhus and Demetrius', which was performed at Vanbrugh's Opera House in the Hay Market in 1709.

Subsequently the Italian went up to Castle Howard, where he painted the magnificent domed hall, the high saloon and the garden room in the winter of 1709/1710, although some accounts give his work in Yorkshire as two years later.

At Kimbolton the theatrical nature of Pellegrini's talent is apparent. A triumph of Caesar glorifying the military victories of William III could easily have been a procession in an opera, and the charming musicians with their little dog on the upper staircase could be sounding the opening notes to send the curtain up on some spectacle at Drury Lane. The ceiling on the main staircase continues the eulogy of William II; two putti hold his portrait to which Minerva is pointing, while Fame trumpets his glory. Touches of rococo occur in the ceiling in the Queen's boudoir, where Venus and Cupid are surrounded by garlands of roses. The topmost ceiling on the staircase has a touch of humour where two cupids play with the family coronets which rise from baron to earl and finally duke against a background of soft clouds and azure skies.

Pellegrini also painted the chapel at Kimbolton. Over the altar is the transfiguration of Christ. While the figures of the three Apostles—Peter, James and John—show the right degree of dramatic astonishment, and Moses and Elijah faithfully represented the tablets of Authority and Revelation, the central figure of the transfigured Christ has a certain latent femininity which is hardly compatible with someone who persuaded twelve men to leave their nets or businesses and follow him into the wilderness. But this is perhaps a charge which could be levelled at many representations of Jesus Christ. The spaces between the windows are enhanced by paintings of the four evangelists, but while Matthew, Mark and John turn respect-fully towards the altar, the figure of St Luke is facing in the opposite direction.

This curious fact has now been explained by Mr C. S. Lewis, Headmaster of Kimbolton, who discovered that it was painted by a Rev. Mr Peters as a replacement for the original apostle who had been destroyed by damp. Presumably the parson did not paint it *in situ*, and the person who commissioned it forgot to tell the clerical gentleman which way the saint should face.

Vanbrugh's work on Kimbolton took some years, but the main body of the rebuilding appears to have been finished by 1719. During all this time Hawksmoor was helping Vanbrugh with the practical details of the castle. In the accounts of the period Coleman mentions 'six large sheets of Drawing Paper used by Mr Hawcksmoore'—at two shillings, and two packets of draughts sent from London by Mr Hawcksmoore witch I paid postage . . . One shilling and fourpence.'

As usual in all these grand house building operations, the flights of fancy of patron and architect outran the supply of money. As Sir Winston Churchill mentioned in respect of Blen-heim, 'by some deep law of nature' everything always cost twice as much as the estimate. Coleman, like the builders of Blenheim, had to wait for his money. He was paid in 1713 for work carried out in 1710. Master masons and foreman builders seem to have been infinitely patient in the eighteenth century.

The great portico on the garden front was added about 1715. This is a classical feature which bears little relation to the rest of the building. The recent discovery of a drawing by Galilei in the Library at Huntingdon showing this portico and the details of the fan-shaped steps leading up to it, as well as drawings for the proposed enriching of the entrance doorway, has cast a slight doubt on Vanbrugh's responsibility for the portico itself. It could perhaps be that Galilei merely designed the steps and that he was putting a suggestion for the doorway to the Duke of Manchester. There is no doubt that Galilei was working at Kimbolton, and a letter to him from the Duke makes this clear: 'I found one pair of Stairs only in ye middle of ye Collonade would not doe well so have ordered two more on each side as you first proposed it.' He also mentioned chimney pieces which the Italian had designed and suggested that the stone cutter should be persuaded to carry them out, and in the marble 'we choosed'.

A sketch by Vanbrugh of his proposed idea of the garden front shows a completely different treatment more in keeping with the rest of his castle design, in which the crenellations are carried on and the central block has three curved archways. It could be that Lord Manchester simply rejected Vanbrugh's first design and had decided that he preferred something more in the Italian taste, of a more strikingly classical order, to finish the garden front with a flourish. There is no doubt that it is a beautiful addition to the façade of the house, and now this east portico is enhanced by an avenue of huge trees own over a hundred years old which draw the eye to its Doric classicism.

Another of Vanbrugh's patrons was Sir Edward Southwell, for whom he designed King's Weston, near Bristol. Edward Southwell was thirty-one when he succeeded his father in 1702, and like many other inheritors of fortunes in his period his thoughts immediately turned to planning an enhanced setting for himself.

King's Weston is one of the smallest of the houses which Vanbrugh designed or re-designed for his patrons. In its heyday it excited the greatest admiration, for the setting was superbly chosen on rising ground, with a view over the Bristol Channel to the Welsh hills. Perhaps the setting reminded Vanbrugh of the view from the walls of Chester. In the eighteenth century the setting of the house was considered by contemporary taste to conform to the idea of landscape as a background to architecture.

The Prince de Ligne, who made a hasty Gallic tour of England at the end of the century, said: 'What is more beautiful than King's Weston, and the view of the river Avon and the whole of Wales spreading out? What is more superb than Windsor? What Majesty—how nature has excelled herself— with what grace the rivers traverse these immense landscapes!'

Vanbrugh, although a man of his time, was in some senses in advance of it. He included the landscape as part of the plan to offset his houses, like a playwright choosing the setting for the people in his play.

The most original thing about the design for King's Weston was that Vanbrugh's treatment of the chimneys made the chimneys part of the design, like a colonnade on the roofscape. Vanbrugh made use of these essential features to dramatise the skylines of his houses, and in the nineteenth century many Victorian houses copied this idea.

Vanbrugh was very conscious of the essential originality and balance of this new treatment and he was anxious about the details. In the autumn, while he was staying at Castle Howard, Vanbrugh wrote to Southwell saying:

'In my last I told you I wished you would not go up with the chimneys till I was with you on the spot, to make tryall of the heights etc. with boards. I am glad to find you now of the same opinion, tho' you had not yet recd. my letter; for I would fain have that part rightly hit off. I likewise think you in the right to clear off the scaffolds, tho' there be more difficulty in getting up the stone for the chimneys.'

He countered some objections which his patron had obviously made about the designs and added:

'I hope, however, at last I shall see you as well pleased as the Lord of this place [Castle Howard] is; who has now within this week had a fair tryall of his dwelling, in what he most apprehended, which was cold. For tho' we have now had as bitter storms as rain and wind can well compose, every room in the house is like an oven, and in corridors of 200 ft. long there is not air enough in motion to stir the flame of a candle. I hope to find the same comfort in your Chateau when the North West blows his hardest; so pray don't think you'll stand in need of a few poor trees to screen you. The post will be gone, if I say anything now, than that I am most heartily your humble sert.'

The interior of the house, especially the beautiful carved staircase, was of great elegance. The walls on the landing were arcaded and the niches painted in grisaille with classical figures or classical urns. The garden, in its heyday, formed a perfect setting for the house and its distant landscape of river and hills.

At about the same time, Vanbrugh sold a property he had acquired at Claremont in Surrey. In an attractively chosen landscape he had built himself what he called a 'little Box'. His mother lived at Claygate in the same county and was then in her eighties, and presumably Vanbrugh had chosen his own country retreat in order to visit the old lady, who in spite of her nineteen pregnancies had survived into a green old age. Vanbrugh had sold his property to Thomas Pelham. Pelham's acquisition of lands, titles and riches proceeded from a complicated web of family relationships and judicious political allegiances.

In July 1711 he succeeded as adopted heir to the bulk of the estates of his mother's brother, John Holles, Duke of Newcastle. In gratitude for favours received, he added his uncle's name to his own becoming Pelham-Holles. When the Hanoverians came to the throne, he immediately and firmly declared for the house of Brunswick. As a result of this excellent decision he was created Viscount Haughton, Earl of Clare, and finally Duke of Newcastle.

Pelham-Holles had already begun to extend and improve Vanbrugh's modest house, with the architect's help, before he had inherited and acquired money and titles. The house was now equally elevated in rank and called Claremont to celebrate his new earldom. The first alterations to the house seem to have been on a small scale, and the letters which Vanbrugh wrote to the Duke were connected with smoking chimneys and the ever present troubles of getting the fabric up in fair building weather. The Duke of Newcastle was apparently a gentleman who fussed and interfered in the details of the building. Vanbrugh wrote reassuringly to him about the operations: 'I am swearing as much as is necessary to get it cover'd.'

Newcastle was known as 'Permis' Newcastle because of his constantly repeated catch phrase *'Est-il permis?'*, brought back perhaps from a short tour on the Continent. He was a member of the Whig aristocracy in which Vanbrugh moved. Though Vanbrugh's profession was architecture, he was used by his aristocratic friends in delicate political negotiations and he moved in the inner Whig circles on a friendly and intimate basis. Permis Newcastle was one of his friends and a fellow member of the Kit Cat, that inner circle of the Whigs. Unfortunately for Vanbrugh this tight intimate circle was already fatally undermined.

The traps were set, and ready to be sprung and the biggest trap of all was the cherished Palace at Blenheim.

CHAPTER XIII

After Victory

'And everybody praised the Duke
Who this great fight did win.'
'But what good came of it at last?'

The glory of the battle of Blenheim was fading, and only the
expenses of the building remained.

The Duchess had always considered the plan for Blenheim
to be 'madde'. Like the Duchess, many people have since
criticised it on the grounds of its vast size, its inconvenience,
and the heaviness of the design. Critics both during Vanbrugh's
lifetime and since have referred to the megalomania of the
architect. It was suggested that everything had been sacrificed
to spreading masses of stone across the countryside.

These criticisms are as irrelevant to Vanbrugh's designs for
his noble clients as are modern criticisms of Victorian houses
as being too big and inconvenient. As Victorian and Edwardian
houses relied on troops of indoor and outdoor servants for
whom extra accommodation had to be provided, so Vanbrugh's
houses were equally carefully planned for the great personages
of his day, and their retinues.

Both Castle Howard and Blenheim were imagined, not as
one large and impressive house, but according to the architect's
idea of State, Beauty and Convenience. The State rooms usually
consisted of two great saloons. Hawksmoor was accustomed to
refer to these as the 'ceremonies'. The State apartments were
not designed as one house, but as a series of linked suites. Each

of these would consist of an ante-chamber, which led to a drawing room, bedrooms, dressing rooms, and a 'cabinet' or study. Guests expected to live their lives independently of their hosts, and to receive their own guests separately. During the seventeenth and eighteenth century guests very often stayed two or three months at a time and separate apartments were more than necessary in order to preserve both amenities and good relationships.

In addition to the guests' suites there were often, as well as the state dining room, small 'eating parlours' for guests and a chapel. Much accommodation had also to be provided for ladies' maids, valets and servants of all kinds, as well as space for coachmen and grooms. The era of the coaching inn had not arrived and travellers on little frequented routes often used the great houses of their friends as hotels. Many inns were not well equipped and some were verminous. The great lords and ladies of the period wisely took their own bedding with them when they went travelling. As late as the 1730s the Duchess of Marlborough, writing to her grand-daughter, begs her to stay at Holywell, her house near St Albans, and to use it as a 'quiet inn'.

Vanbrugh's houses were designed with many eventualities in mind. He was of the opinion that his houses were conveniently and carefully planned, even to the extent of providing a way out of each separate apartment, so that the great man or his guests could slip out without the necessity of encountering un-welcome petitioners waiting in the ante-room.

The way of life represented by these houses must be taken into account if Vanbrugh's planning is to be sympathetically understood. In the same context, the fact that the kitchens are often some way from the central block of the house was also carefully thought out. The kitchens at Blenheim, when the house was filled with family parties including children and nursemaids, troops of house servants, as well as guests, the ser-vants of the guests, visiting coachmen, ladies' maids, valets and grooms, must have had to provide meals on the scale of a large ocean-going ship.

Sarah, when visiting a house of which she happened to approve, wrote:

'The offices were in a manner I liked better than any I have seen, not wings, for they are very seldom set on agreeably, only to make a show, and sometimes inconveniently done. But at this place there is a very large building for servants, and all manner of offices put so near the back of the house that the meat may be brought into it as easily as from the wings; which prevents all stinks and noise of every kind.'

It was more than necessary that the noise, bustle and confusion which accompanied cooking on such a large scale should be separated from the noble rooms of parade.

The age was ritualistic, and the rituals of a great man's daily life demanded a setting commensurate with his standing. This was a point on which the Duke of Marlborough and his architect thought in unison.

The 'haut standing' of the Duke of Marlborough was European, and on this account he had the status of a Prince.

Vanbrugh himself, when writing to Lord Ryalton, Godolphin's son, whose wife Henrietta afterwards succeeded her father as Duchess of Marlborough, sketched out his ideas on the subject:

'As to the Offices in the Out Courts I here inclose a Copy of a Paper I sent my Lady Dutchess, And to my Lord Duke. I hope it will satisfy both them And your Lordship that there is nothing more than is necessary to all Houses of *much less rank than this*. And if your Lordship will Observe other Houses where you go, You will find hundreds that have more out buildings a great deal. All the Difference is, That they are generally ill favour'd by Scrambling about, And look like a Ragged Village Whereas these being all Compriz'd within

One Regular Handsome Wall (And being likewise regularly dispos'd within) Form a Court, which by this means Adds to the Magnificence of the Dwelling, but not to the Quantity of it. Tis impossible this can be thought a fault, if seriously thought of at all.'

In the same letter he also pointed out quite logically, if gently, that it is not possible to build a house so that every attractive prospect can be seen from every room. He argued for the building of what he called a 'greenhouse' or orangery, and in graceful charming language sketched out his feelings for it.

'The water (where it will Appear to the best advantage) whether Lake or River is full in View. There is another thing which I think worth Your Ldships remarks in this Case, which is, that this Greenhouse will keep off the Westerly sun from that end Garden, and Grott under the Gallery, at a time in the summer evenings when the West Side of a house is intollerable. And there will not be so agreeable a place in the whole Garden, as that will be towards six o'clock, provided the Sun be schreen'd a little off; Nor will there be so pleasant a room for View Nor so cool (yet all the Same Gay and light) in the whole house, as that Greenhouse or Detach'd Gallery, for that indeed is what I take it to be, And not a Magazine for a parcell of Foolish Plants.'

Vanbrugh found it easy to imagine himself taking a glass of wine, surveying the prospect of the lake which was to be conjured up, all the while sheltered from the fierce rays of the westering sun.

This letter of Vanbrugh's was tersely endorsed by the Duchess: 'The second green house, or a detached gallery, I thank God I prevented being built; nothing, I think can be more mad than the proposal, nor a falser description of the prospect.' The Duchess was not interested in pleasing prospects or charming lakes; she preferred the speedy and economical completion of building operations. She conducted her campaigns as the Duke did his battles and drove on furiously in spite of the odds provided by architects, artists, masons and carpenters.

A week after his letter with the airy plans for his greenhouse, Vanbrugh was forced to bring his ideas down to the Duchess's level and wrote on more practical matters. He was glad that the Duke might return earlier if the treaty was signed. Meanwhile he reported that the middle part of the building had advanced very fast. Unfortunately the weather which Vanbrugh had imagined in his letter about his greenhouse had not been forthcoming, and he spoke of the 'Cruell Wett Season' which had stopped the stone.

Vanbrugh was worried because, owing to the Duchess's low prices the carters had refused to bring the stone in. They did not consider it to be worth their while. In fact they would not consider bringing it in at all, 'except when the ways are perfectly good, And that they have nothing else to do, as may possibly fall out in October.'

There are some economies which turn out to be expensive. In spite of all the frustrations which Vanbrugh was forced to recount to the Duchess, he remained her Grace's humble and obedient servant.

The Duchess was waging a war on two or three fronts, and one of the recipients of her salvoes was her long suffering husband.

'I am much obliged to you,' wrote the Duke in September 1709, 'for the account you give of the building of Blenheim in yours of the 21st and the farther account you intend me after the Duke and Duchess of Shrewsbury have seen what is done.' The Duke went on to assure his wife that he can take pleasure in nothing so long as she continues 'uneasy and think me unkind, for I am fonder of my happiness than my life which I cannot enjoy unless you are kind'. In spite of the years which had passed since their courtship he was still the suppliant.

The Duke of Shrewsbury referred to in the Duke's letter

14a. Sarah, Duchess of Marl-
borough (painting after Sir
Geoffrey Kneller; National
Portrait Gallery)

b. Queen Anne (on her great seal)
(from G. T. Wilkinson: *History of England*, 1834)

15a. Arthur Maynwaring (ing by Sir Geoffrey Kneller National Portrait Gallery)

b. Marlborough House, designed by Wren (from *Vitruvius Britannicus*)

had visited Blenheim while building operations were going on. His house at Heythrop was near to Blenheim. Shrewsbury had married an Italian wife who was a Papist. Sarah had made some of her usual 'Mrs Candour' remarks about the lady. It was generally believed that Lady Shrewsbury, before she changed her name and nationality, had not been shrouded in the white garment of a blameless life. But she was determined to shine in the highest circles in England, and felt that political influence was the key to gain these social ends. It is suggested by Sir Winston Churchill that because of Lady Shrewsbury's influence her husband was gently pushed towards the Tory camp. Lady Shrewsbury was another in the coven of quarrelling and envious women. Sarah's sharp tongue raised enemies as quickly as the Duke's sword subdued them.

About this time my Lord Duke of Shrewsbury came no more to the site at Blenheim and another potential enemy was added to the Duke's difficulties. From the battlefields where men were dying, the Captain-General had to waste time writing soothing and useful advice to the battlefields of the boudoir and the drawing room. Already in the summer of 1709, Marlborough wrote to Sarah counselling caution: 'It has always been my observation in disputes, especially in those of kindness and friendship, that all reproaches, though ever so reasonable to serve to no other end but to the making the breach wider.' He suggested being obliging and kind to all her friends and to avoid entering into cabals. But pessimism now began to slip into his thoughts:

'I can't hinder being of opinion, how insignificant soever we may be, that there is a power above which puts a period to our happiness or unhappiness; otherwise, should anybody, eight years ago, have told me, after the success I have had, and the twenty seven years' faithful services of yourself, that we should be obliged, even in the lifetime of the Queen, to seek happiness in a retired life, I should have thought it impossible.'

The Duke had profited by his own talents, but he had also benefited by his wife's long intimacy with the Queen. Now that intimacy was nearing its end and his wife's character was doing as much to destroy his influence as it had done previously to promote it. The clash between the two women was not only a clash of personalities, it was also a clash of political allegiances.

Sarah was, and would always remain, like Vanbrugh, a confirmed Whig. Neither the Duchess nor her architect had ever wavered from their steadfast belief in the tenets of freedom from papist influences, detachment from the king over the water, and the right of every true born Englishman to a Protestant sovereign. The Duke's allegiances had always been more evanescent. He is always described as 'courteour like' and had lived in and about courts since early manhood.

Sarah's views were clean cut and uncompromising, like Vanbrugh's. She was not prepared to give quarter either to the Queen over her Tory sentiments, or to architects over her view that all that was needed in Woodstock Park was a neat plain house. It was unfortunate for Vanbrugh that he was never able to get the Duchess to see the palace from his point of view, or that with his pleasant personality he should never have been able to achieve an easy working relationship with her despite her first favourable impressions of him.

Vanbrugh's problems as artist and architect were linked with the Duke's. If the wars in Europe had been prolonged, the building of Blenheim was equally prolonged, and the expenses mounted daily. These were to provide an excellent excuse for the Tory attacks on Marlborough. In many senses the Duchess was right in feeling that the palace had been a mistake. Its grandeur was to prove her husband's Achilles Heel.

Up to this time, although the payments for the works had been tardy, they had been forthcoming. Vanbrugh had been the Queen's choice as architect and she had from the outset taken a keen interest in her presentation of a palace to her victorious general. But five years is a long time for the gratitude of Queen and nation to endure. The continual payments and demands for money for the 'golden mine of Blenheim' were becoming tedious to Parliament and people alike. The palace was providing his enemies with room for treacherous manoeuvres.

Although the building of Blenheim was fraught with political problems, the Duchess was driving on with Marlborough House, with the able help of Sir Christopher Wren, though even he was to be dismissed before the building was completed and accused of accepting bribes. Nor was the Captain-General to be left in peace over his wife's house. He was used as an agent to buy Dutch tiles (14,000 of them), as well as Dutch bricks, Italian mirrors and statues from Florence, all these sent back in Her Majesty's ships and passed through the customs duty free. There was nothing of which the Duchess did not manage to make economical use.

The Duchess's drive to get Marlborough House finished seemed in some senses to be a way of showing Vanbrugh, and others of his craft, what a good plain house should be. She was encouraged in his new venture, as always, by her faithful friend and amanuensis Maynwaring. About this new building he remarked: 'If the house be set in an equal line with her Majesty's Palace, it will have a view down the middle walk of her Garden and being remov'd from all manner of dust and from the smoke of the houses in Pell-Mell, you will live and sleep as it were in the middle of a great Garden.'

It was a garden in which the serpent Mrs Masham was already a tenant. Maynwaring also seems to have taken Vanbrugh to see the new building, which was perhaps not the essence of tact. Maynwaring reported to the Duchess that Vanbrugh had praised the interior, 'but I must own for the outside he found several faults there that were very obvious when he shewed them.'

Maynwaring was an agreeable gentleman who liked to see all points of view, and he added a few words of soothing syrup for the Duchess: 'He has talk'd me into an opinion that he is an able architect as to what relates to the Fabrick without.' He ended with the pious hope that the Duchess and Vanbrugh might work together to make 'the best house in the world'. Logically this ought to have been a possibility. But many different causes were to combine to prevent this happy conclusion.

In the autumn of 1709 the decline of the Whigs was helped by a happy accident for the Tories. Dr Henry Sacheverell, D.D., Fellow of Magdalen College, Oxford, chose 5 November, the day of gunpowder, treason and plot, to promote a few useful plots for the Tories. He picked St Paul's Cathedral, recently finished by Sir Christopher Wren, as the venue for his harangue on the evils of what was known as 'occasional conformity'. This strange phrase meant that Dissenters and low church Whigs would occasionally drop into their Parish churches in order to avoid being prosecuted as non-jurors (that is, men who refused to take an oath of loyalty to the Crown). With fiery eye and impassioned voice, the doctor preached his sermon on 'Perils of False Brethren in Church and State'.

In the popular mind the Whigs had always been seen to be aligned with the forces of atheism, if not revolution. Here was a passionate cleric suggesting that they were not only Whigs, but broods of vipers who were encroaching on the rights of 'Her Majesty God Bless Her! Whose Hereditary Right to the Throne, They have had the Impudence to Deny and Cancel, to make Her a Creature of their own Power'. The essence of his attack was that the Whigs were using the Queen as a tool, and that the English church, by law established, was in danger. This was the nub of the fight between Queen Anne and the Whigs, who were represented by the Marlboroughs.

In the Augustan age the throne still had power to dismiss ministers or to listen to intriguers who wished to form an alternative government. The functions of Parliament and Cabinet were not clearly defined, and although Queen Anne might represent a Protestant monarchy restored by the Whigs, the 'patriots who saved England', she was herself a pious High Tory who saw herself as the nursing mother of the English Church.

Dr Sacheverell was blowing a trumpet call alike to the old followers of the Martyr King Charles I, to the Tory hunting squires, and to those remaining followers of the king over the water. Within a few short weeks Dr Sacheverell's sermon had been printed by an enterprising bookseller, Henry Clements, and had sold, it is estimated, 100,000 copies. This made it the outstanding political best seller of the age.

The Whigs could hardly take this challenge to their authority and their patriotism lying down. They decided to impeach Dr Sacheverell, who no doubt relished this exhibition of his importance. Westminster Hall was newly decorated by Sir Christopher Wren for the trial with hangings and scaffolds. Tickets were at a premium, and Colley Cibber, ever conscious of pit and gallery, complained that the three-week trial was emptying the theatre. The doctor himself rode in a glass coach to and fro to his trial 'like an Ambassador making his entry rather than like a Criminal conducted to his Tryal.'

The Whig complaints were loud and prolonged, for while the pious doctor declared that he abhorred all disorders, his followers were apt to bludgeon down any passing Whig who did not immediately declare himself for High Church and Sacheverell.

Even the Queen was drawn to the trial and sat in a box designed for her by Sir Christopher Wren, with a discreet curtain hiding her sentiments and her expression from the popular gaze. The Duchess of Marlborough, also present, managed to pick a quarrel with a fellow Duchess, Lady Somerset, about etiquette. Obsessed with her position at Court and the possible loss of her gold key—emblem of her position as Groom of the Stole—Sarah seems for once to have been totally unseeing as to the final outcome for the Whigs of the pseudo martyrdom of the doctor.

The trial ended on 21 March 1710 and the martyr parson received a nominal sentence. He then set out for further triumphal progresses about the country, like a pious pop star, sowing the seeds of the electoral triumph of the Tories and the True Church in England.

The sands of political favour, like the supply of money to Blenheim, were running out. If the Masham intrigues at Court were the cause of the rise of Harley and the Tories, there were other undercurrents in the country which were undermining the foundations of Whiggery in general, and the building of Blenheim in particular. Vanbrugh had ridiculed churchmen in his plays; they were to prove stronger than his jokes.

Another parson, Dean Swift, the ambitious Irishman, now made his appearance in the wings and was prepared to play the part of the demon king. He had been rebuffed by the Whigs, and when dealing with him the Lord Godolphin had been 'altogether short, dry and morose'. The Dean went away enraged and prepared to unsheath his sharp quill for the use of the Tories. He wrote to Stella: 'The Whigs were ravished to see me, and would lay hold on me as a twig while they are drowning.' Like many others of his age, the Dean was not over particular which side he joined so long as he could obtain some patronage for himself. Vanbrugh was one of the few men who stayed faithful to his Whig principles, sometimes to the detriment of himself, and his work.

Swift's pen was more easily available to his patrons. Everything was changing. The impossible was happening and the great Duke's power was waning politically at home, although he could still be made use of on the European battle front.

At the beginning of 1710 Marlborough was back from fighting his country's enemies abroad and was confronted by his political enemies at home. He wrote to the Queen suggesting that she should either dismiss Abigail Masham or himself. The Whigs took fright at this uncompromising attitude and the sentence in his letter which made his position crystal clear was expunged. The Whigs were weakening and indecisive. At this crucial point came the trial of Dr Sacheverell, and in the spring of 1710 a mere two months afterwards, came the final break between the Queen and Sarah.

It is hard to read of the final interview between Sarah and the Queen without feeling that, in spite of her difficult nature and badgering character, she had perhaps deserved better of the Queen. Whatever the Duchess's shortcomings may have been, in the end the punishment meted out was severe. To all her protestations of calumny the Queen returned but one single phrase, 'You desired no answer and shall have none'.

Sarah herself recounted the incident: 'When she [the Queen] came to the door, I fell into great disorder; streams of tears flow'd down against my will, and prevented my speaking for some time.'

It was all in vain. The friendship was dead. Its disappearance was to involve the grand alliance of the Marlboroughs and Godolphin. Sarah never saw the Queen again. Blenheim had become a monument to a vanished friendship, and a victory long ago.

But Vanbrugh still struggled on with its building, and with all the details of its embellishment. In April 1710 he wrote very earnestly about some statues which had been made in Florence and which, as was usual, had not been paid for.

'For God's sake Speak to My Ld. Ryalton about it, that a Remittance of £300 more may instantly be made out . . . The giving leave from the Great Duke to make these Statues was a very great Compliment meant to Ld. M. And obtain'd by Application from the Envoy there, so that you may judge how it must sound in the Court at Florence to hear the Statuarys who are employ'd can't get their money.'

It was not only the Italians who were not being paid; the financial position on the home front was as frail as the political balance.

In June, Vanbrugh still wrote, cheerfully to the Duchess about the progress of his palace, although he must have known that the whole project hung precariously in the balance.

'I left things in such a Way Madam when I came from Blenheim that I believe I may assure you the Whole House will be covered in this year. The Bridge quite got up, And the Great Court in a manner finish't: I mean as to, Leveling, paving and enclosing. And I think I may now Venture almost to Assure your Grace Likwise (As I have already done my Lord Treasurer) That the whole Expence, of House, Offices, Bridge, Avenues and Gardens will not *exceed* Two Hundred and Fifty Thousand Pounds. Tho' I find I shall have the Satisfaction of Peoples thinking it had Cost Double that Summ.'

It was not the moment either for satisfaction, or for speaking frankly of large sums to the Duchess. Two weeks later when the news of the dismissal of Lord Sunderland, the Marlboroughs' son-in-law, from his post as Secretary of State, reached Vanbrugh he wrote to the Duchess in some alarm.

London June 24th 1710.

'Madam, your Grace will not wonder that some of the People at Blenheim who trust the works with very great sums (some of them more than they are really worth in the world) should be a little frightened with the news of my Lord Sunderland, and other things they daily hear. And this apprehension I find is like to prove a great hindrance to the very hopeful progress this summer, unless something be done to encourage 'em; which I believe a Letter from your Grace would do, either to Mr Travers or to me, by which you shou'd give us commission to declare to them that whatever happen'd you wou'd take care they shou'd not suffer. I believe such a letter wou'd be sufficient; and I suppose your Grace will have no objections to it, since Tis only what you have on your own accord often said. If your Grace be pleased to do something of this kind, the sooner the better; because there is such a quantity of Materials got in, and such a number of men at present engag'd that the work of his summer will be surprising, if no unlucky cheque be put to it.'

Vanbrugh carried on as if a 'cheque' to the building was not be thought of. 'Square blew paving' was ordered for the completion of the Great Court, and pebbles 'to pitch ten thousand yards'.

To the Duke, on 1 August 1710 he reported the progress of the building, coupled inevitably with the difficulties about the supply of money.

'I am heartily touched with the thoughts your Grace should (after the great Services this barbarous nation is indebted to you for) meet with any sort of trouble that may allay the satisfaction, I flatter myself I else would find, in the great progress we have and shall make here this summer. The rest of the House to the Westward is now out of all danger of being uncovered.'

A week later Lord Godolphin's dismissal followed that of Sunderland. At the end of August Vanbrugh decided to make a circuitous approach to the formidable Duchess about money. He had apparently been using the ubiquitous Maynwaring as a go-between.

'Mr Maynwaring shew'd your Grace the copy of a letter I was forc'd to trouble my Lord Duke with in May last. Tis easy to imagine the change of My Lord Treasurer (Lord Godolphin) must bring some people very hard upon me, who with great difficulty were prevail'd upon to wait before. But now seeing me totally disappointed on all sides there is nothing but money will satisfy 'em; of which I have none to give 'em.'

News about the need for money was something which the careful Duchess preferred not to hear.

Apart from writing to the Duke and Duchess, Vanbrugh had also written to Lord Poulet, outlining the bad situation which the workmen found themselves in. He said that things at Blenheim are 'falling into a Distraction not to be Expressed, from the Great Arrears due to a vast Number of poor familys.' The complications of the Duchess's fall from the Queen's Grace now spread their nets wide, and were actually causing local families in Oxfordshire to starve.

The Duchess paid no attention to the imploring letters. She had deeper problems to ponder—her own diminished glory, the loss of her power, and most important of all the preservation of her husband's influence, if that were possible. A further complication was now added. The Whigs had chosen the wrong moment to appeal to the electorate, and Dr Sacheverell's propaganda was doing its work all up and down the country, to topple the hated Whigs, and return the one true Church to its former glory and power. Blenheim had become a very minor incident in the Duchess's grand strategy.

On 30 September the worried architect wrote to Robert Harley, the begetter of all these disasters, the relation of Abigail Hill, who had brought about the 'Great Change' in the fortunes of the Marlboroughs and of Blenheim. In this letter Vanbrugh said that although it was not strictly his province to 'solicite the mony for it, but to take care of the Designe, the Execution, & ye contracts' he hoped that he will not be blamed for regarding Blenheim more as a monument to the glory of Queen Anne rather than a mere house for the Duke himself.

The trouble was, as always, the 'extream necessity' of covering up the stone against the winter frosts and rains. Local stone in Oxfordshire, when it is in a raw state, was and still is extremely porous and easily destroyed by the weather flaking it away. Vanbrugh could visualise his masterpiece, half built, falling into a ruin, like Rosamund's Bower, before it was carried to its longed-for triumphant conclusion.

To the copies of the letters which Vanbrugh had written

trying to save his palace from destruction, he added a note: 'Three days after I had sent these letters, there came an Express Order from the Dutchess of Marlborough to put a general Stop to the Building till money should be Order'd from the Treasury to go on with it, and a Stop was put accordingly.'

A note of bitterness creeps into Vanbrugh's letter to Mr Joynes at Blenheim written on 7 September 1710: 'I have a letter from you with an Acct: of what pass'd with My Lady Dutchess. I think She has given Orders she'll repent of, but be it as she thinks fitt. If she orders the House to be pull'd down, I desire you'll comply wth. her.' His bitterness was mitigated when he arrived in London and found a letter from Mr Taylor of the Treasury, which said that although the Queen found herself temporarily short of revenues and unable to carry out the work as fast as she would wish. 'Yet her Majesty wou'd by no means, have what is so far Advanc'd left in a Condition to be injur'd by the Approaching Winter.'

Vanbrugh was asked to give an estimate of how much it would cost to cover the building against the winter. His estimate was £8,000. In the event the Treasury later gave him £7,000.

Behind these simple facts of covering the half-finished building lay many political manoeuvres. The Duke was still needed by the Harley Ministry to fight on the Continent. Should he leave the Queen's service they would have been disgraced in the eyes of the nation to whom he was a popular hero. They wished to make use of him and to discard him only when the time was ripe and his European work was done. The stopping of the work and the possible decay of the gift of the Queen would not burnish the bright image of the Tories. Seven thousand pounds was a small bone thrown to keep the Duke happy and to prevent his resignation.

There were other pressing considerations. On the day that the Duchess had stopped all work on the palace, Vanbrugh wrote to the Duke outlining the plight of the workmen. He wrote that although the principal stonemasons and carpenters could perhaps weather the temporary financial storm, 'yet the labourers, Carters and other Country People, who us'd to be regularly paid, but were now in arrear, finding themselves disbanded in so Surprising a Manner without a farthing wou'd certainly conclude their Money lost; And finding themselves distress'd by what they ow'd to the People where they lodg'd & c.'

Joynes was equally alarmed: 'We fear it may be of Ill Consequence in turning off such a body of poor Necessitous people without paying them.' He added that they have begun their 'pranks' already and have been breaking some of the capitals of the columns.

Vanbrugh made the same point to the Duke. 'Numbers of them having their Familys and Homes at great distances in other Countys, twas very much to be fear'd such a general Meeting might happen, that the Building might feel the effects of it.' Blenheim was not only in danger of being destroyed by frost, but by its own builders. Behind the letters lurked the humiliations of the architect and his clerk of the works.

The labourers were not only in a destructive mood but, Vanbrugh wrote, 'I had for some days past observed 'em grown very insolent, and in Appearance kept from Meeting only by the Assurance we gave them from one day to another that money was coming. But all I had to say was cut short by Mr Joynes' Shewing me a Postscript my Lady Dutchess had added to her Letter forbidding any regard to whatever I might say or do.'

'My Lady Dutchess' liked subservience and obedience to her will. As she wrote: 'I am very fond of my three dogs, they have all of them gratitude, wit and good sense. Things very rare to be found in this country. They are fond of going out with me; but when I reason with them, and tell them it is not proper, they submit.'

Vanbrugh was no dog to the Duchess. After her insulting postscript, he wrote to the Duke: 'Your Grace won't blame me, if asham'd to continue there any Longer on such a foot; as well as seeing it was not in my power to do your Grace any farther Service.' He ended by remarking that as small a sum as six or seven hundred pounds would have paid off the poor labourers, and added that 'notwithstanding all this cruel usage from the Dutchess of Marlborough' he will receive with pleasure 'and Obey and Commands your Grace will please to lay upon me being with the Utmost Defference I ever was, your Grace's most Humble and most Obedient Servant.'

Sir Winston Churchill in his account of the monetary mazes of the building of Blenheim states that the Tory parliamentarians, who had always harped on the 'golden mine of Blenheim', had suspended payments and laid traps to make John and Sarah responsible for the expenses of Blenheim, a trap which the Marlboroughs were trying to avoid. It is a charitable viewpoint.

Godolphin, out of favour, and out of office, merely remarked, 'Let them keep their heap of stones.'

Marlborough wrote, as always, urging discretion on his wife: 'My opinion is that you and I should be careful of leaving the disposition of carrying on the building at Woodstock to the Queen's officers. It is our best way not to give any orders, but to let the Treasury give what orders they please, either for its going on, or standing still.'

He did not agree with Sarah's peremptory order for the stopping of all the works or for the dismissing of the workmen.

To the Marlboroughs, their conduct may have seemed prudent husbandry, but to the architect, watching his cherished dream in danger of falling into ruin, and the workmen with no money for lodgings, food, or transport to return to their homes, the problem presented itself in a less academic way.

William Stratford, of Christchurch, Oxford, wrote in August of 1710:

'The debt to the workmen at Blenheim—that is known is

above £60,000. They owe to Strong the mason for his share, £10,500. It will go hard with many in this town and the country who have contracted with them. Their creditors begin to call on them and they can get no money at Blenheim. One poor fellow who had £600 owing to him for lime and brick came on Saturday to Tom Rowney (the Member for Oxford) to ask for a little money he owed him. It was about £5. The fellow thanked him with tears and said that the money, for the present, would save him from gaol.'

Heavy debts were nothing less than damnation, starvation and imprisonment in Vanbrugh's day. It was only too easy for comfortable craftsmen—or even architects—to slip into the pit of the debtors' prison which yawned below.

Vanbrugh kept his courage up, and tried to work for the good of the enterprise and for the people who were carrying it out. The Duke was less optimistically inclined. He wrote to his wife:

'It no way becomes you or me, to be giving orders for the Queen's money. Neither you, nor I, nor any of our friends ought to meddle in their accounts, but to let it be taken by the Queen's officers, as they always ought to be. She is mistress of her own money, and consequently of the time of finishing that house.

'Whilst Lord Godolphin was in, and I had the Queen's favour, I was very earnest to have had it finished; but as it is, I am grown very indifferent. For, as things are now, I do not see how I can have any pleasure in living in a country where I have so few friends.'

Time had not modified Sarah's views of the palace project. The weakness of the Duke for this great monument to his glory was something which she had never understood. She was disposed, as always, to take the troubles of others lightly. Strong the mason was quite happy putting on the roof, she noted, and the fact that he was owed £10,000, a vast fortune at the time, she ignored. As for the threats of the workmen to destroy the house, she merely remarked: 'Pulling down the house will be of no great use to the workmen, or to the towns about that have so much reason to hope to live by it.'

Sarah was intent on pursuing her own private feuds, and enmeshed in them was her ultimate plan to dispense with Vanbrugh, whom she had come to regard as the source of all the extravagance and useless grandeur of Blenheim. But the Duke was Vanbrugh's friend, and had great regard for him both as a man and as an architect: 'I am very sure I am a well wisher and faithfull friend of Mr Vanbrughs and tho' I am at this time very much out of fashion, I will flatter my Self that I may yet live to have it in my power of being useful to those I have obligations to.'

The Duchess did not admit obligations, she liked her rights— to the last penny of them. But the Duke was trying to use his diplomatic practice, so long useful to his country abroad, to soothe the savage breast of his wife.

'I beg of you to let Mr Maynwaring know that I beg the favour of him to *manage* Vanbrugh, so that he may not be angry; for that would be a pleasure to those that wish us ill. Upon the whole we live in a very disagreeable age in which we must expect no favour.'

Vanbrugh had dubbed Blenheim a 'monument of ingratitude': The Duke's glory was passing; only the monument to it remained unfinished.

CHAPTER XIV

Tory Triumphs

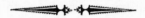

The Duchess had stopped the building, but the implications of her action remained. She brushed aside the possible effect on her elections that the sight of so many starving people might have: 'As I never gave a bribe for the elections I trust the Town of Woodstock with that, for besides it is certainly their interest not to disoblige the Duke of Marlborough.'

Mr Travers, sometimes styled the Duke's agent, went down to Woodstock and found the situation in the town was not to be taken as lightly as the Duchess would have preferred. The poor workmen were unable to pay their lodgings in the town and had no money to travel back to their homes.

Travers wrote to the Duke on 8 October outlining the events at the Woodstock Election: 'When I came hither on Friday morning I found the scene much changed from what Mr Vanbrugh and Mr Hawksmoor had told me. The people who had been turned off without their wages were full of complaints and tears, and then threats and violence—'

There was another threat—other candidates than the Duke's might be brought in, 'Blenheim indeed being under a cloud.' But Travers wrote: 'to prevent any tumult that might be set on foot at the Election and in compassion to so many poor starving people, I borrowed £300 here on my own credit and ordered the Comptrollers to pay off the poor labourers and to divide the overplus among the most necessitous of this town.'

Travers' three hundred pounds saved the election at Woodstock, although the Whigs were defeated over most of the country, sometimes by defections and sometimes by treacheries. At Woodstock, in spite of the difficulties with the workmen, Lt. General Cadogan and Sir Thomas Wheate were elected without opposition. It is hard not to draw the conclusion that the Marlboroughs, especially the Duchess, were better served by the electors than their actions merited.

With Sunderland and Godolphin irrevocably removed from the Queen's Government, the position of the Marlboroughs was totally undermined, and with them the financial situation of Vanbrugh, and all at Blenheim. It was like a town under siege, waiting for starvation to do its work.

At this point Dean Swift, who had ever been willing to wound the Whigs who had done him few favours, by the autumn of 1710 was gathering his forces to strike.

In November 1710, a month after the election had pointed the way for the aspiring Irish clergyman to climb his way up the ladder of worldly preferment, he wrote to Stella: 'I dined today at Sir Richard Temples with Congreve, Vanbrugh, Lieutenant General Farrington & Co. Vanbrugh I believe I told you had a long quarrel with me about those verses on his house; but we were very civil and cold. Lady Marlborough used to tease him with them, which had made him angry, though he be a good natured fellow.'

Swift had written some verses in 1703 in mock heroic style on the small house which Vanbrugh had built for himself out of the rubble of Whitehall Palace.

In 1698, due to a domestic's fervour for drying linen, which was left too near a fire in Whitehall, the Palace caught fire and as a result none of Wren's buildings was saved. Only the passion of Wren himself, and the quick action of his helpers, saved the Inigo Jones Banqueting Hall. In the immediate post-fire euphoria King William had decided that Wren should design him a splendid new classical palace to rival the Louvre. But like the ashes of the fire, the enthusiasm for this soon cooled.

The designs for this projected palace were lost for over one hundred years, but in 1930 they were discovered in the Library at All Souls College, Oxford. Inigo Jones' Banqueting Hall was to form the centrepiece of a huge building with a portico one hundred feet high in the Italianate style. The palace remained only a plan.

A year after the fire John Vanbrugh was granted leave to build himself a lodging in Whitehall upon ground where Mr Vice Chamberlain's stood before the fire. He was further given permission to make use of such bricks and stone out of 'ye rubbish of the said Palace as he should have occasion for.' It was against the anti-climax of this small house instead ot the grandiose palace that Swift's contemptuous lines were written:

> 'At length they in the rubbish spy
> A thing resembling a Goose-pye
> Thither in haste the Poets throng
> And gaze in silent wonder long
> Till one in raptures thus began
> To praise the pile, and builder Van.'

Not unnaturally the Duchess with her hatred of architecture enjoyed the verse, but equally it was not surprising that Vanbrugh, who had haunted the palace of his imaginings like a ghost, should have been discomforted. His precarious position, and the mountain of building and monetary difficulties of Blenheim did not make his architecture a subject for raillery. Swift's jokes were not good humoured, especially as he had included in them charges that Vanbrugh's talent for comedy was purely that of a plagiarist.

Encouraged by the success of his first set of verses Swift repeated the dose in 1708, suggesting that it was purely on the 'grandeur' of Vanbrugh's ridiculous Goose Pie house that he had been raised to fame as an architect.

> 'For building famed and justly reckon'd
> At court Vitruvius the second.

No wonder, since wise authors show,
That best foundations must be *low*;
And now the Duke has wisely ta'en him
To be his architect at Blenheim.'

The last couplet of the verse gave the final twist to the carefully barbed shafts:

'We might expect to see next year,
A mouse-trap man chief engineer.'

In November 1710 Swift was dining in the inner Tory circles,
receiving compliments for his attacks on Vanbrugh, the protégé
of the Whigs. He rejoiced that he had been at Court, 'where the
Queen passed by us with all the Tories about her; not one
Whig, and I have seen her without one Tory.'

Swift was using a little blarney on his Tory friends: 'Prior
was damped until I stuffed him with two or three compliments.'
Although the Dean was in a rising way and quite prepared to
relish the fall of the Whigs, including Vanbrugh, he still hugged
the bitterness of the past to his bosom: 'It is hard to see these
great men use me like one who was their better and the puppies
with you in Ireland hardly regarding me.'

The envious Casca had not forgotten past slights. It is possible that Vanbrugh's strictures on the clergy were included in
Swift's unhappy rememberings. Had not Sir John Brute,
dressed as a clergyman, confessed to a talent for drunkenness
and simony? No quarter could be given amongst wits.

In the *Examiner* of 16 November 16 1710 Swift struck his
decisive and brilliant blow against Marlborough himself. In a
long attack, he commenced by writing: 'I said in a former Paper
that the one specious Objection to the late removals at Court,
was the fear of giving Uneasiness to a General who has long
been successful abroad.' Swift then went on to ask a long series
of rhetorical questions dedicated to the proposition that the
General had enriched himself from the Wars. That the glory

was not so much the country's but the personal perquisites of the Marlborough family:

'Will the accusers of the Nation join issue upon any of these Particulars, or tell us in what Point our Damnable Sin of Ingratitude lies? Why tis plain and clear; For while he is Commanding abroad, the Queen dissolves her Parliament at home: In which *universal calamity* no less than *two persons* allied by marriage to the General have lost their places.'

Lord Sunderland was, of course, the Marlboroughs' son-in-law, and Godolphin's son, Ryalton, was married to their daughter.

While attacking Marlborough, Swift interlarded his prose with compliments to the Queen.

'This is not an age to produce Favourites of the People, while we live under a Queen who engrosses all our Love, and all our Veneration; and where, the only way for a great General or Minister, to acquire any degree of subordinate Affection from the Publick must be by all Marks of the *most entire Submissions and Respect* to her Sacred Person and Commands; otherwise, no pretence of great Services, either in the Field, or the Cabinet, will be able to skreen them from universal Hatred.'

This was the perfumed incense of the Divine Right of Kings. The 'patriots who saved England' were in eclipse.

The sharpest strokes of all came in an inventory which Swift drew up, comparing the cost of a General's triumph under the might of Rome and the 'golden mine of Blenheim'. He dubbed this 'two fair accounts.'

A bill of Roman Gratitude	l	s	d	*A bill of British Ingratitude*	l	s	d
Franckincense &				Woodstock	40,000		
earthen Pots to burn it in	4	10	0	Blenheim	200,000		
A Bull for Sacrifice	8	0	0	Post Office Grant	100,000		

A bill of Roman Gratitude				*A bill of British Ingratitude*	
An Embroidered				Mildenheim	30,000
Garment	50	0	0	Pictures, Jewels	
A Crown of Laurel	0	0	2	& C.	60,000
A Statue	100	0	0	Pall Mall Grant	10,000
A Trophy	80	0	0	Employments	100,000
A thousand copper					
medals value half pence				Sum Tot.	£540,000
a piece	2	1	8		
A Triumphal Arch	500	0	0		
A Triumphal Carr valu'd					
as a Modern Coach	100	0	0		
Casual charges at the					
Triumph	150	0	0		

Sum Total   £994 11 10

Swift had been carefully nurtured by the Tories, and his writings were the fair fruit of their husbandry. The attack was anonymous, like so much of the scurrilous journalism of the period. The piece ended with the suggestion that the Duchess had misappropriated the Queen's funds in her capacity as Mistress of the Robes. Whatever faults the Duchess may have had, and Vanbrugh had suffered from most of them, careful management of money, whether it was her own or the Queen's, was one of her virtues. Possibly care with money is not considered a virtue by many. Swift had written of the Duchess: 'Three furies reigned in her breast, the most mortal enemies of all softer passions, which were sorded Avarice, disdainful Pride and ungovernable Rage.'

This last passion caused her furiously to try to discover the author of the underhand attacks on the Duke. But journalists of the early eighteenth century covered their snail trails carefully. The penalties for writing pornography and libel could be the loss of their ears, the pillory or prison. It was as well to conceal one's identity and one's sources.

While the Tories, Harley and St John would have liked to have dismissed Marlborough, their position on the Continent would have been precarious. The Elector of Hanover, the heir to the British Throne, the King of Prussia and the Dutch all made it clear that Marlborough must be retained as Commander in Chief.

Although Marlborough was occupied in his campaigning, and in spite of the fact that he expressed indifferences as to the fate of Blenheim, in his secret thoughts the image of his palace still remained. He wrote: 'I think that those that take care of the building at Blenheim, when the winter season and the want of money makes the work to cease, should take care to cover the works, so as what is already done may receive no prejudice, and then it may remain as a monument of ingratitude as Mr Van calls it in his letter.'

Sarah remained staunchly in her uncompromising mood when she wrote to Godolphin.

'My lord Marlborough approves very much of all that I said to Mr. Travers upon the subject of Woodstock, and I suppose will not be less of that mind when he sees the letters that Mr. Joyns writ, to fight me into sending them money. He adds that they may pull down what they have built, if they please, he will never contradict it, which I was glad to see; for I think that building was the greatest weakness my lord Marlborough ever had, and, being his passion, I am pleased he has over-come it; and I believe, these Ministers thought to ensnare him by it.'

In the autumn of 1710, when the libels had done their work, Harley and the Tories were still playing a double game, and Blenheim was one of their pawns. The Duke had not given up his monumental dream, in spite of all Sarah had to say on the subject.

Vanbrugh wrote to Joynes at Blenheim that he was in 'daily Expectation of my Ld. Dukes directions about money.' In October he was very glad to find that 'no mischief has happened to the Building, which I know there was a good deal of reason to apprehend, how light soever My Lady Dutchess might make of it.'

The Duke was not the only man to have to serve Harley. Vanbrugh, too, was under the necessity of paying service to his new master. He wrote urgently to Joynes, asking him to send estimates of the money required to secure the building against the winter and the weather, adding, 'I waited on Mr. Harley today, who told me that I might depend upon the Treasurys taking care of the Building, they having receiv'd the Queens Directions for it, and that they would do what they cou'd at present, and continue to forward it as Money cou'd be spar'd.'

Harley at the Treasury was at long last disposed to send the seven thousand pounds for the securing of the building, Vanbrugh asked Joynes again for the accounts, and also requested that he might have his papers which 'I left in the Right Hand Drawer of the Little Table I us'd in my Bedchamber'. He also asked Joynes that if, and when, the money should be forthcoming he would keep two or three hundred pounds in a private bank for emergencies which the Duchess might nor forsee. 'But make no mention of this to any body.' It was perhaps a precautionary sum against favourite workmen being again reduced to penury.

On 19 October the good news was announced. At last the money had arrived, but by the beginning of the year following, most of the cash had disappeared. Vanbrugh wrote urgently to Mr Joynes. 'Mr Parker tells me you have paid away the whole £5,000 which I am sorry to hear and hope is a Mistake.'

Apart from the swift sifting away of the money, more important happenings had flung the fate of Blenheim once more into the balance. When the Duke returned from the wars at the end of the year, the Queen had completed Sarah's degradation and dismissed her from all her employments. Abigail had done her work well. The Duchess, not to be outdone, threatened to publish all Anne's intimate letters which contained many disparaging remarks about her own sister, Queen Mary, and her brother-in-law, William III.

The Duke was past sixty. He had been campaigning for ten years, and now he was faced with the wreck of all his cherished dreams of retiring with his power and prestige unimpaired. He had said that he would 'go on all fours' if he could restore his wife's credit with the Queen. Even Sarah wrote a letter of apology to the unrelenting Anne, hoping by this means to avoid her husband's resignation. The Queen read it but remained obdurate.

The Duke then tried to remedy the matter with a personal appeal, falling on his knees in front of the Queen to ask her to let his wife at least retain her gold key as Groom of the Stole.

Churchill records this incident with distaste: 'This obsequious grovelling to royalty was an essential part of the pathway to the bright fields of power and action in an age when royal favour dominated all.'

If Vanbrugh kowtowed to the Duke, the Duke in his turn had to kneel to the royal prude. It was a useless exercise, the Queen demanded her gold key and within three days. The Duke pleaded for ten, but Anne, to show her power over him, then demanded the key in two days. Sarah, when she realised that the last bastion to her influence with the Queen had fallen, sent the key back at once. Abigail was created Keeper of the Privy Purse, and the gold key of Groom of the Stole went to the Duchess of Somerset.

A week before this final crumbling of his wife's power, the Duke's sudden arrival at Blenheim had been announced by Vanbrugh. He was concerned that the bridge should be shown to the Duke to its best advantage. 'An other thing I desire may immediately be gone about is the striking the Centers under the Great Arch of the Bridge, and pray let them be lay'd so out of the way as not to confuse the View of the Bridge in any part of it.' Vanbrugh concluded by wishing Mr Joynes and Mr Bobart a happy New Year which, in the event, was unlikely to materialise.

In February, Vanbrugh again wrote to Joynes about his hopes for money to carry on. 'My Ld Duke go's in a day or two, And Mr. Harley has assur'd me yesterday we shall have money to proceed this year, but wt. the Sum will be, I don't yet know, but he said 'twoud be Issu'd by weekly Payments. I hope they'll begin soon after my Ld. Duke go's.'

He ended by asking Joynes to 'ask Kitt Cash if the French book of Paladio be not in Mr. Strongs Shedd; I thought we had it in Towne but dont find it.'

Vanbrugh obviously attached some importance to this book which he had written to Tonson to buy for him when Tonson had been on one of his continental journeys. The architects of Vanbrugh's period were much influenced by one another's ideas, and cross-fertilisation of imagination produced subtle changes in the carrying out of their huge building operations. When Wren, Hawksmoor and Vanbrugh himself worked together on architectural projects, it is often difficult, even for the experts, to disentangle the influences which were brought to bear on the final result.

But subtle influences were not in Vanbrugh's mind in the spring of 1711; money for the workmen was his principal concern.

Before he sailed for the Continent the Duke had interviewed Harley about the essential cash for carrying on with the building. Vanbrugh later wrote to the Duke that he had been told by Harley that he (as architect) would have 'no directions but from your Grace alone, nor the money to be accounted for in any other Place.'

This was perhaps a pious hope that the Duchess could be prevented from interfering. But once the Duke had been safely induced to sail off to the wars to take up his command, the whole question of finance for Blenheim became less urgent to the Tories. The Blenheim affair had been used as bait to keep the Duke happy. Now he was once more where the Ministry wanted him—overseas and in harness.

In March Vanbrugh was still 'in daily hopes of money being order'd for Blenheim—which had been done ere now but for this accident to Mr Harley.'

The 'accident' to Mr Harley had been a murderous attack by a Frenchman who had ennobled himself with the false title of Marquis de Guiscard. The Frenchman had been the companion in profligacy of St John, but when the latter had achieved power he had cast the Frenchman aside and reduced his pension. Smarting from this double insult de Guiscard had taken his revenge by getting in touch with the French enemy. As a result he was about to be arrested for treason, and sent to Newgate.

His appeals to his former companion in venery, St John, had fallen on deaf ears. He preferred to forget that they had shared the responsibility for a bastard child. Infuriated, de Guiscard attacked Harley with a penknife and wounded him. The thickness of his embroidered coat saved the Treasurer. His slow recovery from his wound, and the fact that the near fatal blow had been aimed by a foreigner, miraculously restored his popularity. He returned to the House of Commons on 26 April amidst universal acclamations and congratulations.

At this point, some dispute arose between St John and Harley. Both claimed the honour and prestige of being the object of the Frenchman's dastardly attack. On points, Harley appears to have won. With all the drama which surrounded the attack, and the recovery from it, the affairs of Blenheim had sunk to a secondary place. Vanbrugh still hoped that he might be able to get the main private apartments in the east wing ready during the course of the ensuing summer.

But even these hopes were struck by the squalls of the Duchess's dismissal from Court. She had been told to leave her apartments in St James's Palace, apartments which she had used and fitted up over the course of many years. She had lived about St James's since she was a child; it was another bond broken. Infuriated by the idea that possibly the hated Abigail might inhabit her cherished grace-and-favour residence, Sarah reacted in the usual way of angry tenants. She began to remove the locks, looking glasses, and marble fireplaces which she had paid for.

The Duke wrote in some agitation, trying to restrain his wife: 'I am sent word the Queen is desirous of having the lodgings at St James's so that I desire you would give directions for the removing of the furniture. I beg you will *not* remove the marble chimney pieces.' As Miss Austen remarked there is nothing like disputes over an inventory to bring out the worst relations between landlord and tenant.

For once Sarah took notice of her husband's request—she left the chimneypieces intact—but the incident of the brass locks and the fireplaces had hardened Queen Anne's feelings against the palace of Blenheim.

Arthur Maynwaring, anxious as usual to conciliate all parties, spoke to Harley and remarked that he hoped that the building of Blenheim could be continued. Harley replied that everything was about to be amicably settled 'till this late bustle about the lodgings. The Queen is so angry that she says she will build no house for the Duke of Marlborough when the Duchess has pulled hers to pieces, taken away the very slabs out of the chimneys, thrown away the keys, and said they might buy more for ten shillings.'

The confusion caused by the coven of quarrelling women had not abated.

In June of 1711, Harley, who as a result of his fortuitous wound had been raised to the splendour of being created Earl of Oxford, asked Vanbrugh if he could give an estimate for the finishing of Blenheim. The answer was that it could cost £87,000. There were provisos. Some expenses the Duke might take upon himself. These were glossed over. Unfortunately for Vanbrugh, and for his army of masons and carpenters, these were merely tentative enquiries. No money was sent. Poor Joynes reported that spirits amongst the Blenheimites, as they called themselves, were low, as well they might be. 'I shall be

heartily Glad to hear of your coming down,' he wrote to Vanbrugh, 'which will give new Life hear.'

Bobart, who does not seem to have had any official position,
had constituted himself the Duchess's spy and was carefully
reporting on any misdoings which he might happen to come
across.

The Duchess was in careful correspondence with him: 'I
wonder much at Mr Vanbrugh for what you write of his orders.
I allways thought him a bold man but I think they are more so
that will worke upon that House unless he would give them
better assurance than I fear he can of ever being paid.' She
added that she hoped that Bobart would continue to report on
any further 'mad things' which were ordered.

While Harley was using Matthew Prior on a secret mission
to negotiate peace with the French, unknown to the Duke, the
Duchess was proceeding similarly, using Bobart to report on
the mis-deeds of her architect, behind his back.

At last in August the money began to arrive. Vanbrugh wrote
happily to the Duke: 'I am glad I can at last acquaint your
Grace, there is a weekly payment begun for Blenheim at 1000 l.
a week to continue for twenty weeks; and my Lord Treasurer
[Harley] told me this morning he would think of a further
supply.' In the same letter he suggested that the Duke might
perhaps let him have a little money on his own account.

The money had arrived as the Duke was advancing on
Bouchain. During the siege itself the Duke wrote on 9 September, the letter was headed 'Camp before Bouchain': 'I cannot omit returning my hearty thanks to your Lordship for the
kind advice you have been pleased to give me by Mr. Craggs
relating to the money issue from the Exchequer for the Building
of Blenheim.' Even in the heat of battle, the Palace was always
in his mind and heart.

Meanwhile the peace negotiations proceeded apace. The
project was so secret that even Swift, the agent of the Duke's
downfall, was not at the centre of the web. While the Ministers

disarmed the Duke by supporting his campaign and soothing him with funds for Blenheim, Grub Street continued its attacks. Mrs Manley, often used, and briefed, by Swift for his more scurrilous attacks on the Marlborough family, in *The Examiner* held up to ridicule what she called 'The House of Pride' (Blenheim Palace):

'This dazzling, unwieldy structure was built amidst the Tears and Groans of a People Harass'd with a lingring war, to gratified the Ambition of a Subject, whilst the Sovereign's Palace lay in Ashes. [This was a reference to the burning of Whitehall.]

'It was dedicated, from the first Foundation to the Goddess of Pride; the Building excessive costly, but not artful; The Architect seem'd to consider how to be most profuse and therefore neglected an advantageous Eminence (made proper by Nature) to build one a quarter of a Mile short of it, at the vain expense of Fifty Millions of Sesterces. There were to be seen Stately Towers, noble Porticos, ample Piazzas and well turned Pillars, without one handsome Room unless you will call the kitchens and cellars such, which part of the house happens to be of little use to the Parsimonious Founder.'

There was little doubt that the expenses of Blenheim were a fruitful source of underhand attacks. From 1705 the estimates had mounted steadily from £100,000 until in 1711 they had reached the heady total of £287,000. Vanbrugh, in his easy way, wrote that although it might be a large sum for a house, it was but a 'poor reward for the services that had occasioned the Building it.'

He had managed to placate the workmen, and they continued their labours, although the past debts still remained unpaid. They were still 'trusting the building', the Queen, and her ministers. The Duke was similarly being duped. The victory he had won at Bouchain, a victory of which he was most proud, had indeed not been entirely to the taste of Harley and St John. It might be to the prejudice of their secret negotiations.

While the Duke dreamed of the final defeat of the might of France, the only thought in the minds of the Tories was finishing the war as swiftly as possible and disembarrassing themselves of the victorious and popular Duke.

But Harley and St John were still covering their tracks with care. They even closed down *The Examiner*. Although this action needed to be compensated in some measure, Mrs Manley, its leading light, applied to Harley for a pension 'for services rendered' which she received.

At the end of the campaigning season the Duke arrived at Greenwich. The Blenheimites expected him to review the progress of the Palace at once, but Vanbrugh announced to Joynes on 22 November, 'My Lord Duke thought to have set out for Blenheim yesterday, but has put it off for ten days.'

As usual Vanbrugh was anxious that the building should appear to the best advantage, and asked that Kitt Cash would get the paving done in the corridor from the Bow Window room, and the 'stairs up that my Lord Duke may go to the Upper Storey that way'.

But my Lord Duke had other troubles on his mind than paving and stairways. On 27 November Swift published his 'Conduct of the Allies and of the Late Ministry in the Beginning and the Carrying on the Present War.' The tenor of the pamphlet was that Marlborough must be destroyed, although this was never specifically stated. The whole of the war had been a gigantic error which had been waged for the glorification of the Duke. His avarice and pride engineered and prolonged the war. 'Ten glorious campaigns are passed, and now at last like the sick man we are just expiring of all sorts of good symptoms.' It was only by a hair's breadth that the foolish policies of the Whigs, and the Duke had been checked. 'By these steps a G—l during pleasure might have grown into a G—l for life, and a G—l for life into a *King*. So that I still insist upon it as a wonder how her

M—y thus besieged on all sides was able to extricate herself.'

By a sleight of public relations, Swift had banished the vision of a patriotic war. The Duke was the traitor and the Tories the patriots and the defenders of Queen and realm.

No wonder my Lord Duke came no more to Blenheim, although Vanbrugh wrote to Joynes about the details of the building and added a postscript asking that a doe should be sent up to him. This would have been considered another abuse by the Duchess.

At the end of December, Queen Anne sent for the Duke and dismissed him from all his offices. The Duke of Ormonde became Captain General, Commander of the Armies and of the 1st Guard. Louis XIV remarked with satisfaction, 'The affair of the displacing of the Duke of Marlborough will do all for us we desire.'

The charge against the Duke of Marlborough was that he had engaged in the peculation of funds. Everyone knew that the allegations were false. The funds had been disbursed in the course of the paying of agents and the collecting of information. It was the Duke's Secret Service Fund. His successor, the Duke of Ormonde, received exactly the same allowances for the same services, which amply underlined the point.

The *Gazette* on New Year's Day announced that the Queen had created twelve new Peers, the exact number to turn the balance in favour of the Tories in the House of Lords. Abigail's husband was one of these, and she became Lady Masham.

The Duke, for once emulating his wife, threw the Queen's letter of dismissal into the fire. His reply to it survived. Considering that he had been the Queen's counsellor, friend, and the founder of her fame, it was dignified, if bitter. Writing on 1 January 1712, he said:

'I am very sensible of the honour your Majesty does me in dismissing me from your service by a letter of your own hand, though I find by it that my enemies have been able to prevail with your Majesty to do it in the manner that is most injurious to me. And if their malice and inveteracy against me had not been more powerful with them than the consideration of your Majesty's honour and justice they would not have influenced you to impute the occasion of my dismission to a false and malicious insinuation contrived by themselves, and made public when there was no opportunity for me to give in my answer . . .'

The letter ended: 'I wish your Majesty may never find the want of so faithful a servant as I have always endeavoured to prove myself to you.' It was the end of thirty years of brilliant partnership. It also made an end to the building at Woodstock, although it had not put 'paid' to the bills that accrued to it.

The Blenheimites were naturally thrown into a state of acute dismay by the Duke's dismissal. What trust could they put in the building, once the Duke, their protector, was gone?

He did not visit Blenheim until August 1712 and then it was only to announce that he and the Duchess were going abroad for an indefinite stay. Joynes later described this visit:

'When his Grace had view'd the Salon talking with Mr. Vanbrugh, Mr. Travers, Sir Thos. Wheate and several of the country gentlemen there to wait on him, he went forward from the Salon as if going through the south front apartments to the Gallery, but stopt short in the Roome next to ye Salon and called me, putting his hand on my shoulder; "Joynes, I have a very good Character of your prudent care and pains taken in this building, in which I am well satisfied and so determine to put the care of this Building into your hands, that if any damage etc. comes to it you are the person I shall call to account for the same and no person else. I am now going abroad. Do you take it into your possession and attend the same till you hear from me to the Contrary".'

It was easy to see why the Duke was popular with his

16a. The Old Opera House, Haymarket, built by Vanbrugh 1785 (Mansell Collection)

b. The Elevation of Kings Weston, Glos., designed by Vanbrugh (from *Vitruvius Britannicus*)

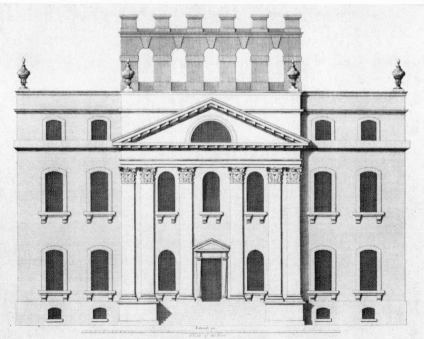

The Elevation of KINGSWESTON in the County of GLOCESTER the Seat of the R.t Hon.ble EDWARD SOUTHWELL, Esq.r Principal Secretary of State for the KINGDOM of IRELAND
Designed by S.r Io. Vanbrugh k.t
Elevation de la Maison De KINGSWESTON dans la Comté de GLOCESTER

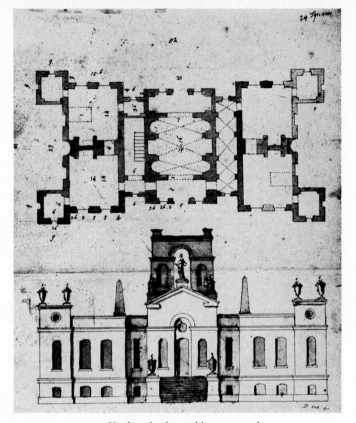

17. Vanbrugh, the architect at work
a. Design for a side elevation of Eastbury Park, Dorset, drawn over part of the ground
plan of Blenheim Palace
(Victoria and Albert Museum)

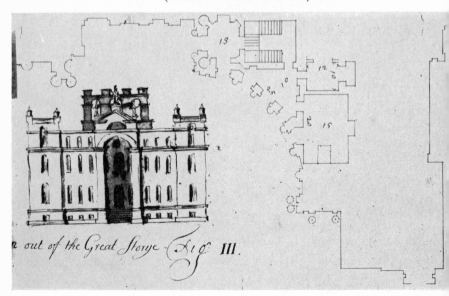

out of the Great Storye Fig. III.

b. Kings Weston on part of a ground plan of Blenheim

soldiers; he was not afraid to delegate responsibility or to compliment on work well done.

In the same month of August Godolphin fell ill, and Sarah, with her usual courage, nursed him till he died on 15 September. She called him the best man who ever lived. 'He was a man of wonderful frugality in the public concerns, but of no great money above his paternal estate. What he left at his death showed that he had been indeed the nation's Treasurer and not his own.' This was a sincere compliment from Sarah, that stern guardian of her own treasure.

In the same month of September Arthur Maynwaring died: 'He caught a great cold by walking too late in the Duchess of Marlborough's garden at St Albans, and that cold encreas'd upon him so fast, that he believ'd it would finish what his former illness began.' Maynwaring was, of course, suffering from tuberculosis. Dr Garth was sent for but could give no hopes for his recovery. The Duchess visited him when he was dying, and according to Maynwaring's biographer, Oldmixon, she 'the greatest lady in England, wept often by the side of his Death Bed, which he water'd, as often with his Tears, being sensible how much he ow'd to such an Illustrious Mourner.'

Mr Maynwaring's death did not scotch the rumours about the cause of it. Some kind acquaintances had suggested that he died of 'the Remains of a Venereal Distemper. His friends and Servants caus'd the Body to be open'd, which was done.' Two doctors, two surgeons, and an apothecary declared that 'there was no Symptoms of any Thing Venereal.'

Arthur Maynwaring left his small fortune to be divided between Mrs Oldfield, his son by that lady, and his sister. The 'Towne' took it very ill that Mrs Oldfield, an actress and an acknowledged mistress, was made executrix. This fact was slightly vindicated by the fact that Arthur Maynwaring left only a very modest competence to his mistress and his son.

The year 1712 had not been a happy one for the Whigs and their remaining friends. On 1 December, the Duke embarked on a packet at Dover, and set sail for the Continent. Before he left he settled his affairs. A memorandum from Vanbrugh stated:

'The Duke of Marlborough (upon his design to travel), made a new Will which he executed at St James's. Mr Cardonel, Mr Craggs and myself saw him Sign, seal, declare and publish it, and afterwards Sign'd it as Witnesses in his Presence with a Codicil. The Duke at the same time burn'd his former Will, cancell'd a former Deed, and executed a new one. The will consists of fourteen sheets, every one of which the Duke sign'd.'

Once the Duke had gone abroad, to be followed by the Duchess at the beginning of 1713, the works at Blenheim dwindled like a small river in a dry summer. In happier days there had been over a thousand men employed in and about the estate, now they had shrunk to a handful. Works were covered. The carvings of Grinling Gibbons and his fellow artists and craftsmen were boarded up. Joynes had taken to fishing, catching a brace of good trouts, a chub and eight dace. Bobart made hay. But peace was not entirely unalloyed: there had been certain difficulties between Bobart and Joynes, perhaps a residual bitterness left from the Duchess's interference. Mr Wise, the chief planner of the Blenheim garden, the doyen of all the gardens of England at the time, was asked to resolve their difficulties.

Joynes, engaged in his peaceful fishing, had been showing visitors round the half-finished house, presumably for a consideration. This had upset Bobart, who had retaliated by refusing him the produce from the orchard and garden. Wise went carefully into the dispute and 'as to your right in having Earbs and Roots out of the Garden in proper seasons, I should not think you were ever refused by anybody'. He suggested that Joynes and Bobart should 'discourse moderately and cooley together about this matter'.

But nothing was ever cool or moderate about the Palace and Park at Blenheim.

Vanbrugh had made the remains of Rosamund's Bower quite safe from the weather, and had built a little tower on the roof. The whole of Woodstock reposed like the palace of the Sleeping Beauty, while the Great Duke and his Duchess travelled on the Continent receiving the courtesies accorded to his former victories.

The Duchess was a reluctant traveller and in her letters to her relative 'Mr Jennens', she reveals herself as a true Briton, prejudiced against all things foreign, and all foreign ways. At first, she was reluctantly compelled to admit, writing from Maestricht, that 'all the Places one pass'd through in these Parts have an Air very different from London' but she noticed that the ordinary people are 'half starv'd'. The Duchess seemed to have developed a more acute social conscience once she had crossed the Channel, than she had showed for her starving workmen at Blenheim.

She was sweetened 'by the Honours they have done me in all Places upon the Duke of Marlborough's Account,' which were 'not to bee imagined, which is not disagreeable now because it cannot proceed from Power, it shews hee made a right use of it when hee was General, and is a short Way of letting you see what People must think Abroad of this Ministry and Parliament'.

Vanbrugh, on his home ground, thought exactly the same as Sarah about both Ministry and Government, and although he was happy to use his little box in Woodstock Park, enjoy the does in season, and contemplate the landscape at his ease, this happy situation was not to be allowed to endure for long.

At the beginning of the year 1713 he wrote to the Mayor of Woodstock about a simple matter—the paving of the market place in Woodstock Town. He had, he said, already spoken to the Duke about it, which my Lord Duke

'seemed well inclined to, and I believe had done ere now, but for the *continual plagues and bitter persecution he has most barbarously been* followed with for two years past. However upon his going away, I mentioned this thing to him again; and he left such directions with those who take care of his affairs, that I have at last commission to tell you it will be done, and that I am desired to take some care of it.'

He added another of his sanguine postscripts to the effect that he has hopes that the Treasury will pay the Blenheim Debt 'My Lord Duke having offered to advance the money if they will give him only tin-tallies, which will not be payable to him in seven years—not sure then.' Blenheim still lived on hopes, and the promise of tin tallies.

Unfortunately for Vanbrugh his letter fell into the wrong hands, having been misdirected. It was used by some anonymous person to destroy Vanbrugh's credit. Like most anonymous letters, it breathes a mixture of piety, treachery and smugness.

The letter was sent to Robert Harley, Earl of Oxford, 'Ye 26th Instant 1713,' which could have been the day after Vanbrugh wrote to the Mayor of Woodstock. It ran:

'Sir, A letter happening accidentally into my hands, Containing the following Lines, I thought it my Duty, out of Ye Obedience I owe to her Majesty and respect to the present Ministry to discover a Person of such trecherous Principles, who altho' being rais'd to such Honour, under Her Majesty, yet makes no scruples of railing against the Church's Upholders, and Owns his Chiefest interest lies in the coming of the Pretender.'

The anonymous writer says that he had not been able to get the letter but had only read it, and now the Mayor to whom it was sent 'hath cut out the Latter Sentence'. It seems unlikely that Vanbrugh, that staunch Whig should have expressed a wish for the return of the Pretender. Possibly the 'latter sentence' had been added by the writer who signs himself *A Well Wisher to both Church and State*. It is strange how often people who sign themselves as well-wishing do so in the context of ill-doing.

The result of the mis-carrying of this letter was disastrous for Vanbrugh. He was not a rich man. His theatrical projects only brought him in a small rent. He had pinned all his hopes on the glittering towers of Blenheim.

The Tories were still pursuing even the smallest quarry with the utmost bitterness. Vanbrugh's letter was printed in *The Post Boy* on 24 March 1713 with the comment; 'The gentleman who wrote the following letter to the Mayor of Woodstock, having met with the chastisement he deserves for it, 'tis to be hoped those who by the extreme lenity of the present Administration are yet suffered to enjoy these offices they obtained under another, will take warning, and keep themselves within the bounds they ought.'

Vanbrugh was dismissed as Comptroller of the Works on 15 April 1713.

Loyalty to the Duke was now a mortal sin against the Administration and Vanbrugh wrote to one of his relatives on 2 April 1713:

'I don't know whether you have heard, that I am turn'd out of my place in the Works, for writeing a letter to the Mayor of Woodstock in which I say the Duke of Marlborough has been bitterly and barbarously persecuted for these two Years past, in which I only meant the Continuall and Daily Libels and Pamphlets which pelted him, but some High Church Members of Parliament wou'd needs have it, I meant the House of Commons and so have push't the matter to my being turn'd out, I believe I cou'd have prevented it, if I wou'd have made my Submission to those High-Church Blockheads, but that I wou'd on no terms do.'

The architect of Blenheim was as uncompromising and straight-forward in his loyalty to the Duke, as he was to his Whig principles. Nor was he prepared to bend the knee to political churchmen.

In October Vanbrugh went up to Yorkshire to stay with his friend Lord Carlisle at Castle Howard, where he happily enjoyed 'the nature of the place, the Works he has done, and the manner of his Living, that I shall have much ado to leave it, till I am forc'd to come to Towne, to take care of several uncomfortable things which I fear, will long be Allays to the Pleasures I cou'd else have some tast of.'

The exile of the Duke was to bring many unfortunate consequences in its wake for Vanbrugh. Trimmers can often exact tributes from both sides. Loyalty must often serve as the sole reward of the loyal.

CHAPTER XV

Under Her Majesty's Displeasure

Unpleasant intelligence travels fast. No sooner had the news of Vanbrugh's fall from favour and dismissal from the Board of Works been spread than his post was being eagerly sought by other claimants. Or solicited by patrons for other protégés.

The Duke of Shrewsbury had been appointed Ambassador to Paris, where possibly his Italian wife was thought to be an asset in a Papist environment. On 6 April 1713, the Duke wrote to Harley:

'I understand Mr Vanbrugg is fallen so much under her Majesty's displeasure that it is supposed he will be removed from his employment in the Works. I think myself obliged, as much in respect of her Majesty's service, as in justice to Mr Thomas Archer to acquaint you that—impartially speaking according to my skill—he is the most able and has the best genius for building of anybody we have.'

The Duke did not speak impartially. Thomas Archer was under his patronage and had designed his country house at Heythrop.

'I mention this,' wrote the Duke, 'in case only that Mr Vanbrugg be removed, and give me leave to add that this is a matter in which I *will* say with Sir Positive, if I do not understand it I understand nothing.'

Sir Positive At-all was a character in Thomas Shadwell's play *The Sullen Lovers*, who dubbed himself an expert in everything from music and statesmanship to Flanders lace and painting. He also admitted to having made seventeen models of the city of London—in pastry. These had unfortunately been devoured by rats. It was probably in the capacity of model maker that the Duke of Shrewsbury remembered the foolish knight.

Whether the Duke emulated Sir Positive or not—he was prepared to profit by the loyalty of Vanbrugh to My Lord Marlborough.

The fall of the Duke was like some great monolith being overthrown. Once his sustaining influence had lost its power, even the lesser followers were bound to feel the sharp attacks of their Tory opponents, who were not slow to rouse the Queen's wrath against any one who should oppose their hatred of the Duke. It has been suggested by some historians that one cause of the extraordinary change in the Queen's attitude, was that her mind had possibly been weakened by the massive doses of laudanum which she took. Laudanum was a medicament in which opium was the active ingredient, and unfortunately it was the only pain killer known at the time.

This may have been true, but there were other factors. Sarah had said that the Queen's whole character seemed to change from the time of the death of Prince George, her husband. Many seemingly stupid men may exercise a restraining influence on the characters of their wives.

It is difficult not to perceive a certain vindictiveness creeping into the Queen's actions after the gradual disintegration of the Whig ascendancy. Another facet of Anne's character was pin-pointed by the Duchess when she shrewdly remarked: 'The Queen could be ruled as much by fear as by flattery.' Like Queen Elizabeth I, she loathed the very idea of her successors, and on several occasions had refused to allow the Hanoverians to visit England. She was at heart a Stuart and, for all her sickly body and inability to bear healthy children, had a dynastic feeling for the trappings and reality of power, and for her divine right to choose Ministers who were to her political liking.

The complications of Tory intrigue had not only destroyed

the Duke's reputation, but that of his admirer Vanbrugh, the architect of Blenheim.

The Duke and Duchess had at least the consolation that their funds were well disposed. To protect their assets they had handed certain sums of money over to their sons-in-law, and in addition the Duke had prudently deposited abroad £50,000 in Holland. Vanbrugh was not so well placed, and now the Controllership, one of the chief sources of his income and influence, had been taken from him.

In November of the year 1713 he wrote to an unknown correspondent, possibly someone who was connected with the theatre.

'I trouble you lately with a Letter relating to the Comedy Stock in Drury Lane. I am since informed you have directed the Present managers to lay before you an Inventory of what was carryed from the Haymarket. I hope they will give you a right one; if they do, you will see, it was the Richest and completest Stock that ever any Company had in England, Consisting of all that was in Lincolns Inn fields (for which I gave £900) All that was added to it upon the first opening the Haymarket house (which came to a great Sum) and what was in the most profuse manner added farther, when Mr. Swiny brought all the Chief Actors thither from Drury Lane and was Oblig'd to gratify them with whatever they would have. There was beside this (by neglect of those Mr Collier employ'd) a great part of the Opera Stock carryed off. So that, there can be no doubt left, of the Stock being far beyond what ever had been known before upon the Stage. And there was no pretences whatever from those Present Managers to a property in one ragg of it.'

Blenheim was not the only place where abuses were rife. Vanbrugh, a wit without resources, was forced to press his claims for the finery which decorated the fine gentlemen of the sock and buskin.

This insistence on grand clothes for stage spectacles was demanded by the public. The contemporary financial accounts for the theatres make it clear that these lavish productions were not only expensive but realistic. Real silver plate was often used in plays. Should the scenes demand beds then it was specified that the bedclothes must be clean at every performance. The materials were of the best quality—satins, gold and silver lace, silken hose, India muslin, white damask, brocades, silver petticoats, and velvet suits and gowns trimmed with Flanders lace.

Conrad von Uffenbach reported on the English theatre that the 'scenery and properties at the Queen's Theatre in the Hay Market had all been made expressly for the opera, and were very fine—though not so costly as those in Italy.'

They had been costly enough to cause losses to Vanbrugh. His £900 represented bills paid to swordsmiths, mantua makers, suppliers of lace, gloves, furs, shoes, wigs and stays. His character, Mrs Amlet in *The Confederacy*, who supplied false hips and stays to the ladies, was obviously drawn from his own experience in the theatre. But it was an experience which had proved expensive, and the disentangling of Vanbrugh's claim was not to prove easy.

In 1700 there had been two wardrobes. One belonged to the nook building Christopher Rich, and the other to Thomas Betterton at Lincoln's Inn Fields. Betterton's company then moved over to act under Vanbrugh's management at the Queen's Theatre, Hay Market. In this way the dresses and props had changed hands several times. It had become increasingly difficult to separate the inventories of furs and furbelows, and to decide which company had owned which embroidered gowns. Vanbrugh applied to the Lord Chamberlain's office to help him with his claim for the payment for costumes now at Drury Lane.

But as costumes were not only costly to make but costly to maintain, and were being constantly washed, cleaned and renewed, a claim of this kind was difficult to establish. Could it have been that the white feather which was washed and mounted for Mrs Porter was a feather paid for by Vanbrugh? Or was the coat remodelled for Wilks with best flannel, and three dozen buttons, originally part of the playwright's hard-bought comedy stock?

Further difficulties were added to the establishment of his claim in that many of the properties were hired. When Cibber tried to charge the theatre with two shillings and sixpence for the hire of a wig for Othello, his bill was endorsed 'Mr Cibber is to pay for the wig himself.'

Two of Vanbrugh's careers, architecture and the theatre, seemed to be in temporary eclipse. Claremont and Castle Howard were continuing projects, but the loss of his post as Comptroller meant that Vanbrugh was no longer at the centre of architectural activity.

It was about this time that Vanbrugh began to think of his other career at the College of Arms. It was nearly ten years since he had been made Clarenceux in spite of the 'saucy opposition'. During that time, although he had been Clarenceux Herald and had been responsible for carrying out many ceremonies, including the investing of the future Prince of Wales with the Order of the Garter, he had never troubled himself to register his own coat of arms.

At the beginning of 1714 Vanbrugh applied to the Deputy Earl Marshal, the Earl of Suffolk, for a confirmation of the arms of his grandfather, Gilles van Brugg, the gentleman who had fled from Flanders during the time of the Catholic persecution. Eventually the arms were authorised, and it was decided they should be quartered with the coat of arms of his mother Elizabeth, daughter of Sir Dudley Carleton. The official description of his coat of arms was: 'Gules, on a Fesse, Or, three Barrulets, Vert: in Chief, a Demy Lion. For a Crest, a Demy Lion, issuant from a Bridge composed of three reversed arches, Or.' The reference to a bridge had formerly been a little joke, a play on the words 'Van Brugg'. Since Vanbrugh's difficulties with the Duchess over his bridge, it had become a joke with a bitter flavour.

Unfortunately for Vanbrugh, his efforts to put himself in a position to be able to claim the office of Garter King of Arms were too late as far as the Queen was concerned. It had been some years since she, writing under her sign Manual at Kensington in 1706, had instructed 'her trusty and well beloved John Vanbrugh one of our Kings at Arms' to invest the Elector's son with the Garter. His jokes in *Aesop* had not been forgotten; 'I know every man's Father, and every Man's Grandfather, and every man's Great Grandfather.' He had now been compelled to emulate his own character Quaint.

All his current efforts seemed doomed to defeat. On 29 May 1714 Vanbrugh, in a postscript to a letter he wrote to the Duke of Marlborough, added: 'The Queen has at last pass'd a Patent (even without my Lord Suffolks concurrence in it) to Mr Anstis for the reversion of Garter. She said she had been under an obligation to consent to it; but my behaviour had been such in writing that Letter to Woodstock, that now she had done with me—That was her expression.'

The Queen's bitterness was seeking out the lesser enemies. While Anstis had managed temporarily to live down the suspicions of Jacobitism—the Tory Administration was engaged in intrigues with the exiled court at St Germains. There was an undercurrent of talk about the return of the Pretender, should he be prepared to forego his damning allegiance to the Pope.

There was no present advancement for Vanbrugh in the College of Heralds. Nor were the difficulties over Blenheim growing any less pressing. Vanbrugh had put in his claims for the back payments due to the craftsmen and to himself in the summer of 1711. Three years later no money had been forthcoming. Even craftsmen like Strong the Mason, were in severe difficulties. With great reluctance Vanbrugh informed the Duke that Strong might have to sue him for a sum 'he and his Family are not able to bear'. The only other alternative was for the men to sue the crown.

If the workmen were undecided whom to sue, the politicians were equally full of distracted alternatives. Even Vanbrugh at this juncture seems to have been dismayed at the divisions and disloyalties which had floated to the surface.

He reported to the Duke abroad that 'it was high time for a little encouragement from Hanover. In a word, one does not know where this thing will go, if something is not quickly done, to give some satisfaction in the Elector's present mysterious proceeding.'

The Elector was not the only one who was proceeding mysteriously. The Tory administration had been actively intriguing for the return of the Old Pretender. There was grave danger that the Whigs and their followers might be in permanent eclipse should the Stuarts return. A simple political fact which would explain the divisions amongst them.

Vanbrugh also voiced to the Duke other rumours which he had heard: 'But one odd thing I can acquaint your Grace of amongst them (at least of my Lord Anglesea in particular) that your Grace is held in strong suspicion of having wholy [sic] embark'd in the pretenders interest; and that you are to bring him over.'

My Lord Anglesea was not very far out in his suspicions, for my Lord Duke had been in correspondence with his nephew, the Duke of Berwick, in France. He had pointed out that the Churchill lands and wealth were in the power of a hostile Tory government, and that possibly the French Government, in view of the imminent conclusion of the Peace, might use their influence in the Duke's favour.

Even Churchill finds it difficult to gloss over the Duke's constant correspondence with the exiled Jacobite court, which lasted from 1689, the year after William III came to the throne, until 1716, when the Hanoverians were already well established as the reigning Protestant succession. Sir Winston advances the ingenious theory that possibly the Duke had used his connections as a source of intelligence and information, both during and after his long years of campaigning. On the other hand, it was also true that the Duke had originally served in the French Army, that he had been friend and adviser of James II, and the Duke of Berwick was his nephew.

Now the Duke of Marlborough, abroad and discredited, and his Tory enemies were both playing the same double game in corresponding with the exiled Stuarts. Whether Harley and the Tories had perhaps swayed the Queen to their point of view, and she was at long last, as she approached her final dissolution, prepared to admit that her half-brother had not been smuggled into the lying-in chamber of her stepmother Mary of Modena in a warming pan, will never be known.

Vanbrugh took his usual uncompromising view about the rumours of the Duke's shifting allegiances, he did not believe them. "Twoud be very hard we should be yet undone by the Meer Tory Mob, Ignorant, furious country Priests, and Stupid Justices, when all their chiefs of any weight have left them.'

He still retained his strong feelings against Justices and Clergymen which had been so apparent when he wrote *The Provok'd Wife*.

He ended his letter to the Duke with a graceful compliment: 'I send with this a Draught of the Obelisk my Lord Carlisle is raising to express his grateful sense as an Englishman, of what he thinks the Nation Owe to your Grace, it is in all one hundred Feet high.'

This was a monument, which unlike Blenheim, was not the subject of dispute. The account was rendered, and presumably paid in 1715, although the inscription was not added until later.

Mr Harvey's account for 1726 lists 'The inscription in ye Obelisque. £1.14.0.'

It could have been that the Earl delayed putting the inscription on to the monument until the Protestant succession was no longer in doubt. There is little point in nailing one's colours to the wrong masthead.

If the Duke's monument lacked its inscription, the Duke's enemies were equally without direction, and confounded by the prospects before them. The Queen was obviously dying, and like the Duke, Harley and St John had been in touch with both Hanover and St Germains during the spring and summer.

Eventually the wrath of the dying Queen fell on Harley. Swift, who had so benefited in influence from the partnership of these two dubious, quarrelling men, tried to reconcile them, but Harley was dismissed. The Queen's reasons for his dismissal were 'that he neglected all business; that he was seldom to be understood; that he often came drunk', and lastly, the most heinous crime of all, 'he had behaved himself with bad manners, indecency and disrespect.' Harley had been betrayed by Lady Masham, the erstwhile Abigail Hill, in the same way she had betrayed the Marlboroughs.

The triumph of St John was to be short lived. Harley had been dismissed on 7 July. But the Queen was sinking into the shadows, in spite of the doctors' remedies. They laid garlic on her feet, they shaved her head, and finally—fearing an apoplexy—they 'caused her to be let blood'. The Queen rallied for a while then slowly sank into unconsciousness again. This caused Abigail to faint, and it was small wonder, for with the ebbing of the Queen's life, her own influence was withering away.

Around the bed of the dying Queen the intrigues still went on. After a few short sweet days of St John believing that power was in his grasp, the Queen recovered sufficiently to slip the white staff of the Treasurer into the hands of the Duke of Shrewsbury.

Dr Radcliffe, who had built himself a mansion in the country at Carshalton in Surrey (presumably on the proceeds of the Queen's frail health), was sent for. He returned a message saying that 'he had taken physic and could not come'. He was prudently avoiding the obvious blame attached to the death bed of a Queen.

Queen Anne died on 1 August 1714. She was only forth-nine. The news took three days to reach Lady Mary Wortley Montagu in Yorkshire.

With Queen Anne died the hopes of the Jacobites, and immediately stocks rose by three per cent in the City.

The funeral took place at night on 23 August. The postponement was due to the fact that her ladies needed time to arrange their mourning clothes. Her body was not followed to her grave by the chief architects of her glory. Godolphin was dead and the Marlboroughs were on their way back from exile. Dean Atterbury, the prebends and the choir walked in slow procession behind the coffin, all carrying lighted candles in their hands.

While the guns of the Tower of London punctuated the last ceremony the Queen would attend, Vanbrugh, in his official capacity as Clarenceux King of Arms, read over the vault the style and titles of the late Queen. 'Thus it has pleased Almighty God to take out of this transitory life to his Divine Mercy that late Most High Most Mighty and Most Excellent Princess Anne by the Grace of God, Queen of Great Britain, France and Ireland. Defender of the Faith.'

The Queen had not, after all, entirely done with Vanbrugh as she had said.

On a more optimistic note Vanbrugh then had to beseech Almighty God to 'bless and preserve with long life, health, and honour and all happiness the Most High, Most Mighty and Most Excellent Monarch Our Sovereign Lord, George.'

No doubt Vanbrugh hoped himself to be included in the worldly honours and joys of George 'now by the Grace of God, King of Great Britain, France and Ireland.'

The Marlboroughs had been staying at Antwerp, but had also been keeping in touch with the way events were moving in England.

'We had a very inconvenient house,' wrote the Duchess,

'and before we could remove from thence the Duke was so weary that took a resolution to go for England.'

The Marlboroughs were not the only people who were well informed. Swift's informants let him know, even before the death of the Queen, that 'The Whigs give out the Duke of Marlborough is coming over, and his house is now actually fitting up at St James's.'

On 30 July, Sarah wrote to Mrs Clayton from Ostend; 'I am sure my dear friend will be glad to hear that we are come well to this place, where we wait for a fair wind.'

The fair wind came and the Duke and Duchess landed at Dover on 2 August to be greeted with the news of the Queen's death. The *Flying Post* reported, 'The Duke and Duchess of Marlborough passed through this city [Rochester]. They were received with expressions of joy from the people, especially those at Chatham who strewed their way with flowers, as they adorned their houses with green boughs and welcomed them with repeated shouts and acclamations.'

Like the restoration of Charles II, the death of Queen Anne had lifted the shadows from the country. But instead of an English King being happily restored to his rightful throne, the King was German. His well-beloved Queen Sophia Dorothea did not accompany him. And for a very good reason. She had been for some years imprisoned by him in the castle of Ahlden for adultery. The King's faithful mistresses—Madame Kielmansegge, created Countess of Darlington, and Madame Schulenberg, created Duchess of Kendal—followed him into his English exile. Kielmansegge, a lady of large size, was dubbed the Elephant, while her thin love-sister was christened the Maypole.

In *The Four Georges*, Thackeray sketched in the scene:

'I am a citizen waiting at Greenwich pier, say, and crying Hurrah for King George; and yet I can scarcely keep my countenance, and help laughing at the enormous absurdity of this advent!

273

'Here we are, all on our knees. Here is the Archbishop of Canterbury prostrating himself to the head of his church, with Kielmansegge and Schulenberg with their ruddled cheeks grinning behind the defender of the faith . . . The great Whig gentlemen made their bows and congées with proper decorum and ceremony; but yonder old schemer knows the value of their loyalty. 'Loyalty!' he must think—as applied to me—it is absurd! There are fifty nearer heirs to the throne than I am. I am but an accident, and you fine Whig gentlemen take me for your own sake, not for mine.'

It was not a far fetched picture. St John had needed but another three or four weeks and he might have managed to turn things differently. As it was, the Duke, and incidentally the architect, were back in favour. The King remarked soothingly to Marlborough: 'My Lord Duke, I hope your troubles are now all over.' Vanbrugh also hoped for a reversal of his fortunes. The King had taken possession of his lucrative inheritance.

The Duke was restored to his country and his fortune.

On 18 September, through Marlborough's influence, Vanbrugh was created Sir John.

Dr Garth, suspected of atheism by the Queen and the Church party, was made Sir Samuel. The tables were slowly turning.

The future looked rosy, and within a few days the Duke was down at Blenheim, and hoping to see, as the Duke's chaplain said: that 'the noble monument of English gratitude gloriously finished, to perpetuate the memory of an action which, in English history has no parallel, and which succeeding generations will wonder at, and be the better for.'

Vanbrugh was equally optimistic that now the clouds about the Palace had lifted he would be reinstated in the favours of the Duchess. The Duke had always seen his good qualities. In the autumn of 1713, long before the happy return of the Duke, this had been in Vanbrugh's mind when he wrote to an unknown friend about the pleasure that Lord Carlisle found in Castle Howard:

'And if you think it proper (as from yourself I cou'd with you wou'd say what you know to be true) That whether I am quite convinced or not of my having been so much in the wrong in my behaviour to her [the Duchess] as she is pleas'd to think me, Yet while she does think me so I can't but set the greatest value upon her Generosity; in urging my Lord Marlborough in my favour; I must own to you at the Same time, That her notion, that I had not done what I did, but upon her declining at Court, has been no Small inducement to me, to expose myself so frankly as I have done, in my Lord Duke's and her particular Cause for tho' I cou'd have born she should have thought me a Brute, I cou'd not endure she shou'd think me a Rascall.'

A forthright last sentence which sets the writer's character clearly in black and white.

Whether he was right in hoping for the Duchess's good offices was doubtful. While the Marlboroughs were still abroad, Vanbrugh, owing to the loss of his office as Comptroller and his disappointment over the hope of the Garter, had found his circumstances somewhat straitened. He had already asked for £200 to be given to him as a travelling allowance and a £400 a year salary. There seems to be no evidence that the Duke had ever paid him the salary. The Duchess wrote that she had persuaded the Duke to pay the £200 travelling allowance when Vanbrugh 'was turned out by my Lord Oxford (Harley), without any reall Merrit to the Duke of Marlborough but an unlucky accident for want of knowing how to Spell a man's name.' The letter having miscarried, the Duchess was not allowing Vanbrugh any merit for loyalty.

The Duke's eyes were still fixed on his noble monument and, after going to Woodstock with Vanbrugh, he had come to a decision about the unfinished building.

Once the Government had paid the debts incurred during Queen Anne's reign, the Duke had resolved to finish the building at his own expense. Vanbrugh gave him an estimate for its finishing, which was £54,000. There was, as always, a proviso. Although the Government was prepared to acknowledge the debt, it was 'adjusted'. Like the unjust steward in the New Testament, the Government scaled the debts down. Any workmen or contractors who were owed less than £10 were paid in full, the others were paid a third of the money owed to them. This meant that Vanbrugh, who was owed £2,463, was only paid £800. For a man who was comparatively poor this must have been a bitter blow after all he had been led to expect. Even this settlement took nearly a year to bring to fruition.

Not only were the workmen expected to forego two-thirds of the money which was owing to them, but they were also expected to resume work at a lower scale of payment. The Duchess had decided that now the workmen were no longer employees of the Crown, they could hardly expect royal rates from private patrons, however noble these might be.

The prospect which opened out was hardly brilliant for architect or craftsmen. Nor had Blenheim acquired a happy reputation in the countryside. Vanbrugh, writing from his Goose Pie House in Whitehall in the spring of 1716, reported the difficulties to the Duke: 'I have acquainted Mr Strong [the Mason] that your Grace does not incline to the last proposal he made about his debt &c upon which I can get no other from him than the first; which was to go on with the Towers upon the foot of the old Contract.'

Vanbrugh pointed out the nub of the matter: 'But as he has so great business here in town, I'm afraid there will be no bringing him to other terms.'

Poor Mr Joynes, when visiting the quarrymen, had received the same stony answer. He had not found that 'there is any likelihood of having Stone but on the former Terms.'

Although the Duke and Duchess had regained and consolidated their fortunes and were one of the richest families in Europe, they still retained their frugal outlook. They were not inclined to dissipate money on the Blenheim project on other than favourable terms to themselves. The guiding hand of the Duchess can be detected in this housewifely approach.

The Duke had promised Vanbrugh 'something substantial'. The brilliance of his reward had appeared in the form of his now being entitled to call himself 'Sir John'. It was a piece of patronage which had cost the Duke nothing except a smile in the right direction. If My Lord Duke's financial uncertainties were over, the same was not to apply to Sir John's.

The Earl of Carlisle proved to be an enduring friend. At the beginning of 1715 Sir John was reinstated in his post as Controller of the Works, in addition a new post was created for him, 'Surveyor of the Gardens and Waters'. This appointment concerned him in all the little details of the Royal Gardens: overseeing rivers, 'conduits, Pipes and Engines', as well as making sure that fountains played, canals were cleaned and that cisterns worked. In his capacity of overseer of gardens he 'brought to the Board the after-mentioned proposals for works to be done in H.M. Gardens'.

Queen Anne had detested the smell of box edging and had had it all rooted out, the new King proposed that 'box should be planted in lieu of Border Boards.' Vanbrugh reported that the amount of box edging needed at Kensington alone would be over 3,000 yards. Changes in taste could be expensive. He was also concerned in providing lists of 'tubbs and pots'. These were presumably the tubs used in the orangery. It was the custom to decorate the formal gardens with tender plants which were put out in summer and then wintered in the orangeries or 'greenhouses' as Vanbrugh called them.

In March 1715 the Commissioner of the Royal Hospital for Seamen at Greenwich met together. Politically they could be said to represent a transitional stage.

They included 'Lord President—Lord Oxford [Harley], Sir

John Vanbrugh, the Duke of Marlborough and the Earl of Halifax'.

This happy state of affairs was not to last. Revenges were preparing between Whig and Tory. But the moment was not quite ripe. In April 1715 Harley's supplanter, St John (Bolingbroke), became frightened. The erstwhile Secretary of State went round to Marlborough's house in St James's in an attempt to ingratiate himself with the great Duke. After this interview St John showed himself smilingly at the theatre. At Drury Lane *Love Makes a Man* was playing for 'the benefit of Mr Penkethman'. There was no benefit for St John.

After the performance St John left abruptly for Dover, disguised as a valet. 'My blood,' he wrote to Lord Lansdowne, 'was to have been the cement of a new alliance.' French sources reported that 'It is taken as certain that it was Milord Marlborough who warned Lord Bolingbroke [St John] of the Cabinet's decision not to spare him.'

In the same year Harley was impeached and committed to the Tower, and the Duke of Ormonde, who had succeeded Marlborough as Commander of the Army, had also fled into the protective arms of the Pretender. Swift, for all the brilliance of his mind, profited little from his attacks on the Duke—he never became a Bishop. He died as he himself had predicted, after thirty years in Ireland, 'like a poisoned rat in a hole'.

The Mashams retreated to live comfortably in the country—it was rumoured on the proceeds of careful milking of the secret service funds. But for the Whigs, and for Vanbrugh walking round Woodstock Park with the Duke, all looked to be set fair.

CHAPTER XVI

Building and Matchmaking

During the spring and summer of 1715 Vanbrugh's affairs went forward happily. He was still building and planning for the Earl of Clare at Claremont. But further honours hovered over the head of this fortunate young man. As a result of his splendid support in raising a troop to fight for King George against the Pretender, he was rewarded by being made Marquis of Clare, and subsequently Duke of Newcastle.

But at the beginning of the year Vanbrugh became involved with Lord Clare in another connection. The Duchess of Marlborough, now happily re-installed in her several houses, the lodge at Windsor, her favourite clean house at Holywell, and Marlborough House in St James', had begun to make plans for her grand-daughters. There was little use in disposing of descendants upon other than favourable terms.

She had approached Vanbrugh as an intermediary about the marriage of the Lady Henrietta (Harriott), who was the daughter of Henrietta, Countess of Godolphin. The Duchess had set her sights on Vanbrugh's friend, Lord Clare, soon to be Duke of Newcastle, who seemed to have suitable credentials to be received into the Churchill family.

Vanbrugh had been proceeding cautiously and he wrote with equal caution to the Duchess in January 1715:

'Sir Samuel Garth mentioning something yesterday of Lord Clare with relation to my Lady Harriott, made me reflect that your Grace might possibly think (by my never saying any thing to you of that matter, since you did me the honour of hinting it to me) I had either forgot or neglected it; but I have done neither—Tis true that partly by company being in the Way, and partly by his illness when I was most with him, I have not yet had an opportunity of sounding him to the purpose. What I have yet done therefore has been only this. I have brought into discourse the characters of several Women, that I might have a natural occasion to bring in hers, which I have then dwelt upon; and in the best manner I cou'd, distinguish'd her from the others. This I have taken three or four Occasions to do without the least appearances of having any view in it.'

This was obviously not an easy assignment for a comedy writer with a keen sense of the ridiculous. He had by a hazard found himself cast in the role of Coupler and could very well have been thinking with Young Fashion: 'Why, how now, Match-maker art thou here still to plague the world with Matrimony?' Lady Harriot although a plain girl, was obviously no Miss Hoyden. Vanbrugh further informed the Duchess:

'I can give your Grace no farther account of the effects of it, than he has seemed to allow of the merit I gave her, tho I must own he once express'd with something joind which I did not like . . . and that was a sort of wish (express'd in a very gentle manner) that her bodily perfections had been up to those I describ'd of her mind and understanding.'

Vanbrugh tried his utmost to advance the merits of the filly he was attempting to sell to the future Duke, saying that although the girl was not strictly beautiful, her face should prove an agreeable one 'which was infinitely more valuable'. He also mentioned 'that her Shape and Figure in general wou'd be perfectly well, and that I wou'd pawne all my Skill (which had us'd to be a good deal employ'd in these kind of observations) that in Two years time, no Woman in Town wou'd be better lik'd.' He may have been thinking of his skill in picking out Ann Oldfield and making her the great lady she had become. Vanbrugh was concerned to try to cast the Lady Harriot in the role of the future Duchess, and felt that perhaps she could be groomed for the role. He ended by assuring Sarah that he was 'truly and sincerely of Opinion that if I cou'd be an instrument in bringing it about, I shou'd do my Lord Clare as a great a piece of Service as my Lady Harriot.'

Nothing pinpoints better the mercenary and dynastic views of the eighteenth century idea of marriage than the correspondence of Vanbrugh with the Duchess over the disposal of her grand-daughter.

A month later Vanbrugh was in some bustle about the arrangements of the Lord Clare's house in Lincoln's Inn Fields, and he assured his Lordships that 'when your l'dship comes to pay the Bills, you will see whether there has been above three or four men a day at Work. They have Appear'd to me a Swarm of Bees, And they have done so much, that I think you may ly in your house the end of this Month if the Upholsterer do's his part.'

As for his Lordship's legitimate lying with my Lady Harriot, this was proceeding at a slow pace. Social occasions were not neglected to bring the party of the first part, the Lord Clare, in touch with the prime mover in the affair, the Duchess of Marlborough. Vanbrugh wrote to Jacob Tonson in the summer of 1715: 'I have just now been with Ld Carlisle, who has named Friday for the Barns Expedition. I have Seen Lady Marlborough since, and she agrees to it, and will order a Bardge at Whitehall. The Company she names are Two Ladys besides her Self. Ld Carlisle, Ld Clare, Horace Walpole, Dr Samll. Garth and Mr Benson.'

During the course of these negotiations, Vanbrugh had ascertained that the price expected by Lord Clare for wedding the Lady Harriot was a mere £40,000. This incensed the Duchess. 'Lady Harriot is not a Citizen, nor a Monster.' As

Vanbrugh remarked acidly: 'As in all her other Traffick, so in a husband for her Grand Daughter, she wou'd fain have him Good and Cheap.' The price of that great fortune, Miss Hoyden, had only been set at fifteen hundred pounds a year and 'a great bag of money'. The Duchess's idea was for a very small bag of money to change hands.

The negotiations lay fallow between Permis Newcastle's desire for a large dowry to compensate for other bridal deficiencies and the Duchess's careful housekeeping.

If the wedding negotiations hung fire, the negotiations for the resumption of the building at Blenheim were under careful scrutiny and ready to re-start when a bitter blow struck the Duke. While he had been abroad in 1714 one of his favourite daughters, Elizabeth, Countess of Bridgwater, died of that eighteenth-century scourge, the smallpox. At that time he was said to have lost consciousness and swooned against the marble chimneypiece. In the spring of 1716 the second blow fell. Anne, Countess of Sunderland, died of what was called a 'pleuritic fever'. This was possibly pneumonia, as she had written of having 'one of mama's colds'. The Duke had already lost his only son of smallpox in 1703, and now his two favourite daughters had followed his son to the grave. Both girls were said to have had sweet natures and have been able to keep their mother's temperament within bounds.

On 28 May 1716 the Duke himself succumbed to a stroke. Dr Garth, now Sir Samuel, was sent for, and in spite of the copious bleedings and cuppings the Duke recovered, and little by little he was able to speak again. But overnight he had become an old man, and although his mind was clear his speech was impaired and never again was he able to take a very active part in public affairs. Born in 1650, John Churchill was already sixty-six and had for some time considered himself an old man. After this severe stroke he became one.

On 25 May 1716 Vanbrugh had still been writing to my Lord Duke about the prices of stone and the wages to be paid to the masons. Three days later the whole of the Blenheim business fell into the hands of the Duchess. The Duke's stroke was a severe blow to Vanbrugh.

The whole of the summer and autumn of 1716 was occupied in complicated correspondence between Vanbrugh and the Duchess about Blenheim. There were the usual detail arguments on the Duchess's side about the masons' price, countered by soft answers from Sir John. Were the towers to be continued during the summer while the good weather lasted? The prices had been reduced from twenty pence a foot to twelve pence.

In June, Vanbrugh expressed his extreme joy at the recovery of the Duke, a joy which no doubt had an added flavour in that it might save him from the Duchess's tender administration.

At the end of June plasterers, pavers and painters were being summoned. Vanbrugh tried to turn the Duchess's mind from her accountancy to a consideration of the beauties which were to greet her when the Palace was ready to become a fitting setting for her magnificence:

'The beauty of this place at this time is hardly to be conceived, which all strangers and Passengers will be ten times more sensible of when the house is inhabited than now; for besides the *additional* beauty of the Furniture, they will then comprehend the cast and turn of the House with the conveniencys which they are now quite ignorant of and see all with confusion.'

The Duchess was disinclined to see anything other than confusion and trickery from her architect and all those he employed. She would have made an excellent company secretary, or income tax investigator.

Vanbrugh ended his letter by wishing that 'the Bath will so thoroughly re-establish my Lord Duke, that he may enjoy the place in the latter season as he returns, when I hope he will see a great deal done to his satisfaction'. He added that 'Mr Thornhill goes on a pace in the Hall; and has begun with a better

Spirit in his paintings than anything I have seen of his doing before'.

Sir James Thornhill, who painted the Hall at Greenwich as well as working at Blenheim, was no better treated by his patrons than Vanbrugh himself. Even at Greenwich his work had been poorly paid and he had put in a complaint about it.

'I have made a demand and valuation of the painting done by me at the said Hospital [Greenwich] and find that when money was at a much greater value greater prices were given and beg leave to instance one, not presuming a parallel. Sir Peter Paul Rubens had £4,000 for his ceiling at the Banqueting House at Whitehall which is a little more than 400 yards of work so was nearly £10 a yard.'

Poor Thornhill had been paid only £634 for what he called his 'great and laborious undertaking'.

He was to fare no better at St Paul's or Blenheim. At Greenwich he had asked £5 a yard, and was paid £3, at St Paul's the fee was £2. At Blenheim he received a *prix de Duchesse* of twenty-five shillings. In compensation he is presumed to have used his assistants to do the grisaille (monochrome) paintings of trophies and decorations on the piers between the windows. The Duchess objected to this as sharp practice—mere monotone paintings should not have been considered to merit the same sum of money as grand historical scenes of my Lord Duke kneeling before an allegorical Britannia with his plan of the battle of Blenheim.

By July, Vanbrugh and the Duchess had descended to the minutiae of housekeeping. He had to explain to her that 'corridore' was a foreign word, and 'signifys in plain English no more than a Passage'. The Duchess could find deceptions everywhere.

The whole of the summer was occupied in complications about prices—prices of stone, prices of marble, prices of mouldings and of beadings. What was the boarding, flooring and roof going to cost? Yet again, the bridge came in for censure from her Grace. Vanbrugh had to write detailed and soothing replies to the Duchess's every objection.

'As for the Bridge I do love it; but will overcome my passion and not be troublesome about it . . . I don't speak of the Magnificence of it, but the agreeableness which I do assure you Madam has had the first place in my thoughts and contrivance about it because I know it won't be understood till 'tis seen.'

His graceful descriptions and the diplomacy he had to use over Blenheim had to be fitted in with consultations with the Prince of Wales and all his other business at the Board of Works. He added in the same letter to the Duchess that he had again been in touch with the Duke of Newcastle (lately Lord Clare). The Duke was still taking a practical view of his projected marriage, although it was sandwiched in between architectural matters as if it were just another piece of business.

The Duke wrote to Vanbrugh: 'Pray cast an Eye backwards and forwards upon Houghton, which I must think of when that great affair of Matrimony is over which I want to talk largely with you. If you have heard anything lately of it, let me know, for I shall come to Town in the Winter with a full resolution to fix somewhere.' If the Marlborough marriage negotiations proved sterile, the Duke was not disposed to be kept on a matrimonial string.

At the end of August, Vanbrugh was staying in his favoured spot with the Earl of Carlisle. The Duchess's instructions pursued him into this green retreat. She had been down at Bath and travelling about. In the course of her travels she had visited King's Weston. The things which interested the Duchess were not the charm of the architecture but the type of stone employed and the prices paid for it. Vanbrugh replied smoothly: 'I am glad your Grace is pleased with Mr Southwell's house; it being the sort of Building I endeavour to bring people to, who are disposed to ask my advice or assistance.'

The latter phrase could hardly be said to apply to his relations with the Duchess. He went on to explain very carefully that although Mr Southwell's stone was cheaper, 'to have sent it by water to Oxford, wou'd have been dearer than to come by land directly from Gloucester which they now do'.

On 21 August Sir John, who was taking the waters at Scarborough, which he probably needed to do, returned to his role of 'Coupler'.

'I can say little more to the other subject till I see the Duke of Newcastle. To whom I design however, in the mean time, amongst other things to mention something of that . . . And I hope the Duke of Marlborough will be entirely of your Grace's opinion. That his money can never be better bestow'd, than to compass the best match in England, for the only Daughter of his next heir.'

Owing to the death of the Duke of Marlborough's heir, the Dukedom had been allowed to descend in the female line, so that the Lady Harriot and her future children were possible heirs to the Dukedom of the Marlboroughs. This was a project which the Duchess did not intend to let slip cheaply.

Apart from the matchmaking which proceeded at a snail's pace, there were other complications for Vanbrugh with the Duchess. The matter of the old Manor had again become a *casus belli*. Although he had pulled down some of the old building, Vanbrugh had in fact made himself a cosy little 'box' in order to be near at hand for his work, and perhaps in the end be able to save at least part of fair Rosamund's Bower. The Duchess soon found out about this, and was deeply incensed.

In October Vanbrugh wrote his explanations of the Woodstock story as he saw it:

'That your Grace might not apprehend there was any thing carrying on at the old Manor against your Orders, I designed

286

to acquaint you before I came away, that I had set three or four men to work, to do some little necessary things without which I cou'd not be there but that they were at my own expence, not desiring to put my Lord Duke to any on my account.'

He went on to explain that he had paved the hall and parlour kitchen and that the few things which he had done had amounted to little more than the rent he would have had to pay for lodgings in the town. These explanations were curtly endorsed by the Duchess: 'Sir John Vanbrugh about his paying for all that ridiculous expence at the Old Manor House.'

The Duchess's detailed account was even more acid.

'He was very fond of an old Building that Stood Awry and Spoiled the view from ye Great Avenue to the House, upon which he laid out a good round Sum of Money to make a Habitation for Himself, and a great Expence there was to lead it, and a Closet in the middle, as if he had been to study the Planets. As soon as I discovered this I put a Stop to it.'

The Duchess had other investigations en train. She had sent for all the account books, and Jefferson, clerk to the patient Joynes, had been ordered to hand them over. He wrote desperately: 'Did all I could to keep my Bookes and Papers but the Order was from the Dukes owne Hand.'

Like so many others of the Blenheimites, Jefferson, whose wages had only been fifteen shillings a week, had asked for his money, but no answer had been received. 'Sir John,' he said, 'has been Extreamly my friend. So has Mr Hawsmoor, Mr Thornhill, of them faith to a wonder.'

The slow campaign being waged by the Duchess against Vanbrugh was coming to a climax, and although Mr Jefferson only rated fifteen shillings a week, he had eyes in his head, and he could see that the Duchess was going in a roundabout way to achieve her ends:

'What disturbs me and what I am heartily sory for, that I believe Sir John will never See Woodstock more, notwithstanding the pretended favour she had for Sir John when he was here. She has alter'd all againe and has put off all the Men at the Mannour house notwithstanding, it was told her that Sir John paid them himself. She carry'd the Duke to the Mannour into Every Roome and Order'd that they shou'd put up no more Hangings nor any thing Else, that Sir John had nothing to Doe there.'

It was quite obvious to Jefferson that, although the Duchess had taken Sir John round the great house and had made lists of all the furniture which was needed, this was a ruse. As soon as 'Mr Hawsmoor had Set Downe everything wanting, she orderr'd Moor to have a Coppy and he had one.' As soon as all the useful and relevant information had been copied down the Duchess was satisfied. She immediately got in touch with her cabinet and glassmaker Moore and said: 'Come Mr Moor, I will leave all to you and you shall Doe every thing as you think fit.'

The Duchess had now all the details she needed from her architect and his assistant Hawksmoor. They had nothing more to give her. Now was the time for the real economies to begin. Jefferson reported her as saying to Moore: 'Tho' Sir John has contracted with Several Workmen, if you Can Get any Body to Doe it cheaper they shall be turn'd out, notwithstanding the progress they have made in the Workes, which makes Sir John of Great Use to 'em. And in order to this he has begun Calling in the Countracts, which has sunk the Spirits of Fletcher, Reader, & every one to a reall flat.'

Although the Duchess had made her plans by October, her architect was still in ignorance of them. The trap was set in the park at Woodstock, but it had not yet been sprung. As late as that month Sir John wrote to the Duchess, in great detail, about the thorny topic of the steps for Blenheim, giving detailed ex-

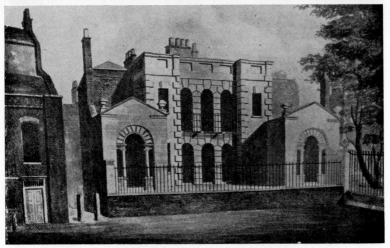

18a. Goose Pie House in Whitehall

b. Mince Pie House at Greenwich, c. 1718

c. Vanbrugh's Castle

19a. First Duke of Newcastle (right) with the Seventh Earl of Lincoln
(National Portrait Gallery)

b. Henrietta Yarbrugh, later Lady Vanbrugh, by Isaac Word
(*The Connoisseur*, July 1917)

planations of why the Duchess's steps had worked out more
expensive than Mr Southwell's. He was still trying to please.
A short postscript to a letter he wrote to the Duke of Newcastle,
'I bought up Peter Walters in my Calash', presaged the final
storm.

Peter Walters was a professional matchmaker and money
lender, he was well known in both these capacities and was
referred to by Pope:

'What's property, dear Swift, you see it alter
From me to you, from you to Peter Walter.'

The Duke of Newcastle had sent for Vanbrugh but he could
not accept the invitation, 'I having engag'd to Mr Walpole to
follow him into Norfolk'.

When Vanbrugh finally went down to Claremont he found
that the urgent topic of the Lady Harriot had come to the fore
again and in a most disagreeable manner. On this visit Vanbrugh
learned that the Duchess, impatient at the protracted and delicate negotiations which he had been carrying on for the
economical bedding of her grand-daughter, had in fact directly
employed Mr Walter in the business.

The Duke began by asking if anything more had passed on
the subject and 'what discourse might have happen'd wth. her
Grace the Duchess'. Vanbrugh remarked that nothing had been
said to him about the marriage negotiations by Sarah. The Duke
was extremely puzzled by the whole thing.

'He said it was mighty strange,' for the Duchess had spoken
to Mr. Walters already about it at Bath, 'and writ to him
Since, in Such a Manner as put him upon endeavouring to bring
on a direct Negotiation.'

If the Duchess was undercutting Vanbrugh on all sides,
Permis Newcastle was still anxious to have Vanbrugh's honest
views:

'He then told me, That before he cou'd come to a resolution

of embarking in any Treaty, he had waited for an Opportunity of discoursing with me once more upon the Qualitys and Conditions of Lady H. For That as I know his whole Views in Marriage and that he had hopes of Some Other Satisfaction in it than many people troubled themselves about, I might Judge what a Terrible Disappointment he shou'd be under if he found himself ty'd for life to a Woman not Capable of being a usefull and faithfull Friend, as well as an Agreeable Companion. That what I had often said to him of Lady H. in that respect, had left a strong Impression with him; but it being of so high a Consequence to him not to be deceived in this Great point, on which the Happyness of his Life wou'd turn, he had desir'd to discourse with me again upon it in the most serious manner.'

The Duke of Newcastle does not seem to have been so foolish a fellow as his fashionable acquaintances made him out to be.

After these preliminary discussions at Claremont, the Duke called in Peter Walters, who was already in the house. Vanbrugh, when penning his account to the Duchess, put down his feelings in his usual forthright manner.

If the Duke of Newcastle had been surprised to find out that the Duchess had approached Walters at Bath, and said nothing to Vanbrugh, Sir John was equally surprised to find out that she was carrying out her negotiations behind his back. As he put it to her: 'After the honour you had done me, of Opening your first thoughts on it to me, And giving me leave to make Severall Steps about it to his Friends and Relations.'

Vanbrugh had been made to look a fool and he made his position quite clear. 'I don't say this Madam, to Court being farther employ'd in this matter; for a Matchmakers is a Damned Trade, and I never was fond of Meddling with Other Peoples Affairs.'

The reasons for her underhand dealings became crystal clear when Sir John returned to town. He met Brigadier Richards, who had received from the Duchess, who never did things by halves, some twenty or thirty pages of complaints. It was a flowering of ten years of spleen and spite against Vanbrugh.

The final break had come. After all the years of toil, explanations, of lack of money and of misrepresentations, Sir John had reached the utmost limit of patience. It was time to make an end. Taking up his forthright pen he wrote to the Duchess: 'Madam,

When I writ to your Grace on Tuesday last I was much at a loss, what cou'd be the ground of your having drop't me in the service I had been endeavouring to do you and your family with the Duke of Newcastle, upon your own sole motion and desire. But having since been shewn by Mr. Richards a large packet of building papers sent him by your Grace, I find the reason was, That you had resolv'd to use me so ill in respect of Blenheim, as must make it Impracticable to employ me in any other Branch of your Service. These papers Madam are so full of *Far-fetched, Labour'd Accusations, Mistaken Facts, Wrong Inferences, Groundless Jealousies, and strain'd Constructions: That I shou'd put a very great affront upon your understanding if I suppos'd it possible you cou'd mean any thing in earnest by them; but to put a Stop to my troubling you any more.*

'*You have your end Madam for I will never trouble you more unless the Duke of Marlborough recovers so far, to shelter me from such intolerable Treatment.*

'I shall in the mean time have only this Concern on his account (for whom I shall ever retain the greatest Veneration) That your Grace having like the Queen thought fit to get rid of a faithfull servant, The Torys will have the pleasure to See your Glassmaker Moor, make just such an end of the Dukes Building as her Minister Harley did of his Victories for which it was erected.'

He had never written a better exit speech for any of his actors as he wrote for himself when quitting the Duchess's service. In one of his short and pungent postscripts he added: 'If your Grace will give me leave to print your paper I'll do it very exactly; and without any answer or remark *but this short letter tack'd to the tail of them, That the world may know I desir'd they might be published.*' His palpable hits at her own great humiliation pinpointed the fact that the Duchess was a woman who had learned little from life but to pass on the blows inflicted by others.

Vanbrugh sent a copy of his letter to the Duke of Newcastle. 'I need make no remarks to your Grace Upon this Abominable Womans proceeding Which shall not however lessen my regard to my Lord Duke, nor good Opinion of his Grand Daughter, who I do not think has one grain of this Wicked Womans Temper in her; if I did, I wou'd not advise you to take her, tho' with the Allay of a Million'.

He stood by his opinions of the Lady Harriot and wished to make it clear that his opinions were sincere and little affected by his relations with the Duchess.

Shortly after Vanbrugh resigned, the Duke had another stroke. It is thought probable that this could have been brought on by the Duchess's railing against Sir John and 'his impertinent letter'. The Duchess had always wanted creatures about her, creatures with no minds of their own who could be employed at rates disadvantageous to themselves. Sir John was not of this company. Nor were the other artists and craftsmen at Blenheim. Once the great days were over, they all faded away one by one, once Sir John had made his sparkling exit. Strong, the mason, 'had great business in town'. Thornhill left to be replaced by the cheaper and more subservient Laguerre, who had painted the staircase at Marlborough House at economical rates, to the Duchess's satisfaction. Hawksmoor was building in London, and even Mr Wise had quit the scene of his 'great Digg' near the disputed bridge.

If Jefferson at Blenheim was so sure in October 1716 that Sir John was to be 'got rid of', Mr Wise was also aware of the undercurrents. Already in the summer of 1716 the Duchess had been trying to get hold of the plans in order to use them without the architect. From Brompton Park on 30 August 1716 Mr Wise wrote, firmly but tactfully:

'I received your Graces of the 26th instant last night and should have been very glad to have given your Grace the Draught or lines of the Court and Causeway which your Grace requires, but these works being Sir John Vanbrugh's and Mr. Hawksmore's design, I never had any perfect Draught of them.'

Mr Wise had been dealing with rich clients for many years and knew their ways. He was not giving away trade secrets so that ideas could be used without payment.

Vanbrugh left the scene of his great masterpiece. Woodstock Manor was pulled down. The Duchess was at last in sole control to do what she liked with the unfinished building with a sick husband at her side. The man who had once dominated Europe was left to limp round the unfinished monument to his former glory.

Vanbrugh went to Blenheim no more. The days of fair weather had departed; he would do as the Duchess desired, and trouble her no more. 'I thought,' he said, 'after this, I cou'd not wait upon the Duke when she was present; And that if I endeavoured to do it at any other time, she wou'd not like it. There has been no other reason whatever why I have not continued to pay my Constant duty to *him*.'

The Duke wondered why his architect had left this child of his brain unfinished and sent a message through the Duke of Newcastle to let Vanbrugh know 'he took notice he had never seen me since he came from Blenheim: I was Surprizd to find he was not acquainted with the Cause, why I had not continued to wait on him as I us'd to do.'

The Duchess had been tactful. She was letting the blame for the break fall upon Vanbrugh—in his absence. If the Duke wondered why his genial architect came to see him no more, she was not to be the one to impart this piece of intelligence. Through all his campaignings in Flanders and France the Duke had prayed for peace to stay in England at Blenheim with his beloved wife. It was perhaps as well for him that the campaigning had not ended sooner. The Duchess was a formidable barrier to pleasant masculine friendships.

But in spite of having to leave his masterpiece to be finished by others, Vanbrugh did not proceed in a mean or unworthy manner over the projected alliance of the Lady Harriot with the Duke of Newcastle. He spoke to various friends about the lady. He interviewed the lady's father, Francis Lord Godolphin, who had presumably had many of Vanbrugh's difficulties over the years with the Duchess, his mother-in-law. Robert Walpole had been consulted.

Godolphin was a man who interested himself in horses and horse racing. He left everything to hazard.

'Nobody can help the Birth forward with the great Lady, but she must be left to her own throws.'

Eventually Newcastle, like the stone masons at Blenheim, was forced to reduce the price of the dowry to £22,000, a net saving of £18,000 to the Duchess.

On 2 April 1717, the Duke of Newcastle was joined in happy and profitable matrimony with the Lady Henrietta. The 'hopes of having a Posterity descend from the Duke of Marlborough' had, as Vanbrugh wrote, 'an extraordinary weight with him.' But the Duke had not only been cheated of his price, he was cheated of his heirs. The birth and fruition of the arranged marriage was projected into sterility. The Lady Harriot never had any children.

CHAPTER XVII

Patrons and
Persons of Quality

Although Vanbrugh had been dismissed from Blenheim, his other projects still continued on the same scale as before. Castle Howard was a continuing source of discussion and invention. The Duke of Newcastle continued to build at Claremont, no doubt helped by his wife's Marlborough dowry.

In 1716 Vanbrugh had been asked by George Dodington to design him a palace which was to rise on the edge of Cranborne Chase, to be of such a size as to rival Blenheim and Castle Howard. It is thought that the drawing entitled 'Design for a Person of Quality in Dorset', which is reproduced in *Vitruvius Britannicus*, may be Vanbrugh's original design for this grandiose building, which was planned to be 570 feet long, enclosing five courts.

All these undertakings were carried on simultaneously, entailing long and gruelling journeys at all times of the year. Vanbrugh was already fifty-two and yet managed to keep up the pace of his work as he had done when twenty years younger. But Blenheim had caused him unusual hardships both financial and physical. The cloud of uncertainties still hung over the unpaid debts. Nor had his expectations of recouping his fortune by being made Garter King of Arms as yet come to fruition. He had been acting as Garter since the Hanoverian, George I, had ascended the throne, his title being 'Clarenceux (nominated Garter).'

In 1716 he officiated at the ceremony of the degradation of the Duke of Ormonde. The Duke had been appointed Captain General following the fall of Marlborough. He had been defeated in Flanders and had fled to the Jacobite Court at the same time as St John, and in 1715 had even been tempted to invade with the Pretender. But the swift defeat of the Jacobites caused him to return once more to France a fugitive. It was no longer fitting that his arms should adorn his stall as Knight of the Garter. On 12 July 1716, anniversary of the Battle of the Boyne, which seemed an appropriate day for the degradation of a Jacobite, Vanbrugh, in his official capacity as acting Garter, went down to Windsor to perform the ceremony. After the reading of morning prayers Vanbrugh repeated the Sovereign's Warrant which lay on the Eagle desk. The Windsor Herald then climbed on to a ladder over the Duke of Ormonde's stall. Sword, banner, helm and crest were officially thrown down. These were then kicked from the choir by all the officers present, beginning with Vanbrugh, officiating as Garter, and ending with a pursuivant. As a final gesture Vanbrugh pulled down the plate over the Duke's stall on which his name was engraved. While the ceremony continued the soldiers stood to attention at the west door and the bells tolled. A Jacobite could no longer desecrate the company of the Knights of the Garter.

John Anstis, Vanbrugh's rival for the post of Garter had been equally suspected of Jacobite tendencies. Sir John had good reason to hope that by the time Sir Henry St George was finally gathered to his fathers the reversion of the Garter would fall to him, especially as he had been acting in this capacity for some time.

Anstis was not popular. It was said 'the trouble and opposition he met with in his business set him so much against the Officers of the College that he did everything to disgrace and ruin it.' Anstis had been imprisoned as a suspected Jacobite when the Whigs came back to power. This did not prevent him from sending a demand from his prison cell for his instatement as Garter King of Arms, putting in what he considered to be his just claim for the reversion of the Garter. The claim was held in abeyance, and for the time being it looked as if Vanbrugh might succeed in his endeavours to become Garter. He had already applied to the Attorney General for a bill granting him the office, but Anstis moved against him and issued a caveat.

The complications of the fight over the office of Garter King of Arms spread out. Anstis insisted that he already had the late Queen's patent, and furthermore that he had been nominated by the Earl Marshal. Lord Suffolk, on the other hand, as Deputy Earl Marshal, was asked to grant the office to Vanbrugh in the King's signature. Anstis did not give up the good fight; he came forward with the fact that he had been previously appointed by Lord Suffolk, who had now in a dastardly manner gone back on his word.

Anstis certainly had the detailed knowledge of geneaology, chivalry and the law, as well as the biographical and topographical details of numerous noble and landed families at his fingertips. But he was not personable. He was dubbed 'sordid, extravagant, and unforgiving' and for good measure it was said of him that 'his principal foible was drinking, which vice descended to his sons who were sots before they were men.'

It was not surprising that Vanbrugh's friends would rather have seen the office fall to him.

The Officers of the College of Heralds were not acting as nobly as their high sounding titles might have warranted. For some time they had not only been selling offices, which happy practice went on till 1763, but the Windsor Herald, who rejoiced in the appropriate name of Piers Mauduit, had been extracting and selling books from the library of the College of Arms to pay his debts.

Although Anstis' claims had been set aside, he continued to battle against Vanbrugh with all the detailed knowledge of law and procedure at his command. Not only was Anstis proceeding to claim the office, but he had also put in a petition for arrears of salary due to him. There was no point in skimping on monetary claims.

By 1717 the matter was still not settled and Vanbrugh himself was not in good health. He wrote to the Duke of Newcastle about a 'feaver I have been ill handled by' which has 'not made me so indifferent to the Misfortunes of others, not to have been struck in the most sensible degree about ten days Since on the News we had delivered for certain of the Dutchess of Newcastle being given over.'

In her grand-daughter's illness, as in her marriage, the Duchess of Marlborough had been her usual busy self. She prided herself on her knowledge and treatment of various distempers, and certainly had great courage in nursing various members of her family through smallpox. In the event the Duchess of Newcastle was not seriously ill, but this did not prevent the other Duchess turning up to give good, if unsolicited, advice. 'The Husband,' she wrote, 'is certainly very kind to her and good natur'd, I believe; but very young and ignorant as to any Thing of Distempers; and tis plain by what I saw when I came that Doctor Mead had frightened him out of his Witts, in order, I suppose, to bee paid the better.'

Everyone, whether doctor or architect, was suspected of malpractices. Vanbrugh, in spite of his own illness, wrote to Newcastle saying 'I am extreamly glad to hear Your Danger is over, of Losing a Wife, whose place you never can supply.' The marriage seemed to have proved the success Vanbrugh had shrewdly judged it might be.

In the middle of October 1717, Sir John wrote to the Lords Commissioners of His Majesty's Treasury from 'the Bath' where he was presumably taking the waters in order to recover his health. The matter of John Anstis was still not resolved.

'I believe it will not be necessary to give your Lordps. ye trouble of a long detail of what has pass'd on this Occasion. But that it will Suffice to acquaint you, That upon an Application to his Majty. in Council from ye Earl of Suffolk . . . he prepared a Bill for his Royal Signature to pass ye Great Seal containing his Majesty's Grant of ye Office of Garter Princ01l King of Arms to me.'

He ended a letter full of complications by saying that the delays had been caused by the other side, and he thought it 'just and reasonable for ye King to keep his Money in his hands, till he see whether a Patent granted by himself, or his Predecessour, determins who is to have ye honour of being his Officer.'

On 12 April 1718 it was decided that the King should sign a warrant against Anstis' right to the patent. Unfortunately for Vanbrugh, the Duke of Norfolk, that old friend of Anstis, had persuaded the Attorney General that the prosecution should be held in abeyance as its successful outcome was in doubt. The question which hung in the balance was whether it was his Hanoverian Majesty who had the right to choose his Garter King at Arms, or whether it was the Earl Marshal. The rights of the Earl Marshal were upheld by default, and the whole matter was dropped.

Anstis had already moved into the College of Heralds, bag and baggage, presumably considering, with his knowledge of the law, that possession was nine tenths of it.

It was another defeat for the agreeable Sir John. The Earl of Carlisle for once had not been able to help him; there were patrons and counter patrons. Possibly the Hanoverian King did not take these petty offices seriously. As Englishmen always consider foreign titles slightly comic, presumably the Hanoverian took the same view of English Heralds. Surrounded by German courtiers and flanked by his fat and lean German mistresses, George I was able to accommodate himself to English money, while remaining insulated to English thought.

Through the mazes of eighteenth century patronage even the most complaisant and easy of men could be ill handled, although Vanbrugh himself was not neglecting the difficulties imposed by the new regime. When writing to the Duke of Newcastle, and regretting that they had missed one another 'at the back stairs', presumably at St James's, he added: 'My Lord Sunderland has told me when your Grace and Lord Stanhope have Spoke, he'll then talk effectually with the Dutchess of Munster.'

This 'Dutchess' was Ermengarde Melusina von der Schulenberg, Duchess of Munster, later to be dubbed Duchess of Kendal, the King's thin mistress called the Maypole, to distinguish her from the fat one called the Elephant.

Lord Sunderland, the Marlboroughs' son-in-law, had risen once more to favour after his fall under Queen Anne, because he spoke German. Nor was Vanbrugh's fluent French unhelpful to him at the new Court, French being the *lingua franca* of the polite world throughout the eighteenth century.

Vanbrugh's negotiations were connected with what he called 't'other unlucky affair', which was a further move against him at the Board of Works. Whether these were in any way connected with the Duchess of Marlborough, or whether they were merely manoeuvres to replace him, taken by other patrons moving upwards in the new reign, is uncertain. But as some of the accusations against him were monetary, it could have been that Sarah's loud complaints had not improved the solid reputation which Sir John had formerly achieved. Other factors could also have contributed. Sir Christopher Wren was now an old man; with Hawksmoor and Vanbrugh they had formed the triumvirate at the Board of Works, but now the feeling was in the air that their style of building was becoming old fashioned. The Earl of Burlington and the pure Palladian school were moving forward. With the beginning of the new reign, change was in the air.

The immediate worry for Vanbrugh was to hold his office and to make sure of his eventually succeeding Wren, when the latter finally retired. In the same letter where Vanbrugh wrote of speaking softly to die Schulenberg, he mentioned that the prices which were charged to the King for work done at the Board of Works had been compared unfavourably with those charged to my Lord Chetwind. The reason for this was obvious: 'My Lord Chetwins work being done, at the lowest rates, paid in the porrest houses in Towne.' An additional difference was that although the King had paid very little more than the Lord Chetwind, allowances had also to be made 'for fees and gratuitys which the King's Workmen are forc'd to allow in the Offices.'

It seemed that the rates paid to the workmen depended partly on the worth and quality of the work they performed, and partly on the grandeur of the client for whom they worked. In this connection Vanbrugh put his cards on the table. He desired to have the King's favour, or he would 'Abandon any pretence to it for ever'. It was the same approach as he had made to Dutchess Sarah. Either he would be considered *persona grata* or he would leave such unprofitable employment.

Some time later he wrote in the same forthright vein:

'I have reason to believe the King has had such an unfair Account given him secretly of my Management, both of his Houses and Gardens; As must make me Appear a very bad Officer in the Employments he has been pleas'd to intrust me with.

'As I am inform'd This Representation has been follow'd with an Attempt to have me remov'd from his Service: And this attempt, is in a way of Succeeding.

'All I beg is, That My Lord Sunderland will please obtain his Direction to the Treasury, To examine into The Truth of My Conduct; and to make an Impartial Report to him, how they find it.'

The cabals against Vanbrugh's post in the Board of Works were carried on by William Benson. His machinations, together with the difficulties over the succession to the office of Garter, seem to have upset Vanbrugh as well as undermining his health. He wrote to the Duke of Newcastle:

'I'm sure your Grace won't easily believe I wou'd invent
excuses to keep away from you, But between those two
Accursed things of determining the Windsor point, and my
friend Bensons, together with ten Summonses a day I have to
Kensington (the royal palace) I am not only divested of passing one moment to my Satisfaction; but am so disorder'd by
the hurry into the bargain That I thought 20 times yesterday,
I must have dropt dead.'

Each patron was disposed to consider himself a special case,
but the lot of the patronised was never easy.

Vanbrugh ended on a note which pinpoints how much his
talent to amuse had helped him in his path upwards into the
higher reaches of Whig patronage. 'Your Grace will therefore
See, tis neither in my power to Attend you as I most heartily
wish I cou'd nor to be in a Condition (in the present way I am)
to be either entertaining or useful to you if I cou'd come.'
Shortly afterwards he wrote about being 'flea'd with Blisters'.
'Blistering' was another of the primitive remedies used at this
time, or it could possibly have been that Vanbrugh was suffering from shingles, which are notoriously caused by nervous
exhaustion and worry.

In 1718, Vanbrugh reached the nadir of his fortunes. The
King had given his decision in favour of John Anstis, who had
slipped comfortably into the post of Garter King of Arms. This
was finally decided on 20 April 1718. A few days later in the
same month, William Benson, a Wiltshire landowner who had
little experience or even talent for architecture, was appointed
to Sir Christopher's old place as Surveyor General at the Board
of Works. This last was an even sharper disappointment. Vanbrugh had previously been offered this post but had declined it, as
he himself said 'out of tenderness to Sir Christopher Wren'. Having made a graceful gesture, he had reason to be sanguine that
when the right time came, the plum would fall to him, but changes
of politics, of sovereigns, and even of taste had intervened.

Hawksmoor was dismissed at the same time. Benson, in the happy way of nepotism at that time, had brought in his nephew to serve under him. The nephew proved totally incompetent. Benson also brought in to the Board of Works, Colin (or Colen) Campbell, afterwards to compile that repository of eighteenth century architectural knowledge, *Vitruvius Britannicus*. In the first volume of this work, Campbell described his patron and his patron's self-designed house in fulsome terms:

'Wilberry in Wiltshire is the Seat of William Benson Esq. invented and built by himself in the Stile of Inigo Jones, who, by his excellent choice, discovered the Politeness of his Taste: and as he is Master of the most refined part of Literature has here expressed a particular regard to the noblest manner of architecture, in this beautiful and regular design, which was executed Anno 1710.'

William Benson, apart from having powerful friends at Court, was a disciple of the school of Palladio. Wren, Vanbrugh and Hawksmoor had not travelled in Italy, so far as is known, and such Italian ideas as they had used had come to them through the book of Palladio or through the influence of French architecture. The new school of amateurs, using the word in the French sense, had taken the pure spring waters of the Italian school to their hearts and the later extravagances of Rome had shocked their Protestant souls. The style later to be called Baroque smacked so far too much of the Church of Rome rising triumphantly from the Reformation to be attractive to the northern soul. Some other Italian influences had to be found, purer, nearer to the Greek ideal than the decadent manifestations of an Italian operatic magnificence. Everything is to be pure and Palladian, and anything which deviated from this mould was suspect.

Wren had been dismissed, and even Vanbrugh was not able to save Hawksmoor from being sent away. So far from being promoted to Wren's old post, Vanbrugh's friends had the greatest difficulty in retaining for him the one which he already had.

But, in spite of the setbacks, he attempted to revive his spirits with social occasions and wrote his thanks to the Duke of Newcastle for his 'most sweet venison, at the eating of which— Ladys (amongst other Folks) drank your health.' The Tate a Tate Club had been reviv'd at the Hercules Pillars Alehouse in High Holborn, at which entertainment, according to Vanbrugh, 'there was stinking Fish, Stale cold Lamb for supper with divers Liquors made of Malt in an execrable manner.'

During the same summer he wrote on several occasions about being 'cruell' bad and again being 'blistered'. Although the Anstis affair had in effect been decided, Lord Suffolk, who had acted as Deputy to the Duke of Norfolk, had died and it might perhaps have seemed to Newcastle that the case could be re-opened. But Vanbrugh said he had no particular interest 'in this thing worth the naming; The dispute with Anstis, being quite out of the Earl Marshal's hand and lying between the Crown and him.'

The cabals at the Board of Works were still giving him trouble and he compared them to his imprisonment in the Bastille so long ago. 'I fear only those same Letters de Cachet, that Surprise folks every now and then.'

A fresh plot had also been set in train at the College of Heralds to make Lord Berkeley Deputy Earl Marshal instead of allowing the Earl of Suffolk to succeed his father. The Earl, although possibly he wanted the honour of the post, appears to have been dilatory in his approach to claiming his rights. Vanbrugh sent a copy of the letter he had written to Lord Suffolk to the Duke of Newcastle. It is a letter which gives many clues to the writer's character, and to the world in which he moved:

'Mr Howard shew'd me to-day the Duke of Norfolk's Answer to your Lordship: but I have some reason to believe that the matter is now however to be dispar'd of, I heartily wish Your Ldship wou'd resolve to hasten up to Town, Not

only as I think it wou'd much Contribute towards the Carrying
this point; but as I think Likewise, it may prove of service to
you perhaps for your whole life; For, give me leave My Lord
to offer to your Reflection, That there are very sharp eyes on
a man's behaviour at his first Appearance upon the Publick
Stage.'

He was passing on the fruits of many years' attending upon
Sovereigns and great Whig lords.

'And tho' the King can have no ground to doubt your good
disposition to his Service and your Country's in Generall; Yet
the Manner of Your expressing it, will give a Deeper or a
Shallower Impression upon him; and by Consequence, turn
more or less to your own service and interest.'

Many hours of patient thought and carefully turned phrases
were in those sentences, and yet they were written by a man
who never deviated from being his own man, who never degenerated into being a creature, or being patronised in the
modern sense of the word. It was a very fine line, but it had to
be drawn in a bold way. He ended his letter to the Earl recommending him to adopt a 'warm and generous appearance at
your setting out', and to caution that the 'least Impression of a
Negligence or Lukewarmness will be very hard to work off.'

The advice he passed on was the fruit of hard lessons
learned in a hard school. But in spite of all his pressing difficulties he was still building and planning for the Duke of
Newcastle.

At the end of 1718 he had been looking over Nottingham
Castle with a view to rebuilding it. In spite of having, as he said,
'being put more out of humour at this Rascally Board of Works
than ever', he approached the possibility of a new commission
with his usual good humour.

Writing from Nottingham on 17 December he said:

'Twas a horrible a day as Storms, hail, Snow and the Divil can make it, I have been over your Castle, inside and out; and am glad I have Seen it at the worst, since it has not alter'd my Opinion of it at all; The Rooms being calm, and warm and all still and quiet within doors.'

Outside, which he referred to as the 'Dehors', his imagination was soon at work. There would be sufficient space for stables and outbuildings, as many as my Lord Duke had a mind to. The park had to be planted but 'there may be a very Noble Pond in it, with small Expence, And the Views from the upper part of it are right.' But he was very pleasantly surprised by the Castle and the fact that it stands 'distinguish'd from the Towne.' He had a conversation with an old retainer who had been living there for more than forty years, and had found out the chimneys were 'not one quarter so faulty as they have been represented'. He ended by congratulating the Duke upon being the master of so noble a dwelling 'which I cannot but think you will extreamly like when a little us'd to it. At first perhaps, you'll think it Stairs you in the face with a pretty impudent countenace.'

He advised the Duke that he would make all the necessary calculations for repairs which ought to be put in hand before his Grace decided to live there. Vanbrugh's idea was to keep the Castle in mind as a whole, not to take notice of the first Mason's estimate which had been sent to him 'it being of very great consequence to have them rightly concerted the wants of which I had Seen a sad experience of . . . I mean what has lately been done by the Duke of Rutland in the Outworks of his Castle; where for want of being rightly understood, the whole grace of them is lost; it looks all like pastboard work, and in reality a great deal of it, is tumbling down already.'

It would be much better, Vanbrugh remarked tactfully, if the work were carried on 'when your Grace is on the Spot and not in a hurry'.

Presumably, as the Duke was known to be fussy and interfering, Vanbrugh was anxious to get things sorted out on the spot, and carefully planned and plotted before being involved in tortuous arguments.

The other reason he put forward against the Duke's leaving for Nottingham gives some insight into his own life, and the travelling conditions at the time.

'Besides; the ways are so execrable and the days so short, that I plainly find, by my own driving (wch is none of the Slowest) you will Not get hither in less than four days; I therefore hope your Grace will resolve, Only to Order the Painting, Glazing, Whitewashing and such things to go on; And leave the rest till I can attend you here in April or May. And then; what is done may be to the purpose.'

Although the roads had improved slightly since Celia Fiennes had embarked on her series of exploratory journeys at the end of the last century, the days of easy coach travel had not yet arrived. Vanbrugh left for Castle Howard, his place of refreshment, light and peace. He wrote from Yorkshire on Christmas Day 1718, saying that he had missed the Duke's letter as he had been three days getting from Nottingham to York 'through such difficultys as the Stage Coach cou'd not pass, which I left over set and quite disabled upon the way. There has now fallen a Snow up to one's Neck, to mend it, wch. may possibly fix me here as long as it did at the Bath this time two years; wch. was no less than five weeks.'

Then, in a quick aside in a letter full of news and political gossip, there comes a sudden sentence giving a hint as to his real plans. 'In short tis so bloody Cold, I have almost a mind to Marry to keep myself warm, and if I do I'm sure it will be a wiser thing than your Grace has done, if you had been at Nottingham.'

Benedick was about to become a married man.

CHAPTER XVIII

The Faithfull Servant as
Married Man

On 14 January 1719 John Vanbrugh, 'Batchelour', aged fifty-five, was married to Henrietta Yarbrugh, spinster aged twenty-six. She was the daughter of Colonel James Yarbrugh, sometime aide-de-camp to the Duke of Marlborough. Her connections were without blemish and distantly aristocratic. Her grandmother Margaret Blagge was sister to the Duchess of Newcastle's grandmother.

In some senses marriage was a curious step to take when Sir John's fortunes had reached a low ebb. In addition to having lost his two possibilities of advancement, there hovered in the background the strong possibility that he might be involved in the law suits preparing over the building of Blenheim.

Sir John Vanbrugh, although he had little to bring to marriage in the way of worldly wealth, was still a man of outstanding merit in a world where talent and manners were assets to be used. The eighteenth century had completely down to earth views about matrimony, well illustrated by Mr Edward Wortley Montagu, who wrote to his future wife, the Lady Mary: 'But is it not wonderful that you are ignorant what the terms are on which you are to be *disposed* of?'

Perhaps Sir John had developed a *tendre* for a girl much younger than himself, perhaps the idea of domestic comfort, coupled with the possibility of a dowry had its attractions.

There were some ambiguities in his attitude, which was not

surprising in view of his previous mocking attitude to marriage. It was awkward to remember his remark like 'that Old Prig Sir Steven Fox has tack'd himself to a Young wench of twenty.' A further ambiguity is lent to the nuptials by a letter written to a friend by Lady Mary, then married to Mr Edward Wortley Montagu. She had been left to moulder in the village of Middle-thorpe while her husband entertained himself in London. At that time she was unhappy, unable to use her talents in any considerable way, and yet determined to put a brave face on a marriage which perhaps she already considered a mistake. She had written, over brightly, to her woman friend in London:

'I return you a thousand thanks for so agreeable an entertainment as your letter. In this cold climate where the sun appears unwillingsly wit is as wonderfully pleasing as a sunshiny day . . . I can't forbear entertaining you with our York lovers (strange monsters you'll think, love being as much forced up here as melons). In the first form of these creatures is even Mr Vanbrugh. Heaven no doubt compassionating our dulness has inspired him with a passion that makes us all ready to die laughing. 'Tis credibly reported that he is endeavouring at an honourable state of matrimony and vows to lead a sinful life no more. Whether pure holiness inspires his mind or dotage turns his brain is hard to find. 'Tis certain he keeps Mondays and Thursdays Market (the days of the Assemblies) constant, and for those that don't regard worldly much, there's extraordinary good choice indeed. I believe last Monday there was two hundred pieces of women's flesh (fat and lean). But you know Van's taste was always odd; his inclination to ruins has given him a fancy for Mrs. Yarborough. He sighs and ogles that it would do your heart good to see him; and she is not a little pleased in so small a proportion of men."

There has been some discussion about this letter in connection with Vanbrugh's subsequent marriage to Henrietta Yarbrugh, especially in view of the fact that her mother died in childbirth a year or so after Lady Mary's letter was written. It has been suggested, which would seem very possible, that he was in love with the mother, and later transferred his affections to the daughter. This does not seem to be unlikely, there is often a psychological link between a man and some particular family of women, an attraction towards a particular physical type, or an easy attitude towards life. Or it could be that it was necessary to court the mother in order to secure the daughter. Lady Mary in her unhappy provincial exile would not have been inclined to look with too friendly an eye on the happiness of others, and the retailing of gossip was a way of proving that she was in livelier spirits than her situation warranted.

Perhaps Vanbrugh's views on marriage were best expressed by himself when defending his views against Jeremy Collier. When referring to the character of Loveless in *The Relapse* he wrote, 'For my part, I thought him so indisputably in the right; and he appear'd to me to be got in so agreeable a Tract of Life, that I often took a pleasure to indulge in a musing Fancy and suppose myself in his place. The Happiness I saw him possesst of, I lookt upon as a jewel of very great worth.'

While on the one hand Vanbrugh was making the best case he could against Collier's attacks, on the other he could have been sincere in his musing fancy. Men who do not marry are often in a better position to indulge their fancy for the ideal woman when they are unencumbered by the possession of the unideal, just as it is easier to indulge poetic fancies about angelic offspring when separated from the every day difficulties of their upbringing.

Yet it was a difficult step for Vanbrugh to take. He had written 'irreverently of Matrimony—because à la Françoise, Bigottry runs high, and by all I see we are in a fair way to make A Sacrament on't again.' His wit now came up to haunt him, and his casual remark about it being 'so bloody cold that he had a mind to marry' was a joke made on the edge of taking his vows to love and cherish. The old Kit Cat friends might have many a laughing reference to his final surrender to respectability. Possibly he felt with Worthy: 'The coarser Appetite of Nature's gone, and 'tis methinks the Food of Angels I require. How long this Influence may last—Heaven knows!'

Two days before the final step was taken he wrote to the Duke of Newcastle from York: 'Lord Carlisle and his family will be here by and by, I came before them a day or two. He treats severall of his Friends today at dinner, and afterwards, we all go to pay Our Respects to York, at the Assembly, Where the Ladys will muster Strong on this Occasion Lord Carlisle being the Idol here. And well deserves their Devotions.'

These must have been Vanbrugh's pre-wedding celebrations, and in a letter written to Newcastle twelve days after his marriage, he makes the best of the situation, by mingling the news with architectural business.

'As I have been the Instrument, of your fixing on this Castle for your Northern Seat, I shou'd have been heartily concern'd to find you disappointed in it. I have no care now left, but to see the Dutchess of Newcastle as well pleased as your Grace is. I hope She won't have the less expectation from my Judgment in Chusing a Seat, from my having chosen a Wife, whose principall Merrit in my Eye, has been some small distant shadow, of those Valuable Qualifications in her, your Grace has formerly with so much pleasure heard me talk of.'

The retreat from being a bachelor was a difficult one to take, and the shadows of the smiles of old drinking companions were perhaps to be feared. It was as well to round off the narrative with a well-turned compliment:

'The honour she has of being pretty nearly related to the Dutchess gives me the more hopes I may not have been mistaken. If I am 'tis better however to make a Blunder towards the end of ones Life, than at the beginning of it. But I hope all will be well; it can't at least be worse than most of my

Neighbours, which every Modest Man, ought to be content with; And So I'm easy.'

He remained his Grace's most faithfull Servant whether a married man or a 'bachelour'.

The most difficult of the old cronies to approach with this piece of intelligence was Mr Jacob Tonson, then again on his travels. 'Jacob will be frightened out of his Witts And his Religion too, when he hears I'm gone at last. If he is still in France, he'll certainly give himself to God, for fear he shou'd now be ravish'd by a gentlewoman. I was the last Man left, between him and Ruin.'

The old Kit Cat days were past and gone, the patriots who had saved England the constitution were falling into the sere and yellow, or into matrimony.

But, as Shaw remarked, marriage often turns out very well indeed—from time to time. This time, as so often with many unlikely unions, it turned to Vanbrugh's happiness and comfort. But six months later he was still uneasy about the opinion of his old friend Tonson. He referred to the great slaughter of all the old friends.

'I don't know whether you'll reckon me amongst the first or the last, since I have taken this great Leap in the Dark, Marriage. Don't be too much dismay'd however, for if there be any truth In Married Man (who I own I have ever esteem'd a very lying creature) I have not yet repented.'

From six months' experience he said: 'I am confirmed my Old Opinion was right; That whatever there was of good or bad in Marriage; it was fitter to end Our Life with, than begin it.'

He was very anxious to reassure Tonson that in spite of the marriage bond he was still his own man: 'for you must know, whatever evils Marriage may design me; it has not yet lessen'd one grain of my Affections to an old Friend.'

Vanbrugh looked back with affection to France, and to Paris where Tonson was on one of his long business trips.

'As to the place you are in; I am so far from being disgusted to it, by the treatment I once met with [his imprisonment in the Bastille] that I think the very thing has doubled a Romantick desire, of seeing it again. In short; I have it so much in my thoughts; that I have talk't even my Gentlewoman into a good disposition of being of the Party if things will fall kindly out for it, next Spring.'

At bottom, in spite of the hard handling he had had in the circles of patronage in which he moved, Vanbrugh was still full of verve and vigour and always ready to plan ahead whether it was a new portico for a Duke, or a trip to Paris with an old friend. Vanbrugh's brother Charles was passing through Paris and he hoped that Tonson would 'drink a Chopine' (half a litre) of wine with him.

During 1719 it was mistakenly reported that Tonson had died abroad. In November Vanbrugh wrote to him in Paris. 'I had one Sensible pleasure from the whole, wch. no Letter from you ever gave me before. it was; From Reflecting on the Change, between mourning a Friends Death, and afterwards receiving a Living Epistle from him.'

From the happy nature of his letters to Tonson after his marriage there breathes the reality of a man who has found a wife who has the secret of bringing ease and pleasure to a man who had approached marriage with a wry smile. He wrote: 'I desire to make no such Correction of your Manners as to stifle one of your Jokes upon Matrimony; for tho' the Chain shou'd happen to hang a little easy about me (by a sort of Messissippy good fortune.)' The reference to Mississippi was to Jacob Tonson's investments in the Mississippi scheme, which was very similar to the South Sea Scheme but based on investments to be made in Virginia. Tonson, who travelled so much in France, was more involved in foreign investments than his friends. Vanbrugh's good fortune was in his wife:

'My Wife returns your compliments. She says she's Sorry she

has not a Sister for you; but she knows them that have. And if you'll give her Commission, She'll answer for't, to provide at least as well for you, as she has done for me. She desire I'll tell you farther, That I have said so much to her of you, while you were alive, after you were dead, and Since you are alive again, That she knows you well enough to desire to know you better, and therefore accepts of your dinner at Barnes, and of your promise to accept of hers at Greenwich where she will treat you with the best of her Good (Yorkshire) Houswifry.'

At this point Harriot, who stood over Vanbrugh as he wrote to his old friend, took up the pen and added a note: 'And if you will make one at cards as I understand you have often done, with much finer Ladys than I am I give you my word that I will neither cheat nor wrangle. Yr. Sern. Hariot V.'

Harriot seems to have been a lively girl with some sense of humour and a modest assessment of her own talents. It could not have been easy to marry a man who had lived amongst 'great folks' for so many years and who had seen, perhaps loved, and been disillusioned by many fine ladies. In addition, he was a man of sharp wit who would not take easily to being bored with female trivialities. She was obviously a girl of character who had taken on a difficult task and carried it off with aplomb, commonsense and housewifely application, all of which are attributes for a happy marriage too often ignored by the romantic school.

Tonson had advised Vanbrugh to put money into the Mississippi scheme, but monetarily the architect's fortunes were at a low ebb:

"'Tis not out of fear I do not follow your advice. But to tell you the truth; I have no money to dispose of. I have been many years at hard Labour, to work through Cruel Difficultys that Hay Market undertaking involv'd me in; notwithstanding the aid of a large Subscription, Nor are those difficultys, quite at an end yet. Tho' within (I think) a tollerable view.'

He went on to mention the 'very hard Disappointment of not being made Surveyor of the Works; which I believe you remember I might have had formerly, but refus'd out of Tenderness to Sr. Chr. Wren.'

Benson, who had been appointed in Vanbrugh's place, had proved so incompetent that both he and his nephew were out of office by August 1719. Once more could Sir John have hoped that his qualifications and the hard work of his constant attendance at the Board of Works might have secured him a post for which he was eminently fitted. 'Mr Benson's reign', as Vanbrugh put it, ended on 4 August, but once again Vanbrugh was passed over in favour of Thomas Hewet, who was even less qualified for the post than Benson. Hewet was Surveyor of Woods and Forests, another post which he had obtained with few qualifications. As Vanbrugh wrote to the Duke of Newcastle with some justified bitterness:

''Tis a very hard matter for me to find out any thing, 'till tis over late to ask for't but they know of every thing time enough to help their humble Servants (without their Aid) when they are quite determin'd to take care of them. Which is Hewets Case now, and was once before, when Ld. Halifax made him his Surveyr. of the Forrests without his ever dreaming of it. I resolve to live in hopes My Ld. Sund. will do the same by me to help this Pill downe, which is a little Bitter, now I come just to the time (and disgrace) of Swallowing it, I don't however blame any body, nor think them wanting. But 'tis one of hardest pieces of Fortune, that ever fell to anybody.'

He went on to add that so far from being found wanting in his office at the Board of Works, he had saved the King ten thousand pounds a year 'And that all his prejudice to me is founded on pure misinformation.'

There was some hint that Vanbrugh was induced to renounce his post in favour of Benson. At this point Vanbrugh suggested that (as the Duke of Marlborough had once done in more exalted circumstances) that he should be awarded the Controllership for life and awarded a sum of money in compensation.

Even Hewet was not yet secure because the Duchess of Marlborough now decided to take a hand in the affair. She and the dismissed Benson, jointly and severally, put forward the idea that the painter James Thornhill should be awarded the post. It is hard not to be of the opinion that Sarah Marlborough was a woman who pursued victims *à l'outrance* and allowed her vindictive feelings full rein. She had managed to induce Vanbrugh to resign from the building of Blenheim, had attempted to obtain his designs without payment, and now she was pursuing him into other fields.

Vanbrugh regarded the new candidate as even more ludicrous than either Benson or Hewet: 'Twou'd be a pleasant Joke to the World, to see a Painter made Surveyor of the Works, in order to save Money.' It is possible that this might be a reference to the fact that Thornhill had been employed at Blenheim and then been passed over in favour of Laguerre, so that perhaps the Duchess was holding out the chance of this appointment as a sweetener which would cost her nothing from her personal fortune: 'But to think that Such a Volatile Gentleman as Thornhill shou'd turn his thoughts & Application to the duty of a Surveyors business is a Monstrous project. I'm so sick of this Rhidiculous [*sic*] Story I can write no more on't.'

It was not surprising that Vanbrugh grew more impatient with the years, the mazes of patronage were full of pitfalls, not only for the unwary but for the sensible and the dedicated. Creatures were the best malleable materials for the majority of patrons, and that was the one role which Vanbrugh would never play.

Apart from the disappointment of his hopes for the post of Surveyor of the Works, Blenheim had again come to the fore. 'I have,' Vanbrugh wrote to Tonson, 'a farther misfortune, of losing (for I now see little hopes, of ever getting it) near £6000 due to me for many years Service, plague and Trouble at Blenheim Which that Wicked Woman of Marlb. is so far from paying me that the Duke being Sued by some of the Workmen for work done there, She has try'd to turn the Debt due to them, upon me, for which I think she shou'd be hang'd.'

The troubles over Blenheim were in part due to the equivocal nature of the original wording of the grants of land and money. Well over £200,000 had already been spent on the Palace, and the contractors had set to work to start proceedings against either the Crown or the Marlboroughs to settle the debts. When the works had been stopped in 1712, at the time of the Duke's disgrace, Vanbrugh had reminded the Treasury that the Queen had authorised the building of the Palace, and that the debts to the workmen were the responsibility of the Crown. When Queen Anne had finally passed beyond the earthly sphere of being able to be sued, half a million pounds was voted to settle her debts. The crown debts at Blenheim were judged to be £60,000. But, in the way of most governments, only £16,000 had been advanced towards the total sum. The contractors who had already waited, like Jacob, for seven years for the consummation of their contracts, decided to go forward and sue the Duke.

Confusion then became worse confounded. Because of the loose nature of the agreements with the Crown, the contractors had always dealt with Vanbrugh, who had acted on behalf of the Duke, who in his turn received the money from the Crown. When the case came before the Barons of the Exchequer, the Court found that the responsibility was the Duke's, the evidence being advanced on the grounds of Vanbrugh's warrant and some of the letters which had been written by the Duke to Vanbrugh.

After this the Duchess became even more bitterly opposed to Vanbrugh than she had been before, on the grounds of the evidence which he had given before the Court.

'The most material witnesses were plainly perjured under their own hands, but most flamingly Sir J. V. . . . because Sir John, by agreeing with any of the works people upon an old dirty piece of paper may yet make whatever contracts he pleased. I have good reason to believe that Bury & Price (the Barons of the Exchequer) were gained by the influence of a very artful man who is a great friend to Sir John.'

The Duchess was incensed that Vanbrugh had changed his views about the debts to the Blenheimites. Previously he had stood firmly on the point that the Crown was responsible. It may have been that Vanbrugh was unwilling to jeopardise his precarious position at the Board of Works. He had already been blackened in the eyes of the world by the Duchess's accusations, and it is very probable that some of these may have infiltrated into Court circles. The very fact that the Duchess had tried to insinuate Thornhill into the Surveyorship showed that she still had some influence. Sir John himself was owed several thousands of pounds which he could ill afford, and the Duke was a rich man, how rich Vanbrugh was not to learn until later. The Duke was perfectly capable of paying his workmen and his architect, and Sir John was possibly at this point in his life not prepared to throw his career into the balance as he had in 1713 by supporting the Marlboroughs, who had hardly proved themselves to be a helpful support to one who had nearly ruined himself by his loyalty to them.

The Duchess was the only client with whom Vanbrugh fell out. All his other building projects ran on concurrently and amicably. In the latter part of his career he was still building at Castle Howard, Claremont, Eastbury, Seaton Delaval, King's Weston and Grimsthorpe. As Vanbrugh continued to build or modify the houses of his noble friends, so the Duchess was to occupy her life in buying land and cultivating quarrels. Her quarrel with Vanbrugh was not to stand in solitary eminence.

But in the comfort of his cheerful marriage Vanbrugh was

able to take his rebuffs from debts and Duchesses more easily: 'I have been so long us'd to attacks of fortune, of these kinds; and found my Self able to bear up against them, That I think I can do so Still, tho' they cost me Some Oathes and Curses, when I think of them; Which to prevent (it being Sunday) I'll say no more of them now.' The portrait of Vanbrugh, in his later years, depicts a man who has lost the easy calm of the Kit Cat days, and has withstood the cold blasts of uncertain patrons.

On another occasion he made his sentiments even clearer on this point: 'Fortunately I am not one of those who drop their spirits at every Rebuff—if I had been, I had been under ground long ago.' It took more than the Duchess of Marlborough to upset the manly spirit of John Vanbrugh. Nor was he without a certain satisfaction in realising that he had remained loyal to the Marlboroughs in the dark days. He owed them nothing in the way of money, patronage, or help. There may have been times when he wished that he had not been chosen to carry out the Duke's grandiose project.

There were always other patrons. During July 1719 he had been to Stowe, where Lord Cobham was planning his park and gardens. Vanbrugh had designed various temples, ruins and pleasure domes to add interest to the landscape, where, as Mr Seeley in his guide to Stowe wrote,

> Here the fair Queen of this heroic Isle
> Imperial Albion, with a gracious Smile
> Confess'd the lovely nature saw at last
> Unite with Art, and both Improve by Taste.'

Gardening, like architecture, has its ebb and flood tides. Vanbrugh visualised the park to be a background like a distant landscape in a painting. But the formalities of his terraces round his houses were rooted in the influences of his French past. The symmetry of the garden front at Grimsthorpe, one of his last pieces of work, has the grace of a French château garden.

At Stowe Sir John collaborated with Bridgeman to produce what the eighteenth century guide book described as a garden and park 'beautifully diversified with Hill, Valley, Lawn, River and a perpetual change of Scene arising from the numerous Buildings intermixt with Wood and 'bosom'd high in tufted trees which strike the Eye with a most picturesque and ever-varying Magnificence.'

William Kent added further temples and archways to those designed by Vanbrugh, and by the middle of the century the guide book listed over thirty of them. Many of these have been demolished or have fallen into real ruins and been forgotten. Some critics have remarked that Capability Brown's views on gardening which overtook those of Vanbrugh, Wise and Bridgman were a reaction from the 'clutter of Stowe'. Now that more than two centuries have passed since my Lord Cobham walked among the noble trees and planned the temples with his architect, the clutter has been softened by decay. On a bright winter day with snowdrops seen through bare branches of trees, the garden has attained that ideal blending of the real with the artificial visualised by its original architect.

Among the buildings which have disappeared is 'St Augustine's Cave'—artfully contrived in the same manner as Shades in a picture, or Pauses in Music. The monkish Latin verse with which its walls were adorned, and the references to the tempting beauty of the 'maid fresh as the Verdure of her grassy bed whose Heaving Globes no sooner struck the eye of the monk but strait the Flames thro' all his vitals fly,' have also gone, as well as Sir John's 'airy building', known afterwards as Nelson's Seat, his Egyptian pyramid, and other buildings devised for amusement and refreshment to the eye on walks and rides.

Vanbrugh's new wife seems to have taken his profession to her heart, for in the month of August he wrote to the Duke of Newcastle: 'I came to Claremont on Saturday last, just after Mr. Forbes was gone . . . I desire to go there again on Sunday

20*a*. Vanbrugh's Rotondo at Stowe   *b*. Vanbrugh's Pyramid at Stowe

c. Seat at Stowe attributed to Vanbrugh

21. The firework display on the Thames, 7 July 1713 (Mansell Collection)

The Exact Draught of the FIRE WORK that was Perform'd on the River of Thames, July 7th 1713; being the Thanksgiving day for the Peace obtained by the Best of QUEENS.

to stay two or three days, And I have a Wife that says She thinks she'll go along with me, Never having seen that place in Beauty.'

Unfortunately, like the projected trip to Paris, this party of pleasure was not possible: 'I have been two days at Claremont: but not *en Famille*, a Bit of a Girle popping into the World, three months before its time. And so the business is to do all over again.'

It was a setback, but in November he was still as happy and easy in his marriage as after the first month. To Tonson he wrote:

'I am much oblig'd to your good wishes, in my matrimonial state; and encourag'd by your opinion that it may be possibly do me as much good as it has mischief to many a one we know, I'll give you however no other account of it till we meet, than that, I have a good humour'd wife, a quiet house, and I find myself as much dispos'd to be friend and servant to a good old acquaintance as ever.'

If his home life was easy, his difficulties at the Board of Works continued. He had tried to get Hawksmoor restored to his old post when Benson had been turned out in favour of Hewet, but with little success. Soliciting the help of the Duke of Newcastle, he sketched in the background 'Mr. Hewet (after ten thousand Assurances to me, of his Friendship to him) may endeavour to promote an Acquaintance of his.'

Vanbrugh was justifiably annoyed that Hawksmoor should be kept out when he himself had had to step down in favour of Hewet. 'I don't in the least desire to invade or Clip, the rights of his Office. I therefore hope, your L'ship will think it wou'd be very hard those Men (Mr. Hawksmoor especially) so Unjustly turn'd out by Benson; shou'd have the double Misfortune of being kept out by him who succeeds him.' Nor was Hawksmoor unaware of the efforts Sir John had made on his behalf. Much later Hawksmoor wrote to Lord Carlisle:

'When Sir Thomas Hewet was made Surveyor General after the dismission of the said Benson, I had hopes of being restored to some at least of my employment, and Sir John Vanbrugh knowing my hardships endeavoured and was very solicitous for me, and had promises from Sir Thomas Hewet in my favour; but he forgot his obligations to Sir John and left me to shift for myself.'

Vanbrugh was, all through his life, quick to sympathise with any form of injustice to real merit, perhaps because his own merits had so often been passed over in favour of nonentities. There are very few men who act 'out of tenderness' to others. The majority who benefit from patronage are quick to convince themselves that their promotion is due to their outstanding merit. Vanbrugh did not have this self-deluding quality. He had constantly supported the workmen against the injustices of the Duchess, the Duke against the underhand attacks of Swift and his fellow libellers, and even on one occasion wrote about the distress of an unnamed gentlewoman which 'comes from her having chang'd her Religion, which has made her Abbandon'd by her friends.'

Vanbrugh would not have been among these.

Some time later he was still trying to get the 'small Office of Clark Engrosser wch. is but £120 a year' for Hawksmoor. His letter was written to the Duke of Newcastle from Greenwich and began 'I hear your Grace was pleas'd to Storm my Castle yesterday.' This is a reference to the house which he had built himself at Greenwich to replace the one in Surrey which he had sold to the Duke of Newcastle. He had interested himself in Greenwich from the time he had first worked on the Royal Naval Hospital with Sir Christopher Wren. It was at Greenwich he had been knighted. In those days Greenwich was a place of repose, a country retreat. He chose for himself a site which had the same appeal for him as King's Weston, high above the river with distant views, where the ground fell precipitously away. In his day the clear air gave a prospect of many ships riding at anchor.

In choosing Greenwich as his country retreat, Vanbrugh showed admirable taste, it was, as Defoe says in his *Tour of Great Britain*, a village where 'there is a kind of collection of gentlemen—rather than citizens—and persons of quality and fashion different from most, if not all, the villages in this part of England. Here several of the most active and useful gentlemen of the late armies, after having grown old in the services of their country are retired to enjoy the remainder of their time.' He went on to note that Greenwich was beginning to outswell its bounds 'and extends itself not only on this side of the Park to the top of the Heath, by the way called Crume Hill, now stretches out on the east-side where Sir John Vanburg [*sic*] has built a house—castlewise, and were in a little time 'tis probable several streets of like buildings will be erected to the enlarging and beautifying of the town.'

The streets were indeed extended, but apart from those built by Sir John they are in the classic eighteenth century red-brick style.

Vanbrugh's house, like Kimbolton, has indeed somewhat of a castle air, with rounded turrets and crenellations like a miniature mediaeval château. Its westward view stretched over parkland to the hospital and the Thames beyond. A winding turret staircase leads from cellar to the roof. Here he carefully provided lead flats so that the magnificence of the views could be enjoyed to their fullest extent. Even today it is a pleasant eyrie lifted above the houses and the traffic. In his own day, with river, countryside and marshes stretching away on all sides, it must have given him the sense of space and distance he had experienced as a child, on the walls of Chester.

Richardson in his *History of Greenwich*, published in 1834, described the house as it was then:

'On the summit of Maize Hill is an irregular castellated

structure of brick called Vanbrugh Castle erected about the year 1717 by Sir John Vanbrugh. At a short distance from this building are Vanbrugh Fields, in which is a singular house, built also by Vanbrugh, and called Mince Pie House. An arched gateway with a lodge on each side, now standing some distance within the principal field, appears to have formed the original entrance from the Heath.'

Although Vanbrugh's house is small, the hall being only twelve feet square, he had given it breadth by the vaulted corridors which opened on each side. From the outside the house towers above the visitor, but inside the rooms are small and welcoming. Outside, the dark brick crenellations and towers seem forbidding; inside the arched windows let in the light and tempt the eye with the distant landscapes. The room which is believed to have been his study appears all windows and land-scape. It is approached by a little ante-room. Like his larger and more grandiose buildings, it is a house built by a romantic who appreciated the feeling of mediaevalism long before Straw-berry Hill Gothick became the fashionable idiom in which to build, or the Victorians re-discovered King Arthur.

Vanbrugh Castle was and is a house full of unexpected twists, of passages, turret staircases and rounded doorways leading to secret quiet rooms. The garden once had a pool, and before the house stood a well which once boasted an elaborate well-head which was the wonder of the neighbourhood. A complicated pumping system, perhaps an elaboration of some engineering feat he had tried out as Controller, brought water up the hill. In its day, with the outworks and fortifications, it must have been a charming miniature folly. Even today un-seeing passers-by describe it as a 'Victorian monstrosity'. But the Victorian additions to it were built with the tenderness and care of builders who saw what he saw—a romantic view of the past.

He had always had a feeling for old buildings, and in the

year he married had attempted to save the old gateway into Whitehall Palace. The letter he wrote to the Duke of Newcastle has a familiar ring to it. It could be a letter protesting about the destruction caused by the motorways.

'Mr Benson's Reign ended . . . but Mr Hewet's Patent not being yet past we have no Board. So that nothing can yet be done about the Gateway. In the mean time I may Observe to your Grace, that I find many people Surpris'd there shou'd be no other Expedient found to make way for Coaches than destroying One of the Greatest Curiositys there is in London as that Gate which has ever been esteem'd, and cost a Great of sum of money the Building; and so well perform'd that altho' 200 Yrs. Old, is as entire as the first day.'

But he was no more successful in his solicitude for the gateway as he had been for fair Rosamund's Bower. A week later he wrote 'If the Saving of the Gate, must Start a new brangle—let it go.'

He was becoming resigned to the stupidities of men, and secure in his castle with his young bride he was able the better to withstand the buffets of fate. Even politics between the malcontent Whigs and the Tories who 'seem good friends in comparison with them' impinged less on his affairs. For he saw no 'great fear of extraordinary mischiefs from these ill tim'd Broyles' and hoped that the want of them may neither disturb Tonson at Barns, 'nor your humble Servant at Greenwich. And so let us be easy.'

CHAPTER XIX

Publick Rubbs
and Private Ease

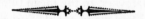

At the beginning of 1720 Vanbrugh's interests in the theatre once more came to the fore. Sir Richard Steele had by this time become involved in the complications over the patents. The upshot of which was that he had 'work'd a Quarrell so high with my Lord Chamberlain' that Wilks, Cibber and Booth were granted a new licence. Vanbrugh was hopeful that this new turn of events might be in his favour, and remarked that he will 'call upon those three gentleman—about the Stock they had of mine, and think they will be willing to come to some tollerable Composition.'

These cabals between the two companies of actors, the patentees and the Lord Chamberlain were further confused by the obvious jealousies of the actors between themselves, and against the Italian opera singers whose pockets were lined with louis d'or by the new found passion of the Quality for music. As Cibber remarked somewhat acidly, 'Although the Opera is not a plant of our native growth, nor what our plainer appetites are fond of, and is of so delicate a nature that without excessive charge it cannot live long among us'.

This view is corroborated by Vanbrugh who wrote to Tonson in 1720:

'The Opera will begin about the 10th March under the Accademy of Musick. It will be a very good one this year, and a better the next. They having engag'd the best Singers in Italy at a great price. Such as I believe will bring the Expences to about twice as much as the Receipts. But the fund Subscribed being about £20,000 may probably Support it, till Musick takes such root, as to Subsist with less aid.'

Vanbrugh, with his liking for Italian Opera, was optimistic —over optimistic; 250 years later the Opera still does not subsist without support.

According to Cibber, who admittedly was a biassed witness, the opera did not remain prosperous for long. 'The opera after one luxurious season like the fine wife of a roving husband began to lose its charms and every day discovered to our satiety imperfections which our former fondness had been blind to.'

The King, according to Vanbrugh, had given £1,000 to-wards the Opera, and the Opera House had been adapted by 1720 so that the acoustics were better suited to both opera and plays. When Cibber had originally returned to the Haymarket he had wished to re-build the interior to the pattern of Sir Christopher Wren's original design for Drury Lane 'before the old patentee, to make it hold more money, took it into his head to alter it.'

Apart from the echoes and the size of Vanbrugh's theatre there were other disadvantages. The actors were too far away from the audience. In Sir Christopher's theatre 'every scene was advanc'd at least ten foot nearer to the audience'. The effect of this was that the weakest voice could be heard in the most distant part of the house. 'A voice scarce raised above the tone of a whisper, either in tenderness, resignation, innocent distress or jealousy suppress'd often have as much concern with the heart—as the most clamorous passions' remarked Cibber, that sage of many theatrical campaigns.

It was well to leave the tearing of passions to tatters to the Italian eunuchs. Good Englishmen preferred their own ways.

Cibber did not have enough time to carry out his ideas, but the echoes were dulled by filling in the width with side boxes, and lowering the height of the ceiling to counteract the echoes.

King George I's fondness for music, apart from his investment in the opera, had also led to the fostering of another new entertainment—masquerades. As a consequence of his patronage, they had become very much to the taste of the 'Towne'. In a letter to Tonson, Vanbrugh remarked,

'The Masquerades go on with their wonted Success, they are limited to Six in a year. The 5th is to-night, and I am going to it, en famille. Neither my Self nor my Gentlewoman having been there before. She calls upon me to come away, and Says she can afford me no more time than to present her humble service to you.'

A letter from Lady Mary Wortley Montagu describes how Vanbrugh's theatre had been transformed to accommodate the guests.

'There was a masquerade on Thursday last at the Haymarket Playhouse. By laying planks over the Pit, they made a continued Floor as far as the Boxes which were blocked up with pieces of fine painting, and two or three of the side Boxes left open for wine and other things. 'Twas of Heidegger's projecting; the price of tickets a guinea and a half, and not only so; but they that took them were obliged to subscribe too for the next.'

Presumably Vanbrugh's gentlewoman had persuaded him to attend the sixth masquerade as well as the fifth.

In August 1720, Lady Vanbrugh was delivered of a son, named Charles, after his godfather, the Earl of Carlisle, that most enduring friend and patron of Sir John.

This was also the year which saw the rise and fall of the South Sea Company. It was a contemporary English parallel to the Mississippi scheme to which Vanbrugh often refers in his letters to Tonson. The French scheme had been based on trading with states around the Mississippi basin. The details of this venture were the brainchild of a Mr John Law, who had conceived the idea of using paper money based on a fixed rate instead of metal money which varied in value. In 1719 the scheme collapsed and Law had to flee from France, afterwards to die in poverty.

The parallel mania for post-war speculation developed in England with the South Sea Company, which had originated with Robert Harley and the desirable object of trading with Spanish South America. A considerable part of the venture was to be in the profitable slave trade. The original scheme had been conceived on the basis of fostering a financial operation which could act as a rival to the Whig-dominated Bank of England. The boom in the South Sea Shares began when the company became responsible for the national debt (always excepting those debts due to the Bank of England and the East India Company). Many investors were even persuaded to exchange their annuities for South Sea Stock. At the beginning of 1720 the South Sea Stock index was 128½, but it began to climb rapidly to an inflated value and by the time Vanbrugh's son was born in August it had reached 1,000.

It is not surprising to learn that the Duchess of Marlborough, with her finely-tuned financial sense, decided that the stock was over-capitalised, and sold out, making a profit of £100,000, while Vanbrugh remarked to Lord Carlisle in the year following the boom:

'The South Sea is so hatefull a Subject one do's not Love to name it; And yet it do's so interfere with almost every body's Affairs more or less, that all they have to do, is in some degree govern'd by it. Even I, who have not gain'd at all, Shall probably be a Loser near £2000.'

Presumably even he had at last succumbed to the speculation fever, or it is possible that he had patrons who had cancelled commissions. The Duchess of Marlborough was one of the few

gainers, as rich people so often are. But many were completely
ruined and fled the country, while others committed suicide
after having lost their only means of subsistence, their annuities.
Several Ministers were implicated and a Committee of the
House of Commons decided that they had indulged in speculation, peculation and had accepted bribes.

Amongst others implicated were both the Craggs—Mr
Secretary Craggs and his father. James Craggs (the younger)
had managed the South Sea stock, not only for his own benefit
but also on behalf of the King's mistresses. James, the younger
Craggs, died of a timely attack of virulent smallpox on the eve
of the report being issued. His father died on the day before
he was to be called to account for his dubious dealings. It was
suspected that he had taken poison.

Even Lord Carlisle's family did not prove immune from the
general disaster. Lord Irwin, the Earl's son-in-law, had been
a heavy loser. Vanbrugh wrote sympathetically to the Earl in
1721: 'Tis with a most Sensible and Sincere concern I condole
with your Lordship, on the Loss of My Ld. Irwin.' He could
have been referring to the financial loss or to the fact that Lord
Irwin had applied for the Governorship of Barbados, presumably in an attempt to recoup his fortunes. Vanbrugh went on:
'If my Lady bears it, better than I fear there's reason to apprehend, I shall be mighty glad of it, both for her own sake and for
your Ldships; who I know have that regard for her, to enter
very far into her afflictions.'

Vanbrugh always seemed more 'sensible' of the afflictions of
others than he was of his own. When he referred to his personal
losses, he dismissed the subject: 'For when I know the worst of
any thing, I can make my Self tollerably easy.'

It was as well that he had attained an even more philosophical attitude towards the buffets of life by his middle age,
for in spite of her gains at the expense of others in the South
Sea disaster, the Duchess of Marlborough was embarking on
her spring campaign.

In the early part of 1721 the Duke had been dropped as Captain-General by the King. As Vanbrugh put it: 'This point of Lord Marlborough's quitting, has hung these two days, upon her Graces opposing it Purely I believe for the money. I suppose she will haggle for a Pention [*sic*] to Support the poor Old Officer and his Wife.' When it came to compensation the Duchess was not prepared to forego the smallest coin. She had written to the Treasury in an effort to prove that Vanbrugh had been well enough rewarded for his efforts at Blenheim.

For good measure she was quarrelling with Peter Walters, the 'coupler' who had involved himself in arranging the marriage of her grand-daughter, and was, at the same time, conducting a dispute with Strong, the erstwhile mason at Blenheim.

Vanbrugh concluded his letter to Lord Carlisle, recounting the list of the Duchess's delinquencies, by remarking that he hoped 'Your Lordship has some Seasonable Frost—as we have here at last, which gives Great Comfort.'

Whether frost was welcome in that it prevented the plague or re-stocked ice-houses is not clear, but one thing was certain, Vanbrugh's relations with the Duchess had suffered a permanent frost.

She was still earnestly engaged in trying to 'turn the Blenheim debt' on to Vanbrugh. It had been finally brought up to the House of Lords. Vanbrugh had been in touch with his old friends and colleagues, the Blenheimites, and he told Lord Carlisle: 'The Workmens Spirits are very Low for the fear they are under, that She and Her Family will at least be able to keep a great many Lords away, who wou'd not Vote for her if they were in the House.'

Her reputation was obviously not in a rising way. Writing a week or so later to Lord Carlisle he remarked:

'I am very glad to find that neither publick nor private Rubbs will discourage you from relying on that ground, that has

331

Supported you hitherto. Tis the same sort of Reflection has enabled me to bear up, as I have done, under things that wou'd else have infaillibly knockt me downe. Of which one has been this Wicked Dutchess, nor has she yet done with me.'

The Judges had given against the Duke in the Exchequer Court and the Duchess had countered by 'handing about' her own account of the Blenheim affair.

As a result of this, Vanbrugh had been finally pushed into replying with a long personal vindication: '*Sir John Vanbrugh's Justification of what he depos'd in the Duke of Marlborough's late Tryal.*'

In a long declaration Vanbrugh included a letter, supposedly written by 'A Gentleman in the Country', in which he puts, with great clarity, his feelings about his treatment by the Marlboroughs:

'Here is the Greatest the Richest and the most powerful favourite that was ever known in England, has the most valuable present made him from the Crown that ever was made here to any subject.

'Those who have had the happy Chance to be employ'd by such favourites (especially in their pleasures) and have been so Successful in their Services, as to give them entire Satisfaction, have never fail'd of making their Fortunes by them.'

The Duke, he went on, had taken more than common delight in work at Woodstock:

'And he was pleas'd from time to time, both by Letters and otherwise to express in the strongest and most affectionate Terms, the great Sense he had of the Services rendred him by Sir John Vanbrugh on this occasion, and the resolution he was in by some manner or other to reward him for it.

'Yet such has been his fate. That after Twelve Years Employment under his Grace . . . and passing Bills for near £300,000.

'And having had the misfortune of being turn'd out of his Place of Comptroller of the Works, and losing that of Garter by offending the Queen, on the Duke's Account; The State he finds himself in at least without one Court favour obtain'd by the Duke for him in this long Tract of Years.

'Or any allowance or Present from His Grace, ever made him, (except a Trifle I believe he wou'd not have him Name.)'

This last was presumably the travelling allowance of £200 a year, which was hardly munificient.

Vanbrugh concluded that he had been left to work upon his own bottom at the tedious Treasury 'for a Recompence for his Services'.

The Duke, and certainly the Duchess, thought the ungilded knighthood sufficient repayment. It seemed a glittering reward to them, for it had cost nothing. Vanbrugh's affection for the Duke was finally ebbing. Possibly he began to believe at last that all the faults were, perhaps, not entirely due to the Duchess. The Duke had a reputation for avarice which was not undeserved. Vanbrugh ended:

'Instead of any reward from the Duke, he finds his Authority for acting in his Service disclaim'd and himself thrown among the Workmen, to be torn to peices [*sic*]. For what his Grace possesses and enjoys, in the midst of an immence Fortune. These (and no other) are the Friendships and the Obligations laid by the Duke of Marlborough upon his faithful and Zealous Servant—John Vanbrugh.'

In the event, the judgment went against the Duchess, but hardly in Vanbrugh's financial favour. 'If I have Strecht my evidence in favour of the Workmen, it has been to cut my own Throat; for my Lord Marlb: being decreed to pay them, I may be pretty sure, he will never pay me whc. will be a Loss of £1600.'

He still remained tolerably easy:

'I have every day of my Life Since twenty years old, grown more and more of opinion, that the less one has to do, with what is call'd the World, the more Quiet of mind; and the more Quiet of mind, the more Happyness. All other delights, are but like debauches in wine; which give three days pain, for three hours pleasure. It has however been my chance, to lead a Life quite against my Sentiments hitherto; But I have made a Virtue of Necessity, from Some Rebuffs I have met with in this Reign, and lessn'd my concern in things I was tempted before to be busy about which has eas'd me a good deal.'

Vanbrugh may have thought he had always had this philosophy, but it was one he had learned late in a hard school. Now with his pleasant detachment from the world with his wife and son he began to see the simplicities of life in a different light. He was still determined to visit his old friend Lord Carlisle in Yorkshire and hoped to set out before Midsummer day 'tho' I am much oppos'd by wise Women in pretending to carry your Ldships Godson such a journey, I resolve to Venture him; for I have a mind to make him as much a Yorkshire man as I can; besides he's so stout, I think he may travel anywhere.'

From Yorkshire Vanbrugh was able to take in new projects for new patrons, and with his usual zest. He wrote to Brigadier Watkins remarking how busy he was with his new commissions. 'I return'd but last night from the North (for here you must know we are in the South) where I have been near three weeks finding a vast deal to do, both at Delavals and Lumley Castle.'

Admiral George Delaval was retired from the navy and having bought the old house at Seaton in Northumberland from his impoverished descendant Sir Ralph Delaval, Baronet, he had decided to consult Vanbrugh about re-building, or planning a new house on the site. Even before Vanbrugh's marriage the Admiral had written: 'I should tell you that Sir J. Vanbrugh

built Castle Howard and it is from thence I hope to carry him.'
A few days later he amplified his plans:

'I intend to persuade Sir John Vanbrugh to see Seton if
possible and to give me a plan of a house or to alter the old
one, which he is most excellent at; and if he cannot come,
he'll recommend a man at York who understands these
matters. So something may be done by degrees and be the
entertainment of our old age, or as long as we live.'

In a postscript the Admiral added that he was much out of
order with the scurvy.

But whether troubled with scurvy or no, he drove on with
the idea. The 'man at York' was Mr Etty. Accounts at Seaton
Delaval list the expenses of the two men's visiting Seaton together. 'Mr Etty 3 days at Seaton with Sir John Van Brough.
27 days boarding at 5d a day'. Included in the bill was 'one
bowle of oats at three shillings and sixpence, and 15 quarts of
ale at 4d.' It is to be concluded that the ale was better than the
food.

Seaton was a site which must have had for Vanbrugh the
appeal of a dramatic stage set. A bleak landscape stretched out
towards the North Sea and the stormy coast. The Admiral was
according to Vanbrugh, 'very Gallant in his operations, not
being dispos'd to starve the Design at all. So that he is like to
have a very fine dwelling for himself, now, and his nephew
hereafter.'

Admiral George Delaval, Vanbrugh's client, had gone very
young into the Service, and owing to the good fortune of serving under his own uncle was, not unnaturally, rapidly promoted. He seems, like the Duke of Marlborough, to have
combined a distinguished serving career with that of a roving
Ambassador. In 1698, while commanding a man of war, he was
negotiating with the Alcaid of Tangier, and later in 1710, having attained the rank of Captain, he became Envoy Extraordinary to Portugal and subsequently to the Emperor of

Morocco. During these missions he was buying provisions and horses for the armies then operating in Spain. It was in 1717 that he bought the estate of Seaton from his impoverished baronet cousin. The shrewd buying of provisions from the Emperor of Morocco, or the treaties carried out with the Alcaid of Tangier, had enabled the bluff Admiral to advance his fortune. In the seventeenth and eighteenth centuries war was considered to be a branch of business where prize money of all kinds could be used for personal advancement. When peace breaks out in modern times, Commanders and Prime Ministers can only look to serialisation of their memoirs to improve their half-pay. Admiral Delaval had richer resources.

In his usual way, Vanbrugh proceeded step by step with Seaton. As the new house went up the old one was demolished, and this demolition started in 1720.

This was to be a vast dramatic house in the operatic vein in which he built his theatre in the Haymarket and his palace at Blenheim. A long avenue leads up to the massive central block, which is flanked by the arcaded east and west wings. The central block has towers on each side, which add to the effect of approaching a castle.

The proportions of the house and its outworks are massive. The great court is 180 feet long and 152 feet broad. Even the stables have the feeling of an echoing mediaeval church.

The interior was on an equally massive scale. The black and white marble hall is 44 feet long, 25 feet broad, and 30 feet high, with a gallery which carries the first floor passage as at Blenheim and Castle Howard, and on a smaller scale at King's Weston. The garden front is equally massive, but less forbidding. A flight of steps leads up to an elegant portico with fluted Ionic columns flanked with towers.

The drama of the house has been matched over the years by the drama of its history. It was ten years in the building, begun in 1718 and finished in 1728. In 1752 the west wing was burned and in 1822 an even more disastrous fire gutted much of the

interior of the central block. The beauty of the interior, before
the fire, matched the strength of the exterior. The rooms were
panelled in mahogany, enriched with painting, stucco work and
statuary. The main saloon was seventy-five feet long and thirty
feet wide and early descriptions of it say that it was painted by
Vercelli. A guide to Northumberland, published before the fire,
described the glories of Seaton: 'At the east end of the saloon a
small antechamber leads into a spacious drawing room'. The
elegant eating room was beautifully ornamented with festoons
of fruit and flowers 'formed of most durable composition and
so admirably painted as perfectly to represent nature.'

The dominating Vanbrugh Hall remains with its niches and
marble floor, but all the elegant decorations of the main rooms
imagined by Vanbrugh have disappeared and can only linger
in the mind of the visitor like the laughter of the people seated
in the elegant eating room.

The main building gives an impression of the massive elegance of Vanbrugh's design.

Undeterred by the setbacks over Blenheim, he took his
usual detailed interest in the building operations, sending the
man on the spot his exact instructions in amplification of the
design. On 16 August 1722 he wrote: 'The answer to yrs
abought keying the circular window to ye north I would have
you break out the 3 keystones, the side keystones 2 inches, the
middle ones 3 inches at least, if too much it may Be taken of.
But never can be added.' The letter indicates his intense pre-
occupation with proportions and he enclosed a rough sketch.

His agent had written in the autumn of 1719 that he would
'continue working the Quarry as long as the weather and the
ways are good'. Fortunately for Vanbrugh, this time he had no
Duchess to survey the prices of carriage of stone, or the plant-
ing of the garden which was done on the usual massive scale.
'1200 trees—£49.10s.' and thousands of 'quicks' (hawthorn
hedging) at 4d per thousand.

The whole project was much to his mind, and he was able to

carry it out to the taste of the Admiral, and with the aid of Mr Etty.

In the summer of 1721 he was at his best and happiest. At Castle Howard the weather was warm and he wished that the Duke of Newcastle could be there to see it in all its beauty. 'Many new Charms open this year . . . of the House I say nothing; The others I may commend, because Nature made them; I pretend to no more Merrit in them than a Midwife, who helps to bring a fine Child into the World, out of Bushes, Boggs, and Bryars.'

In spite of his new found delight in solitude and quietude he had been at York for a week attending a race every day and a ball every night. The Duke of Wharton was the 'Top Gallant' and 'treated the Jockeys with a Plate, The Ladys with a Ball, and all together with a Supper.'

He had also been up to Durham to survey Lumley Castle, which he decided 'well deserved the favours Lord Lumley designs to bestow upon it'.

Vanbrugh stayed there for a week 'to form a General Design for the whole, Which consists, in altering the House for State, Beauty and Convenience, And making the Courts, Gardens, and Offices Suitable to it.'

He was sure that all this could be done for a sum which would not lie too heavily on the family. He had a keen appreciation of the grandeurs of the north. 'There being many more Valluable and Agreeable things and Places to be Seen, than in the Tame Sneaking South of England.' Lord Lumley was Lord of the Bedchamber, and Master of the Horse to the Prince of Wales, afterwards George II. He formed part of the Whig entourage in which Vanbrugh moved.

Like the different veins on an ancient rock face, Lumley Castle had been changed and altered over the centuries. Originally built for defence, with battlements and four towers running round an interior courtyard, the house had been altered in Elizabethan times. Vanbrugh added new and elegant saloons and reception rooms while managing to keep the battlements which brooded over the ravine. Some critics have considered that Sir John spoiled the castle by his 'improvements'. But although the nineteenth century may have over-valued the splendour that falls on castle walls, the Whig grandees of Vanbrugh's day demanded comfortable and magnificent settings for themselves and their families. These Vanbrugh designed at Lumley Castle, and he was able to do it with taste and perception without destroying the dramatic effect of the brooding towers and battlements of the original fourteenth century Castle.

Lumley Castle was being rebuilt in 1721 and about the same time, Vanbrugh drew up his designs for the replanning of Grimsthorpe for the Duke of Ancaster. Lord Lindsey had been created Duke of Ancaster by George I, and he also was part of the Whig circle.

Vanbrugh appears to have been used as a political ambassador to the Duke to canvass his support at the time when the Occasional Conformity Bill was repealed in 1718. He took a letter from Lord Sunderland to Grimsthorpe and reported back to the Duke of Newcastle:

'I am very glad I brought Ld. Sunds. letter, it was very well read and I did my best to make the most on't. Both Father and Son are good in the Main. The latter will I believe be soon in Towne & Vote right even in the Occasional Bill. The Former has Some sighs & Groans about it. Tho'—to give him his due, not so much for fear of the Church, as for fear it shou'd not turn to the King's Service so much as he wishes & expects.'

The Duke was apparently jibbing at the fact that he had voted with Lord Nottingham on a former occasion, and felt that a man of honour should not 'go back and forward'. Vanbrugh put the case delicately. It was not, he said, a matter of honour or Conscience, but 'purely political and discretional'.

The fact that Vanbrugh was in this case being used as a

canvasser and sounder of political opinions, lends some credence to the fact that he had indeed been used as a spy when he was imprisoned in the Bastille by Louis XIV. On the earlier occasion an interest in the charms of capitals, columns and façades was an excellent excuse for the sketching of fortifications. In Lincolnshire his reputation as a fashionable architect gave an equal excuse for visiting a duke and his son in order to make sure their sails were trimmed in the right political direction.

Owing to his friendship with the Duke of Ancaster, which burgeoned from this visit, Vanbrugh was asked to redesign the Duke's house. Grimsthorpe Castle had had a chequered history. It had been sacked by the Roundheads during the Civil War and subsequently restored during the reign of Charles II, though some of the original Elizabethan house remained. The plan given by Colin Campbell in *Vitruvius Britannicus* shows that Vanbrugh intended to rebuild the whole house round a central courtyard. Perhaps because only one side of the house was ever finished according to Vanbrugh's plan, Grimsthorpe has mellowed into that happy blending of different styles which gives so typical, heartwarming, and enduring a quality to many English country houses. On a spring day, with sunshine and shadow lending emphasis to Vanbrugh's design of a central block with flanking towers, the whole has a château effect. The flat, wide blue skies and soft distances could be the Touraine instead of Lincolnshire. Vanbrugh's additions to the house were the hall and the two towers which enclose the chapel and the state dining room.

The vast and beautiful hall, with its arched recesses, gives a view of staircases with delicate filigree balustrades which could be the setting for an Italian opera. The rounded recesses enclose grisaille paintings of the English Kings who had given added glory and lustre to the Ancaster family. Vanbrugh's additions to the house have a delicacy and charm which is perhaps lacking from his more grandiose designs; or maybe with his marriage his ideas had become more mellow.

In 1721 there was a spirit of rebuilding abroad which Vanbrugh remarks on in a letter from Castle Howard to Brigadier Watkins at Scotland Yard in London. 'Here are Several Gentlemen in these parts of the world that are possess'd with the Spirit of Building.' As he wrote about building, the idea of the Board of Works came into his mind. If there could be a Board of Works in the North, who better to conduct it than his old friend and colleague Nicholas Hawksmoor? The supplanting of his friend still rankled in his mind. He referred ironically to 'that excellent architect Ripley', the man who had succeeded Hawksmoor, and wrote, 'When I met with Ripley's name (and *Esquire* to it) in the Newspaper; Such a laugh came upon me, I had like to Beshit myself.' Ripley had been appointed through the influence of Robert Walpole and was said to have begun life as a country carpenter.

Vanbrugh's frustrated endeavours on Hawksmoor's behalf still caused him bitterness. 'Poor Hawksmoor, What a Barbarous Age, have his fine, ingenious Parts fallen into!' He could not help contrasting the philistine attitude of the English to artists, with that of the French, 'What wou'd Monsr. Colbert in France have given for Such a Man. I don't speak as to his Architecture alone, but the Aids he cou'd have given him in almost all his brave designs . . .'

Most men, he said, thought of little more 'than getting a Great Deal of Money and turning it through their Guts into a House of Office. And now I think of eating pray do me the favour to get a Warrant from his Grace, for an other Buck, instead of a Stag for I find that will be of no use to me here. The Buck I have had, and very good.'

With fine weather, a good humoured wife, a thriving son and a warrant for a fine buck on the way, life could be enjoyed day by day and vexations forgotten.

CHAPTER XX

In Spite of the Huzzy's Teeth

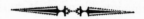

By November 1721 Vanbrugh was back in Whitehall from his pleasant stay in Yorkshire. The journey had been a lengthy one, and he and his little family had stayed at several places on the way. 'We lug'd the heavy Coach—and what was in it.'

Lord Carlisle had asked Vanbrugh for his opinions about the new inoculation for the smallpox, and perhaps because he now felt the responsibility and parental fear for the life of his new son, Vanbrugh had been enquiring about it for his patron. The original idea had been brought to England by Lady Mary Wortley Montagu whose husband Edward had been Ambassador to Turkey. While she was there she had found out much about the life of the country, and incidentally discovered that the Turks gave small doses of the disease to their children and so were able to preserve their lives from the scourge. She remarked: 'The faculty rose in arms, foretelling failure and the most disastrous consequences; the clergy descanted from their pulpits on the impiety of thus seeking to take events out of the hand of Providence, and the Common People were taught to hoot at an unnatural mother, who had risked the lives of her own children.'

In much the same way the Victorian clergy opposed anaesthesia for childbirth, alleging that the Bible stated that a woman should bear her child in pain and suffering. The clergy in our own day seem to have lost this gift for prophetic and didactic pronouncements, which has passed into the sphere of the psychologist and the sociologist.

Vanbrugh reported his discoveries about inoculation to Lord Carlisle, and unlike Lady Mary had not found the doctors un-receptive:

'I have seen some of the Physitians and askt them how in-oculating had really Succeeded, and they assure me, not one Single Person had miscarried, nor that they find any Sort of ground to fear that those who go through the Small Pox that way, will have them again; and one pretty Strong proof they have, by a Young Woman, who ever Since She has had them given her, is employ'd to look after people who get them by the natural course, and yet is not hurt by them.'

Inoculation was in general use by 1740, although Edward Jenner did not begin to inoculate with cow pox until later in the eighteenth century. Vanbrugh was, as always, receptive to new ideas, whether they were Italian opera, architecture, or ways of avoiding smallpox.

Once he was back in London, life from the Goose Pie House took on a less roseate hue than from the windows of Castle Howard. There were other plagues than smallpox on his horizon, the chief of which was the Duchess of Marlborough. She had now decided to bring a Bill in Chancery 'against every-body that was ever concern'd in the Building of Blenheim downe to the poorest workman'. Vanbrugh wondered how much trouble the roguery of the Law would cause the Blen-heimites, 'But all the mischief they and the Devil can do, She'll pay them (the lawyers) for, tho' She'll pay nobody else.'

A week later he had decided that a conference with the Blenheim survivors was essential. He wrote to Mr. Joynes 'at the Pallace at Kensington', asking him if he could find out where Mr Bobart was, because it was absolutely necessary that they should all talk a little together. 'Before any of our Answers are given in order to recollect Such facts, as else we may all make Some mistakes in—after so many Years.'

Vanbrugh was right to be circumspect. He had a formidable

opponent, in what Joynes called 'The Great Cause against Everybody that Had been Concern'd in that Building'.

He was also right to call it a Great Cause. The Duchess had named no fewer than 401 people, alleging that they had 'combined and confederated together to load the Duke of Marlborough with ye payment of the debts due on account of ye Building before her late Majesty putt a Stop thereto'. For good measure she alleged that they had 'charged excessive rates and prices for the same'. The Duchess's list of delinquents began with Vanbrugh, descending right down the scale of the building hierarchy, and ended with the widows of former workmen, who had passed to that bourne where no further stones are cut. Once engaged upon a task the Duchess neglected no detail, nor skimped a single allegation.

It was right that the surviving Blenheimites should talk together and mobilise their defence. The Duchess would not easily be baulked of her financial prey. The Duke was by now little concerned in the campaign which was being waged. There are constant references to his ill health in Vanbrugh's letters and he had suffered two or three strokes. In his age and his weakness, the Duke fell more than ever under the dominating sway of his wife. The spring and summer campaigns on the Continent had been long ago.

In 1721, while Vanbrugh marshalled his tattered forces against the Duchess, the Marlboroughs were living in their several houses, the Lodge at Windsor, where Sarah retained her rangership, Marlborough House, and above all at Holywell. Holywell House, near St Albans, had always been the Duke's favourite retreat. Here it was that he had planted trees and collected the trophies of his long campaigns. Blenheim was to be his enduring glory, Holywell was the house which conformed to Sarah's views of a neat, clean sweet house, and was the Duke's real home.

But in spite of her lawsuits, Sarah was driving on with the building of Blenheim, and in 1721 one wing was finished, and

Letter from Vanbrugh giving detailed instructions about the building of Seaton Delaval including sketches illustrating his points.

(For a transcription of this text see p. 363)

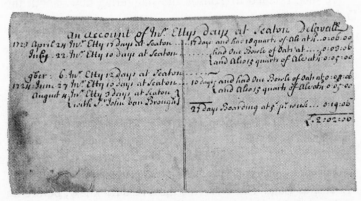

An Account of Mr Etty's days at Seaton Delaval with Sir John Vanbrugh.

year by year the great Palace was rising. The fact that its architect was no longer there to supervise it did not concern the
Duchess. She had never approved of the 'madde' scheme but
there was no sense in wasting money, and once it was begun it
must be finished, and in the most economical manner possible.
The Duke had even been able to live in the house, and there
Sarah had staged an amateur production of the play *All for
Love* (Dryden's play on the theme of Anthony and Cleopatra),
with some expunging of the more dubious passages.

While the building went on, the lawsuit was prepared, the
accused of the former builders marshalled their facts, but on
16 June, two days before the seventeenth anniversary of the
foundation stone being laid at Blenheim, the great Duke died
at Windsor. A mere two days later, Vanbrugh seemed to be in
possession of all the facts about the will and wrote to his old
friend Tonson about it. Jacob Tonson had by this time retired
into Herefordshire where he had bought himself a comfortable
property.

Vanbrugh began his letter, in his characteristic breezy way,
by thanking Tonson for the 'best Sider I ever drank since I was
born', adding that he would have appreciated the cider more if
Jacob had sent him an accompanying letter.

He then retailed to Tonson the staggering news about the
Duke's fortune:

'I can regale you with nothing in return but a short account of
what I was e'en now told by one that knows of my Lord
Marlborough's Treasure which exceeds what the most Extravagant Believer I ever heard guess at it.

'The grand Settlement (which 'twas Suspected her Grace
had broken to pieces) stands good. And hands on Immense
Wealth to my Lady Godolphin and her Successors. How much
I can't yet say; but a round Million has been moving about in
Loans, as Land Tax &c. This the Treasury knew, before he
dy'd; and this was exclusive of his Land, his £5000 a year

upon the Post Office, his Mortgages upon many a distrest estate, His Southsea Stock, his Annuity, which was not sub-scrib'd in, and besides what God Almighty knows of in Foreign Banks.'

This gargantuan appetite for wealth at last broke Vanbrugh's declining regard for the Duke's memory and he commented bitterly:

'And yet this Man wou'd neither pay his Workmen their bills nor his Architect his Salary. But he had given his Widdow (may a Scotch Ensign get her) £10,000 to Spoil Blenheim in her own way. £12,000 A Year to keep her Self clean and go to Law.'

Even in Vanbrugh's listing of the sonorous drum roll of the great General's assets, he spared a thought for injustice. 'And to Lord Godolphin only £500 jointure, if he outlives my Lady. This last is a wretched Article. The rest of the Heap (for these are but the Snipings) go's to Lady Godolphin and so on. She'll have £40,000 a year in present.'

He wrote in much the same vein to the Earl of Carlisle but added that the clipping of Lord Godolphin's fortune was pos-sibly due to the fact that he had not voted for the Duchess—presumably in the Blenheim dispute. Godolphin was consider-ing the manner of the Duke's funeral. It occurred to Vanbrugh that it might be possible to erect a noble monument to the Duke, much in the manner which had been planned at Castle Howard. 'The Place I propose is in Blenheim Park with some plain, but magnificent & durable monument over him.' Whether Van-brugh thought he would have a chance of designing it in his official capacity at the Board of Works is not clear. If he had such an idea he was speedily disabused, for the late Duke had decided to be buried in the Chapel at Blenheim.

A pompous funeral was being prepared 'curb'd and Cripled by her Grace; who will govern it by her fancys'. There was

only one good point about the funeral, 'that is that She'll pay
for it. I don't know whether it won't cost her Ten Thousand
pounds. What a Noble Monument wou'd that have made,
wheras this Idle Show, will be gone in half an hour and forgot
in Two days. The other, wou'd have been a Show, and a Noble
one, to many future Ages.'

Even the Duke's pompous funeral, with its black plumes,
crêpe hat bands and funeral car, was not without its ennuis for
the Duchess. When the accounts came in, she at once began a
dispute with the funeral furnishers, alleging that the forty-eight
yards of black cloth which had been charged for covering the
mourning coach and harness was 'enough to cover my Garden',
and that seven trumpeters and two chaplains charged for had
not been supplied, and that the plumes for the horses had been
listed twice over.

In contrast, Vanbrugh had been talking to the young Duchess
of Marlborough and told her of the Earl of Carlisle's fears of
so great a fortune 'falling into such Generous hands; which she
took mighty well'. The Duchess had replied that covetousness
was very odious to her 'in some other people that she is sometimes frightened lest she shou'd have seeds in her blood, that
may Spring up one time or other. I tell her, now is the time if
ever, Since it generally go's along with great Riches.'

He had certainly had enough experience of that article as he
had once remarked.

'The Towne' had supplied further details about the main
topic of its gossip—the Will. 'Her Grace has by this Will (for
to be Sure that it was her doing) made my Lord Blandford
Independent of his Father and Mother, Depriv'd her Daughter
of the Jewells, and Cater'd bravely for herself I being told
yesterday by a good hand, that one of the Executors has said,
they know of Six Hundred thousand pounds, She had of her
own besides what the Duke has dispos'd of which I have seen
vallu'd by way of money and amounts to almost £140,000
besides Jewells, Plate, Pictures, Houses & Furniture. So that,

at this reckoning the whole amounts to a great deal above two millions.'

The grand total made to the struggling architect a trumpet blast to avarice.

The Marlborough estate was part of the past, currently Vanbrugh was continuing with designs for the great house which Mr Bubb Dodington proposed to build in Dorset. The building would start at once and 'would go on without any Stop as fast as the Revenue the Southsea has left will allow of, which will be about £1800 a year'.

George Bubb Dodington, Baron Melcombe of Melcombe Regis, son of a Weymouth apothecary, had inherited Eastbury Park from his uncle, George Dodington. Although George Dodington had died in 1720, two years after the project was started, he left the property to George Bubb with money to complete it. George Bubb gratefully added 'Dodington' to his name and went on with his uncle's grand design. In the beginning the castle was still an airy dream, although Bubb Dodington spent his holidays from politics down in Dorset. Here he entertained minor poets and writers.

> 'While with your Dodington retired you sit
> Charm'd with his flowing Burgundy and wit
> Or bid your eyes o'er Vanbrugh's models roam
> And trace in miniature the future dome . . .'

Vanbrugh had made the model, but the building was not begun until 1724. When finished in 1738, the interior was as splendid as the exterior and well suited to the host's ideas of his own magnificence. 'The interior of his mansion was as proud and splendid as the exterior was bold and imposing. All this was exactly in unison with the taste of the magnificent owner, who had gilt and furnished the apartments with a profusion of finery that kept no terms with simplicity, and not always with elegance or harmony of style.' His house was planned according to Vanbrugh's ideas of State, Beauty and Convenience, and it was said 'he was not to be approached but through a suite of apartments and was rarely seated but under painted ceilings and gilt entablatures.' He had travelled a long way from the pharmacy.

It is thought that the drawing in *Vitruvius Britannicus*, 'A New Design for a Person of Quality of Dorsetshire', represented the original design for Eastbury, although it was afterwards modified. The whole was massively Roman and yet Vanbrugh added the Gothic touches of castellation which had always pleased him. The entrance to the Park was dramatically solid, and the gardens blended formality with vistas, groves, glades and walled gardens.

New buildings and old friendships occupied Vanbrugh. To Tonson, the eternal bachelor settled in Herefordshire on his pleasant fortune, he wrote reporting on the progress of his family. He was now 'two boys strong in the nursery, but am forbid getting any more this Season for fear of killing my Wife'. In the old Kit Cat days, he added, this would have been a good reason for it. 'But let her live, for she's Special Good.' It was difficult not to continue to make jokes about marriage, but he warned his old friend 'have a Care of this retir'd Country Life, we shall hear of some Herefordshire Nymph in your Solitary walks; bounce out upon your heart from under an Apple Tree and make you one of us.'

He took a great pride in his son, now rising two, and wrote to Lord Carlisle about his godson's progress. He painted a charming picture of himself, the middle aged man, still full of ideas and imagination in the process of handing on his gifts and enthusiasms to the child.

Architecture, he remarked, was not a trade for anybody to recommend themselves by 'at Court'.

'However, I fancy your Lordship's Godson will be a Professor that way, for he knows Pillars and Arches and Round Windows & Spare Windows already, whether he finds them in a book or in the Streets and is much pleased with a House I am building him in the Field at Greenwich it being a tower of White Bricks and a Closet on a floor. He talks of every thing, is much given to Rhyming and has a great turn to dry joking. What these Seeds may grow to, God knows, they being of a kind that may do his business, uphill or downe hill, so perhaps upon the whole, he were as well without them.'

It was a wry comment on his own talents, which had led him uphill and downhill by turns. Not that he begrudged his friends their good fortune, although he was sorry not to see Tonson more often in town. 'I can't blame you however, for you Spend your Life I believe much as I wou'd do, had I made a good Voyage to the Messissippy.' Tonson was obviously, like the Duchess, a prudent stock-watcher. The Mississippi had provided him with his house and apple orchards in Herefordshire.

Vanbrugh still retained his small interest in the theatre, but as this was set at a fixed sum, the prosperity of the theatre and the success of the Opera did not affect it, which was an irony.

'In Spight of all the Misfortunes & losses, that have occasion'd more crying and wailing, than I believe was ever known before; the Opera has been Supported at half a Guinea, Pit and Boxes and perform'd 62 times this last Season. And with all this, the fine Gentleman of the Buskin in Drury Lane, ride about in their Coaches. The Remnants of Rich have play'd Something and Somehow Six times a Week. And Aaron Hill has set up a New Playhouse, to come in for a Snack with them in the Hay Market where the French acted. But with all this encouragement from the Towne, not a fresh Poet (playwright) Appears.'

Cibber had sounded Vanbrugh about the chance of a new comedy from his hand. 'They are forc'd to act round and round upon the Old Stock, though Cibber tells me, 'tis not to be conceiv'd, how many and how bad Plays are brought to them.'

It is the perennial cry of managements down the centuries.

There was some hope that Richard Steele might write a comedy for next winter, and Congreve had sent a message to Tonson 'that he'll poke out a letter to you, to thank you for his Syder too.'

It could possibly be about this time that Vanbrugh started to compose in his mind an idea for a new comedy, which might serve to repair his fortunes and help his old friend Cibber. *A Journey to London* is as lively and cheerful a piece of writing as Vanbrugh ever composed. It never gives the impression of having been written by a man in his sixties and is as full of meat as the first comedy he wrote in the Bastille. The general plot of the play is that Sir Francis Headpiece, having become a 'Parliament Man', is about to leave his Yorkshire home to make his fortune. As in his earlier play *The Confederacy*, where the City Wives are corrupted by the manners and modes of the 'Towne', so in this later piece the country folk are similarly at risk.

His descriptions of the journey of the family up to London have the racy feeling of Smollett: the old coach with four Geldings, to which have been added 'two Cart Horses so that my Lady will have it said, she came to Town in her Coach and Six—with George the Plowman riding Postilion', also Doll Tripe, the Cook who 'had puked with sitting backward'. The provisions, 'Baskets of Plumbcake, Dutch-Gingerbread, Cheshire-Cheese, Naples Biscuits, Maccaroons, Neats-Tongues and cold boyl'd Beef—and in case of Sickness such bottles of Usquebaugh, Black Cherry Brandy, Cinnamon-Water, Sack, Tent and Strong beer as made the old coach crack,' paint a Hogarthian word picture of the country coming to town.

Nor are his observations about the conduct of the town any less biting than those in his earlier comedies, although they have a deeper and more philosophical vein. Lord Loverule and Sir Charles seem older and wiser than Heartfree and Constant, yet in some way they retain a few illusions, if only in a battered form.

Lord Loverule remarks that 'there was a happy time when

The South front of Seaton Delaval in the County of Northumberland the Seat of Francis Delaval Esq.r. defign'd by S.r John Vanbrugh K.t 1721

22a. South Front of Seaton Delavel, designed by Vanbrugh in 1721

The North front of Grimsthorp in the County of Lincoln the Seat of his Grace the Duke of Ancaster and Kesteven He reditary Lord great Chamberlain of England. Defign'd by S.r John Vanbrugh K.t 1723

b. North Front of Grimsthorpe (Lincoln), designed by Vanbrugh, 1723
(both illustrations from *Vitruvius Britannicus*)

23. Sir John Vanbrugh in middle age (portrait by J. Richardson;
Coll. of the College of Arms)

both you and I thought women cou'd never be vicious—nor never cou'd be old.' Sir Charles, perhaps speaking for Vanbrugh, replies, 'The beauteous Form we saw them cast in seem'd design'd for a Habitation for no vice, nor no Decay—but where's that Adoration now?' To which Loverule replies, 'Tis with such fond young Fools you and I were then,' and he adds, 'The pleasure is so great, in believing Women to be what we wish them to be that nothing but a long and sharp Experience can ever make us think them otherwise. That Experience, Friend, both you and I have had; but yours has been at other Men's Expence; mine—at my own.'

Sir Charles then replies with the mellow feeling of Sir John's about his own marriage:

'I still have so much of my early Folly left, to think, there's one Woman fit to make a Wife of; how far such a one can answer the Charms of a Mistress; marry'd Men are silent in, so pass; For that, I'd take my chance; but cou'd she make a Home easy to her Partner by letting him find there a Cheerful Companion, an agreeable Intimate, a useful Assistant, a faithful friend, and (in its time perhaps) a tender Mother such a change of Life from what I lead seems not unwise to think of.'

Nor had it been unwise for Vanbrugh.

In the same comedy he makes a joke about drunken driving which has a modern ring: 'He Drives best when he's a little upish.' It is an illusion which persists.

Poor Sir Francis Headpiece suffers from the illusion that he will be given a place worth a thousand pounds a year, and in a short speech Vanbrugh paints all that he had learned from a dozen humiliations and disillusions:

'My Lord, says I, beggars must not be chusers some place about a thousand a Year, I believe might do pretty well to begin with. Sir Francis, says he, I shall be glad to serve you in any thing I can; and in saying these Words he gave me a

Squeeze by the hand, as much as to say 'I'll do your Business' and so he turn'd to a Lord that was there—who look't as if he came for a place too.'

It is pertinent to wonder how often Vanbrugh himself had felt that squeeze of the hand which promised so much, and fulfilled so little. Was this a comment on his relations with the great Duke, who with his courtly grace had promised him 'something substantial' and left him with an empty title, a debt, and a lawsuit from the widow?

Even the sharpest disappointments can be turned with a joke, and make good material for a comedy, and a cheerful wife form the living material for a tender passage.

In the summer of 1723, as he was about to set out for Castle Howard for his annual refreshing visit, he had the news of the death of the Duke of Ancaster, the hereditary Great Chamberlain. He was naturally concerned, both for the death of his old friend, and for his work at Grimsthorpe: 'I have no particulars how matters are left, but I think the Son he has left, will prove the best Sovereign that has sate upon that Throne, and I hope all reasonable means will be us'd to Cultivate him, for I don't take him to be of an Ungratefull Soyle.'

Nor was he. Vanbrugh informed Lord Carlisle, 'I shall wait upon his new Grace of Ancaster in my way, having the honour of an Invitation from him, to consult about his Building; by which I believe he is inclin'd to go on upon the General Design I made for his father last Winter and which was approv'd of by himself. He certainly has the honest heart your Grace says.'

Vanbrugh had been at Scarborough taking the waters for three or four days, and said that after visiting Castle Howard he would be returning there with Lord Carlisle for a 'Weekes Swigging more', after which he would be pointing towards London. His health was not as rugged as it had been and yet he continued to work hard at his post, and to take as detailed an interest as ever in the intricacies of planning drains for Windsor,

redecorating the rooms at Hampton Court, and designing anything from kitchens, offices, and chimney pieces, or sending
models over for the King's inspection at Kensington.

It would have been a heavy schedule for a much younger
man, given the hard travelling conditions of the day and the
exigencies of patrons. In spite of everything, his work went on.
He occasionally excused himself, as when he begged the Duke
of Newcastle's indulgence for not attending him, but 'I am so
much out of Order, 'twas with no Small Difficulty I went today
to Kensington by appointment from the Vice-Chamberlain.'

In February 1724 he was out of bed, but not downstairs, and
told Lord Carlisle he was not in order 'to form designs', but in
spite of his illness he managed to send detailed instructions
about the carrying out of 'the first Design I sent, with the 4
porticos' which will be found, he thought, 'to be very near
(perhaps quite) as cheap as any Gothick Tower, that has yet
been thought of'.

His thoughts were as vigorous and as forthright as when he
was thirty years younger. And he was as disposed to make jokes
about the clergy who were trying to stop Heidegger's masquerades. In this they had been thwarted by the King, who 'took
occasion to declare aloud in the drawing room that whilst there
were Masquerades he wou'd go to them . . . The Bishop of
London preached one very Spiritless Sermon on the Subject
which I believe has not lost Heydegger one Single Ticket.'

Yet he was not entirely at peace to give his mind to his
designs, for at the beginning of 1724 the Duchess had again
appealed to the House of Lords. Like a ferret, she did not
easily relax her hold. Vanbrugh was not unprepared for her new
assault and had told Joynes to send his solicitor to see him. Sir
John had written a long justification of the actions of himself
and his employees. It was all to be gone into once again, although the facts remained unchanged. Sir John put the conclusion of his Case succinctly: 'From all these things I conclude
that there never was so much as the appearance of a doubt

Whether this Debt of Blenheim was part of the Civil List Debts till the late Ministers thought fit to change their Stile and instead of a Debt—to call it a Claim.' He ended with humbly hoping that 'your Majesty the fountain of Justice and the Guardian of the Rights of the subjects will relieve the Distress of the Numerous Familys of poor Workmen employed in the Building'.

All through his career, perhaps because of his own disappointments, he remained acutely aware of the needs and distresses of others. Equally firmly was he on the side of justice. The Royal Gardener, Wise, had made a contract with the Crown which stated that he must replace 'at his own cost and Charges all plantations that at any time happen to dye.' He put it to the Treasury that the replanting of the Wilderness at Hampton Court had already been done, and that as the destruction of the old one was due to the overflowing of the Thames, it could hardly be claimed that it was due to the neglect of the contractors. Fair is fair, and Mr Wise and his men were not in charge of the floodwaters of old Father Thames.

Vanbrugh might plead well for others, but he had only himself to rely on when it came to his lawsuits with the Duchess. The final outcome of the Duchess's claims and counter-claims was that she managed to extract from the Lord Chancellor Macclesfield a declaration that Vanbrugh had, in fact, never been employed by the Duke of Marlborough. This decision must have afforded Vanbrugh some bitter amusement. He now found that, in spite of all his designs, drawings, models, consultations, and years of work on the Palace of Woodstock, twenty years later the surprising fact came to light, that he had never been employed at all. The decision was the Duchess's revenge for the fact that Vanbrugh had supported the contractors' claims against the Duke. It had the effect of losing him his fees of £1,600.

When the summer came he was in good spirits, having 'newly return'd from a good agreeable Expedition I have been making for Six weeks past'. Lord Carlisle had been in town with his daughters and, his gout being better, Vanbrugh and his wife set out with the party. Their journey had not been a hurried one, 'a piece of husbandry that usually spoils all Journeys of Pleasure'. They had taken in Oxford, where they stayed in a Whig Inn and so proceeded to Woodstock because the Earl and his daughters had a fancy to view the great Palace of Blenheim.

Here there was a check in the party of pleasure.

'But for my own Share, there was an Order to the Servants, under her Grace's own hand, not to let me enter any where. And lest that shou'd not mortify me enough She having some how learn'd that my Wife was of the Company sent an Express the Night before we came there with Orders, if she came with the Castle Howard Ladys, the Servants shou'd not Suffer her to see either the House, Gardens, or even enter the Park, which was obey'd accordingly and She was forc'd to Sit all Day and keep me Company at the Inn.'

It was perhaps not surprising that a woman who could deprive the widows of workmen of their just dues should stoop to humiliate the wife of one of the few men who had stood out against her. But the Duchess's explanation to Lord Carlisle showed that Vanbrugh's stoutness still rankled with her:

'I should not do this upon the worthlessness of his character, nor for any abuses in the building occasioned by him, but in the life of the Duke of Marlborough he had the impudence to print a libel both of him and me for which his bones ought to have been broke, but I did not think it worth the trouble of giving any directions about such a fellow who by it added to the contempt everybody had for him before and did not hurt me; besides this his behaviour was so saucy to me both in his letters and everything he said to me and of me, that one should wonder at any other person should desire to come within my walls.'

357

Possibly Vanbrugh had hoped that his visit might pass unnoticed, and that if the Duchess was from home he could have been allowed a chance to give his wife a glimpse of his masterpiece. Nor was Vanbrugh the only one to suffer this veto: 'The Dutchess has given out a list of persons who may not see the house, among whom are two—her own daughter and Sir Jo Vanbrugh. It is very hard that ye Dutchman may not visit his own Child, who, however he may appear a meer lump and mishapen to others, may seem beautifull in the eyes that begot him.'

Being confined at the Bear Inn for two days did not put Vanbrugh out of spirits with his expedition, for the whole party then went on to Lord Cobhams, 'eating a Chearfull Cold Loaf at a very humble Alehouse, I think the best meal I ever eat except the first Supper in the Kitchen at Barns'.

After this interlude they drove to Stowe, where the Earl and his daughters stayed four days. Vanbrugh told Tonson that his name had often been mentioned during the journey and at Stowe. 'Our former Kit Cat Days were remembered with pleasure. Both Lord Carlisle & Cobham exprest a great desire of having one meeting next Winter, if you come to Towne, not as a Club, but old Friends that have been *of* the Club, the best Club that ever met.' Many of the old friends had gone, but there were still a few left to enjoy a bottle and a laugh together in cheerful company.

Vanbrugh and his wife stayed on at Stowe for another two weeks and left with regret 'a place, now so agreeable that I had much ado to leave it at all'. He had more reason for cheerfulness at the end of the year, for, as he remarked to Lord Carlisle. 'I have given my everylasting Friend the Dutchess of Marlb. great trouble laterly.'

Vanbrugh's friendship with Sir Robert Walpole had enabled him to prevail upon the Treasury to pay him £1,700 out of moneys due for the payment of the Blenheim debt.

Writing to Tonson he was more explicit:

'Since being forc'd into Chancery by that B.B.B.B. Old B. the Dutchess of Marlb. and her getting an Injunction upon me, by her friend the late Good Chancellor who declar'd that I never was employ'd by the Duke and therefore had no demand upon his Estate my hands were tyed up from trying by law to recover my Arrear, I have prevail'd with Sr. Rob. Walpole to help in a Scheme . . . by which I have got my money in Spight of the Huzzy's teeth, and that out of a sum She Expected to receive into her hands towards the discharge of the Blenheim Debts, and of which she resolv'd I shou'd never have a farthing.'

Vanbrugh had no need to add that the Duchess was enraged. He was particularly pleased at this success because this sum was as he put it 'of considerable weight in my Small Fortune, which She has heartily endeavour'd so to destroy as to throw me into an English Bastile to finish my days as I begun them in a French one.'

His thoughts ranged back to his youthful escapades and mischances; in just the same way, when writing to Lord Carlisle, he recalled in his imagination his childhood in Chester: 'I think the Spire that Mr Etty sent will by no means do, a Cap is all that those sort of Towers shou'd have, and I have seen one upon a round Tower on the Walls of Chester, that I thought did extremely well.'

In the autumn of 1725, in the same letter in which he regaled Tonson with his successful foray against the Duchess, he wrote: 'I have pleasure in believing you may have so much friendship for an old and intimate Acquaintance as to take some small part, in the good or ill that attends them, and therefore it is . . . through great difficultys and very odd oppositions from very odd folks, I got leave to dispose in earnest, of a Place, I got in jest, Clarx. King of Arms and I sold it well.'

He remained truly grateful to Lord Carlisle for his gift. The Earl had been one of the few men who had always lived up to his promises and had not merely contented himself with speaking looks and friendly touches on the arm: 'I don't remember whether I acquainted yr. Lordship in my last that I had made an end of my affairs at the College, and rec'd my money—£2,400. Only there remains Still a dispute about £300 in fees which Mr. Anstis will Cheat me of, if my Lord Sussex will let him.' Vanbrugh's affairs were never concluded in a simple way, but possibly in an age when patrons were as will-o-the-wisps this was true of all lucrative offices. 'My parting with that office, while I am still Living had made your Ldps. Gift of it to me Still the More Valluable, and for which I have therefore the more Acknowledgement to return you.'

If he was not afraid to return thanks for favours given, he never gave up trying to obtain favours for his friends. When the unqualified Sir Thomas Hewet died in September 1725, he wrote immediately to Lord Carlisle asking him if it would not be possible to get Hawksmoor restored to his position at the Board of Works before a new Surveyor was appointed, who might bring his own 'creatures' with him. Vanbrugh added that Sir Robert Walpole was of the opinion that the present clerk, who was merely a country joiner, had been put in by Hewet, who was suspected of pocketing most of the fees, and giving the clerk a small allowance. There ought, said Vanbrugh, to be no difficulty 'in sending him home again to his Wife, who keeps an Alehouse in Nottingham.'

Few men are as solicitous for favours to others as they are for themselves. Vanbrugh was one of those men, who could be 'reckoned a masterpiece of nature' and yet could 'crack a bottle Or treat unmoneyed men.'

Just before Christmas in 1725 Vanbrugh wrote to Lord Carlisle to thank him for an excellent Windsor Doe 'which had prov'd good, tho not over Fat as indeed none are this Season, from the Great Rains that have fallen.'

The building of Castle Howard continued as it had done for twenty years past. Vanbrugh tried to convince the Earl that he should finish the West Wing and not build his Temple in the Park. Perhaps because he had never been allowed to finish Blenheim, he was the more anxious to see Castle Howard in its elegant and finished state. In spite of his disappointment about the West Wing, he sent further designs as 'I can't say I like what Mr Etty has sent.'

Some three months later he amplified his ideas about the work going on and sent further instructions and ideas for Mr Etty's guidance. In the last paragraph of his letter he recorded how the Duke of Grafton, my Lord Bathurst, my Lord Binny and My Lord Stairs are all vastly surprised over Castle Howard 'and taken with the Walls and their Towers, which they talk much of.' The last sentence in the letter expresses a jovial satisfaction with his own work: 'I always thought we were Sure of that Card.' That was the last picture of him, sure of his architectural cards, with a cheerful but unfinished comedy on his desk with Cibber ready to stage it. Sir John remained as critical and careful of his last work as he had been of his first.

Cibber reported, 'Yet when I own, that in my last Conversation with him (which chiefly turn'd upon what he had done towards a Comedy) he excus'd his not shewing it me, till he had review'd it, confessing the Scenes were yet undigested, too long and irregular, particularly in the Lower Characters.'

On 26 March 1726 Vanbrugh died of a quinsy in his house in Whitehall. He was sixty-two. To his very last day he had remained the strong, virile artist, both in his architecture and in his unfinished comedy. There was no sign of decline or of a slackening of his powers. He had always produced to others that virile effect which he admired in a building. There must have been many who felt on hearing of his death, 'How often are we to die—before we go quite off this stage? In every friend we lose a part of ourselves, and the best part.'

He left his widow a small competence and his two boys 'strong in the nursery'. One of these children hardly survived him. The remaining son, Charles, godson of the old Earl, followed his father's first profession, and went into the army. By a melancholy mischance he was killed near Tournai at the battle of Fontenoy. There were no direct descendants. His widow survived him by many years and lived to the ripe age of eighty-two. She never remarried. Vanbrugh would have been a difficult man to replace.

By a curious irony, Blenheim was the building which was to be finished most nearly to his ideas, and one of the few to survive as a private house. Kimbolton is now a school, Lumley Castle is an hotel with a gothic crenellated bar, and King's Weston is a police college. Eastbury remained empty for many years and, about the year 1775, it was decided to destroy it. The walls being of Vanbrugh's usual massive construction, the undertaking presented certain difficulties. The house was eventually blown up with gunpowder. Grimsthorpe retains its charm, but it is only partially the child of his imagination.

After his death *A Journey to London* was adapted and finished by Colley Cibber, who sentimentalised the piece. He paid due tribute to Sir John's characters as 'strongly drawn, new, spirited and natural'. But he baulked at the plot. 'All I could gather from him was that the conduct of his Imaginary Fine Lady had so provok'd him, that he designed actually to have her husband turn her out of his Doors.' Mr Cibber preserved the lady's chastity and the piece ran to full houses. Ann Oldfield played Lady Townly and outdid her usual out-doing, according to Cibber.

To the present day Sir John's comedies can still draw the town. His jokes are much to the taste of a modern age, which likes to see the clergy routed, and does not take it to heart if ladies should lose their virtue—or their purses.

Blenheim stands as Vanbrugh's greatest memorial. Yet it was finished by his greatest opponent and the woman who tried to destroy him. It stands in spite of the hussy's teeth, for his design was greater than the woman who drove the workmen to finish it.

'In Spite of the Huzzy's Teeth'

The Duchess lived on to quarrel with her children—and her grandchildren. As Smollett succinctly put it: 'A.D. 1744. In October the old Duchess of Marlborough resigned her breath in the 85th year of her age, immensely rich, and very little regretted either by her own family, or the world in general.' She had outlived the Duke by twenty-two years and her architect by eighteen.

At the time of writing, Vanbrugh's old house in Greenwich is a boys' preparatory school, sixty strong, and at the local theatre *The Provok'd Wife* was playing. And the bridge at Blenheim, that child of architectural contest, spans the lake created by Lancelot Brown. On a June day, when the Park is 'in Beauty', it could be said that he was also sure of that Card.

Transcription of the text of Vanbrugh's letter on p. 345

George Cansfield
August ye 16 1722.

In answer to yrs. about Keying ye Circuler Window to ye North I would have you breke out the 3 Keystones the side Keystones two inches $\frac{1}{2}$ the Middle one 2 inches att least if to much it may be taken of but never can be added. I have sent you a sketch as I have it drawne if it will answer you may do itt in this Nature. Otherwise follow after ye Designe we allways went by. The facio which is in the North Front cannot stop till it comes with ye angle so the window facing the East stand upon it.

I am afraide you Cannot get the Window underneath the architrave for the overture in the Hall rises too high. If that you cannot key to appear very strong; We must leave of the Entablature on ye Return Column from thence have only the facio as you see it done over the Square Window, the inside Overture must guide you this affair.

Written along the side of the letter.

If the inside will allow you to spring lower you may Key the better. That you apprehend very well.

BIBLIOGRAPHY

A. GENERAL

ARBER, E. A.: Term Catalogues, 1668–1711.

ASHTON, J.: *Social Life in the Reign of Queen Anne.*

AUBREY, JOHN: *Brief Lives.*

BAGSHAW, SAMUEL: *History, Gazetteer and Directory of Cheshire.*

——: *History, Gazetteer and Directory of the County Palatine of Chester.*

BARBER and DITCHFIELD: *Memorials of Old Cheshire.*

BINGHAM, Hon. D: *The Bastille.*

BURNE, R. V. H.: *Chester Cathedral.*

DEFOE, DANIEL: *A Journal of the Plague Year.*

——: *A Tour through the Whole Island of Great Britain.*

GRIERSON, EDWARD: *The Fatal Inheritance.*

GROOMBRIDGE, MARGARET: *The City Guilds of Chester.*

MACAULAY, LORD: *The Four Georges.*

——: *A History of England.*

MACKY, —: *Characters at the Court of Queen Anne.*

PEPYS, SAMUEL: *Diaries.*

PEVSNER, NIKOLAUS: *Cheshire.*

RAVAISSON, FRANÇOIS: *Archives de la Bastille.*

ROBERTS, H. D.: *Matthew Henry and his Chapel, 1662–1900.*

SPENCE, JOSEPH: *Anecdotes, Observations and Characters of Books and Men.*

TREVELYAN, G. M.: *England Under Queen Anne.*

VANBRUGH, SIR JOHN: Letters to Tonson in *The Gentleman's Magazine,* 1802, 1804, 1815, 1816, 1831, 1836, 1837, 1839, 1857.

VOLTAIRE, —: *Lettres écrits sur les Anglais.*

WHISTLER, LAWRENCE: *The Imagination of Vanbrugh and his Fellow Artists.*

——: *Sir John Vanbrugh.*

Bibliography

Assembly Records of the City of Chester.
The Chester and North Wales Architectural and Archaeological Society Journal.
The British and Gloucester Archaeological Society: Correspondence; Transactions, Vol. 76.
Society for the Publication of Original Documents relating to Lancashire and Cheshire: Records.

B. THE THEATRE

ADAMS, DAVENPORT: *Dictionary of the Drama.*
AVERY, EMMETT L.: *The London Stage, 1700–1929.*
AVERY, EMMETT L. and SCOUTEN, ARTHUR: *The London Stage, 1660–1700.*
BEHN, APHRA: *Works* (Ed. Montague Summers).
BERNBAUM, ERNEST: *The Drama of Sensibility.*
BURNIM, K. A.: *David Garrick, Director.*
CIBBER, COLLEY: *An Apology for his Life.*
CLINTON-BADDELEY, V. C.: *The Burlesque Tradition in the English Theatre.*
COLLIER, JEREMY: *Short view of the Profaneness and Immorality of the English Stage.*
——: *Defence of the Short View.*
CONGREVE, WILLIAM: *The Comedies* (Ed. Bonamy Dobrée).
DIBDIN, CHARLES: *Complete History of the English Stage.*
D'ISRAELI, ISAAC: *Curiosities of Literature.*
DOBREE, BONAMY: *English Literature in the Early Eighteenth Century.*
——: *Essays in Biography.*
——: *Restoration Comedy.*
——: *Three Eighteenth Century Figures.*
DORAN, J.: *Their Majesties' Servants.*
DOWNES, J.: *Roscius Anglicamus, or An Historical Review of the English Stage.*
EGERTON, WILLIAM: *Faithful Memoirs of the Life, Amours and Performances of Mrs Ann Oldfield.*
FOSS, MICHAEL: *The Age of Patronage.*
GENEST, —: *Some Account of the English Stage.*
GOSSE, EDMUND (Ed.): *Restoration Plays from Dryden to Farquhar.*
HARRIS, BERNARD: *Sir John Vanbrugh.*
HAZLITT, WILLIAM: *Lectures on the English Comic Writers.*
——: *View of the English Stage.*
HUGHES, L.: *A Century of English Farce.*

Bibliography

LOFTUS, JOHN C.: *Comedy and Society from Congreve to Fielding.*

MILES, DUDLEY HOWE: *The Influence of Molière on Restoration Comedy.*

MOORE, W. G.: *Molière, a New Criticism.*

MORLEY, HENRY (Ed.): *Plays from Molière by English Dramatists.*

NICHOLL, ALLARDYCE: *History of the English Drama, 1660–1900.*

PALMER, J.: *The Comedy of Manners.*

PERRY, HENRY TEN EYCK: *The Comic Spirit in Restoration Drama.*

POPE, ALEXANDER: *Works* (Ed. Elwin and Courthope).

RUSSELL, W. C.: *Representative Actors.*

SHADWELL, THOMAS: *The Complete Works* (Ed. Montague Summers).

SMITH, JOHN HARRINGTON: *The Gay Couple in Restoration Comedy.*

SPRAGUE, A. C.: *Beamont and Fletcher on the Restoration Stage.*

SUMMERS, MONTAGUE: *The Restoration Theatre.*

THORNDIKE, ASHLEY H.: *English Comic Drama, 1700–1750.*

VANBRUGH, SIR JOHN: *The Complete Works and Letters* (Ed. Dobrée and Webb).

WARD, A. W.: *A History of English Dramatic Literature.*

WARD, W. C. (Ed.): *Sir John Vanbrugh.*

WYCHERLEY, CONGREVE, VANBRUGH and FARQUHAR: *Dramatic Works* (Ed. Leigh Hunt).

C. ARCHITECTURE AND GARDENING

ACKERMANN, JAMES: *Palladio.*

BLUNT, ANTHONY: *François Mansart and the Origin of French Classical Architecture.*

BRIGGS, MARTIN S.: *Wren the Incomparable.*

BUSCH, H., and DOHSE, B.: *Baroque Europe.*

CAMPBELL, COLIN: *Vitruvius Britannicus, or the British Architect.*

CASATI, —: *La Renaissance Française.*

CLIFFORD, DEREK: *History of Garden Design.*

CONNOISSEUR PERIOD GUIDES to the house, decoration, furnishing and chattels of the Classic Periods; Stuart; Early Georgian.

COUNTRY LIFE: 18 June 1910, 5 December 1968, 19 December 1968.

DOWNES, KERRY: *English Baroque Architecture.*

——: *Hawksmoor.*

DUTTON, RALPH: *The Age of Wren.*

FIENNES, CELIA: *Through England on Side Saddle.*

GENTLEMEN'S MAGAZINE: December 1815 and January 1816 (Greenwich and Blenheim).

GREEN, DAVID: *Gardener to Queen Anne.*

——*Grinling Gibbons.*

HYAMS, EDWARD: *The English Garden.*

LEES-MILNE, JAMES: *Earls of Creation.*

LOUDON, —: *Encyclopaedia of Gardening.*

MACDONALD, ALEXANDER: *Compete Dictionary of Practical Gardening.*

MARSHALL, EDWARD: *The Early History of Woodstock Manor.*

NICHOLSON, NIGEL: *Great Houses of Britain.*

POPP, HERMANN: *Die Architektur der Barock und Rokokoze in Deutschland.*

RENDEL, GOODHART: *Masters of Architecture.*

SEELEY, B.: *Description of the Magnificent House and Gardens of the Rt. Hon. Richard Grenville Templer, Earl Temple.*

SITWELL, SACHEVERELL: *British Architects and Craftsmen.*

——: *Great Houses of Europe.*

SWITZER, STEPHEN: *The Nobleman, Gentleman and Gardener's Recreation.*

TIPPING (H. A.) and HUSSEY (C.): *English Homes; the Work of Sir John Vanbrugh and his School, 1699–1736.*

WEIDLICH, WOLFGANG: *Schlosser und Herrensitze in Niedersachsen.*

WHINNEY, MARGARET: *Wren.*

WHINNEY (M.) and MILLAR (O.): *Oxford History of English Art, 1625–1714.*

WREN SOCIETY: Papers, IV, VI, VII, XII, XVII, XIX.

D. POLITICS

BELJAME, ALEXANDRE: *Le public et les hommes de lettres en Angleterre au dixhuitième siécle, 1660–1714.*

BUTLER, IRIS: *Rule of Three.*

FOOT, MICHAEL: *The Pen and the Sword.*

FOSS, MICHAEL: *The Age of Patronage (The Arts in Society, 1660–1750).*

GRAMMONT, COMTE DE: *Memoirs.*

HAMILTON, ELIZABETH: *The Backstairs Dragon, a Life of Robert Hardy.*

——: *William's Mary.*

HOLMES, GEOFFREY: *The Trial of Dr Sacheverell.*

MONTAGUE, LADY MARY WORTLEY: *Letters and Works.*

NICHOLSON, SIR HAROLD: *The Age of Reason.*

OLDMIXON, J.: *Life and Posthumous Work of Arthur Maynwaring Esq.*

SWIFT, JONATHAN: *Journal to Stella.*

E. THE KIT CAT CLUB

ALLEN, ROBERT J.: *The Clubs of Augustan London.*

CAULFIELD, J.: *Memoirs of the Celebrated Persons composing the Kit Cat Club, with a Prefatory Account of the Origins of the Association.*

GEDULD, HARRY: *The Prince of Publishers* (Jacob Tonson).

Bibliography

PAPALI, G. E.: *Jacob Tonson, Publisher: his Life and Work, 1656–1736*.
RANSOME, MARY: *Kit Cat Club Portraits*.
TROYER, HOWARD: *Ned Ward of Grub Street*.
WARD, NED: *The Secret History of Clubs*.

F. COSTUME AND HERALDRY

CUNNINGTON, —: *Handbook of English Costumes in the Seventeenth Century*.
NOBLE, —: *History of the College of Arms*.
STEBBING, SAMUEL: *Official Account of Vanbrugh's Visit to Hanover in 1708 sent to the College of Arms* (BM. Add. Mss. 6321).
STRUTT, J.: *A Complete View of the Dress and Habits of the People of England*.
WAGNER, SIR ANTHONY: *Heralds of England*.

G. THE MARLBOROUGHS

CHURCHILL, SIR WINSTON S.: *Marlborough, his Life and Times*.
FIELDING, HENRY: *A Full Vindication of the Dowager Duchess of Marlborough*.
GREEN, DAVID: *Queen Anne*.
——: *Sarah, Duchess of Marlborough*.
KRONENBERGER, LOUIS: *Marlborough's Duchess*.
ROWSE, A. L.: *The Early Churchills*.
——: *The Later Churchills*.
THOMSON, GLADYS SCOTT: *Letters of a Grandmother*.

An Account of the Conduct of the Dowager Duchess of Marlborough from her first Coming to Court to the Year 1710.
Letters of Sarah Duchess of Marlborough from the Originals at Madresfield Court.
Opinions of Sarah Dowager Duchess of Marlborough (published from the original MSS. 1788).
Private Correspondence of Sarah Duchess of Marlborough.

H. THE ARMY

CLODE, CHARLES M.: *Military Forces of the Crown, their Administration and Government*.
FORTESCUE, HON. J. W.: *History of the British Army*.
MCGUFFIE, T. H.: *Rank and File; the Common Soldier at Peace and War, 1642–1914*.
TREVELYAN, SIR CHARLES: *The Purchase System in the British Army*.

INDEX